PROFESSIONAL

Flash® Mobile Development

CREATING ANDROID™ AND IPHONE® APPLICATIONS

Richard Wagner

WILEY

Wiley Publishing, Inc.

Professional Flash® Mobile Development: Creating Android™ and iPhone® Applications

Published by
Wiley Publishing, Inc.
10475 Crosspoint Boulevard
Indianapolis, IN 46256
www.wiley.com

Copyright © 2011 by Wiley Publishing, Inc., Indianapolis, Indiana

Published simultaneously in Canada

ISBN: 978-0-470-62007-6
ISBN: 978-1-118-03731-7 (ebk)
ISBN: 978-1-118-03732-4 (ebk)
ISBN: 978-1-118-03733-1 (ebk)

Manufactured in the United States of America

10 9 8 7 6 5 4 3 2 1

For general information on our other products and services please contact our Customer Care Department within the United States at (877) 762-2974, outside the United States at (317) 572-3993 or fax (317) 572-4002.

Wiley also publishes its books in a variety of electronic formats. Some content that appears in print may not be available in electronic books.

Library of Congress Control Number: 2010926881

To Kimberly and the boys.

CREDITS

EXECUTIVE EDITOR
Carol Long

PROJECT EDITOR
Sydney Jones Argenta

TECHNICAL EDITORS
Drew Falkman

PRODUCTION EDITOR
Rebecca Anderson

COPY EDITOR
Karen Gill

EDITORIAL DIRECTOR
Robyn B. Siesky

EDITORIAL MANAGER
Mary Beth Wakefield

FREELANCER EDITORIAL MANAGER
Rosemarie Graham

MARKETING MANAGER
Ashley Zurcher

PRODUCTION MANAGER
Tim Tate

VICE PRESIDENT AND EXECUTIVE GROUP PUBLISHER
Richard Swadley

VICE PRESIDENT AND EXECUTIVE PUBLISHER
Barry Pruett

ASSOCIATE PUBLISHER
Jim Minatel

PROJECT COORDINATOR, COVER
Katie Crocker

COMPOSITOR
Jeff Lytle,
Happenstance Type-O-Rama

PROOFREADER
Nancy Carrasco

INDEXER
Robert Swanson

COVER DESIGNER
Michael E. Trent

COVER IMAGE
© Hedda Gjerpen/istockphoto.com

ABOUT THE AUTHOR

RICHARD WAGNER is Lead Product Architect, Web/Mobile at MAARK and author of several Web- and mobile-related books, including *Safari and WebKit Development for iPhone OS 3.0, XSLT For Dummies, Creating Web Pages All-In-One Desk Reference For Dummies, Web Design Before & After Makeovers*, and more. Richard has also authored several books outside of the field of technology, including *The Myth of Happiness* and *The Expeditionary Man*.

ABOUT THE TECHNICAL EDITOR

DREW FALKMAN has been developing web applications since it was standard practice to test for Mosaic and Netscape. He rode the dot-com wave through growing a startup and achieving venture funding, and he is now happy to consult and train through his own company, Falkon Productions. Over the years, he has architected and worked on sites for customers from startup cattle auctions to Fortune 500 companies using a host of technologies including Java, ColdFusion, JavaScript, Adobe Flex/Flash, PHP, and WordPress. Also a writer, Drew has authored two books on Java for Adobe Press and done technical editing for Que Publishing and Wiley. He has been published in developers' journals and online, including on Adobe.com. He is an Adobe Certified Instructor and Developer and has spoken at conferences around the U.S. He currently resides in Santa Monica, CA.

ACKNOWLEDGMENTS

THIS WRITING OF THIS BOOK has reflected the stormy seas that Adobe has battled in order to release Flash and Adobe AIR for mobile platforms. It started off as an iPhone-based book for Flash developers until Apple infamously changed its terms of use to exclude Packager for iPhone as being a valid way to create iPhone apps. So, we shifted course, transforming the book into an Android-focused book. However, when I was about 80 percent done with the writing, Apple changed its restrictive policy on Packager for iPhone, opening up Flash development once again to the iOS platform. In response, we changed the focus of the book yet again to account for both Android and iOS devices.

On this stormy, but amazing adventure, I was blessed with as good of an editorial team as I have ever had. Major kudos to Sydney Jones Argenta who was project editor. Sydney was diligent, kept me on track, and always kept things positive and forward-thinking. Also thanks to Drew Falkman for his close attention to the technical details as well as many suggestions that improved the quality of the book. Finally, thanks also to Karen Gill for her editing prowess. It was a joy working with this amazing group of editors.

CONTENTS

INTRODUCTION

THE WORLD IS NO LONGER FLAT for Flash developers. While Flash may have originated for running inside the browser, there are now many more dimensions on which to deploy Flash-based applications. The desktop came first with the Adobe AIR runtime environment. The mobile world follows, with Adobe providing solutions for most (though not all) mobile devices you can think of, starting with Android and iOS.

In this book, I explore all aspects of developing mobile applications using Flash CS5 and Flash Builder for Android and iOS apps. You'll discover how to build an app, and install, and debug it on your mobile device. I then walk you through each key topic related to mobile Flash app development, including multitouch events, motion sensor, accelerometer, GPS, mobile services integration, and persistent data storage. Finally, because a mobile device has far less processing power than the desktop does, you learn how to optimize your app to provide the level of performance your users will expand and demand.

WHO THIS BOOK IS FOR

This book is aimed primarily for Flash and ActionScript 3 (AS3) developers experienced in Flash/AS3 development who want to move that base of knowledge to the Android OS or iOS platforms. You may be creating completely new applications or migrating existing web or desktop AIR apps to run on Android or iOS. In general, readers should have a working knowledge of the Flash authoring environment or Flash Builder as well as AS3.

WHAT THIS BOOK COVERS

This book introduces you to AIR for Android and Packager for iPhone. It walks you through the process of developing new mobile applications from scratch and porting existing Flash and AS3 apps and media to the Android platform.

Here's a summary of what each chapter of the book covers:

➤ **Chapter 1, Introducing Flash Development for Mobile Devices** — Explores AIR for Android and Packager for iPhone and how mobile programming is different than developing for the Web or desktop.

➤ **Chapter 2, Setting Up Your Development Environment** — Guides you through the process of getting all of the necessary tools in place to install your app onto your Android or submit to the Android Market. What's more, it guides you through the sometimes confusing process of getting all the necessary approvals, certificates, and profiles you need from Apple to be able to install your app onto your iPhone or submit to the App Store.

➤ **Chapter 3, Building and Installing VanillaApp** — Takes you on a whirlwind tour for creating your first Android or iOS app and installing it on your mobile device.

➤ **Chapter 4, Rethinking ActionScript Programming** — Shows you how programming for Android requires a new mindset and completely new "best practices" in order to create a successful app for mobile operating systems.

➤ **Chapter 5, Multitouch API** — It's no exaggeration to say that the heart and soul of an Android is its touch screen interface. This chapter explores how to work with single- and multitouch events as well as more advanced multitouch gestures.

➤ **Chapter 6, Detecting Motion with Accelerometer** — Introduces you to motion sensor detection and how to create apps that respond to accelerometer events.

➤ **Chapter 7, Implementing Auto Orientation** — Mobile devices have a rotating viewport that has no desktop equivalent. In this chapter, you'll discover how to detect orientation changes and how to reorient your app's UI to respond effectively.

➤ **Chapter 8, Geolocation API** — Guides you through the process of capturing GPS data and utilizing it inside of your application.

➤ **Chapter 9, Service Integration Using URL Protocols** — Discusses how you can take advantage of URL protocols to integrate with core mobile services, including Phone, SMS, Mail, and Google Maps.

➤ **Chapter 10, Android Camera, Camera Roll, and Microphone** — Dives into how you can integrate with Android's camera, CameraRoll, and microphone.

➤ **Chapter 11, File Management** — This chapter helps you understand how to work with files on Android and iOS.

➤ **Chapter 12, Local Databases** — Discusses how you can integrate your app with a local SQLite database.

➤ **Chapter 13, Remote Debugging** — Discusses various methods and SDK tools that you can use to debug your apps, both on the desktop and on Android and iOS devices.

➤ **Chapter 14, Submitting Your App to the App Store** — Walks you through the process of submitting your app to the Android Market and Apple App Store, so you can begin selling your wares.

IOS OR IPHONE?

Let me add a note on how I am using the terms iOS and iPhone in this book. iOS is a newer term that refers to the operating system (version 4.0 and higher) that runs on iPhone, iPod touch, and iPad devices. Previously, that operating system was known as the iPhone OS (versions 3.1.3 and lower).

At the time I am writing this book, Adobe refers to its support for Apple devices as "iPhone" not "iOS". I expect Adobe to change its terminology in the future to be in sync with the newer vernacular.

Throughout this book, when I refer to iOS, then I am talking about what will run on an iPhone, iPod touch, or iPad. When I refer to iPhone specifically, then I am referencing something specific about the iPhone (such as the phone) that is not available on other iOS devices.

WHAT YOU NEED TO USE THIS BOOK

To work through the examples of the book, you need the following:

➤ Android and/or an iOS device

➤ Flash CS5 and/or Flash Builder 4 (optional)

The complete source code for the examples is available for download from our website at `www.wrox.com`.

CONVENTIONS

As you read through the book, you'll note that I use several conventions throughout to help you get the most from the text.

➤ *New terms* are italicized when I introduce them.

➤ URLs and AS3 code within the text are given a monospaced font, such as `Accelerometer`.

SOURCE CODE

As you work through the examples in this book, you may choose either to type in all the code manually or to use the source code files that accompany the book. All of the source code used in this book is available for download at `www.wrox.com`. You will find the code snippets from the source code are accompanied by a download icon and note indicating the name of the program so you know it's available for download and you can easily locate it in the download file. Once at the site, simply locate the book's title (either by using the Search box or by using one of the title lists) and click the Download Code link on the book's detail page to obtain all the source code for the book.

Available for download on Wrox.com

Code snippets that are downloadable from wrox.com are easily identified with an icon; the file name of the code snippet follows in a code note that appears after the code, much like the one that follows this paragraph. If it is an entire code listing, the filename should appear in the listing title.

Code Filename

 Because many books have similar titles, you may find it easiest to search by ISBN; this book's ISBN is 978-0-470-62007-6.

Once you download the code, just decompress it with your favorite compression tool. Alternately, you can go to the main Wrox code download page at `http://www.wrox.com/dynamic/books/download.aspx` to see the code available for this book and all other Wrox books.

ERRATA

The editors and I worked diligently to ensure that the contents of this book are 100 precent accurate and up to date. However, since future AIR for Android and Packager for iPhone updates from Adobe as well as Android OS or iOS updates could potentially impact what's been written here, I recommend making a visit to wrox.com and checking out the Book Errata link. You'll find a page which lists all errata that has been submitted for the book and posted by Wrox.

However, if you discover an issue that is not found on our Errata page, the editors and I would be grateful for you to let us know about it. To do so, go to www.wrox.com/contact/techsupport.shtml and provide a description of the issue in the form. We'll will double check your information and, as appropriate, post it on the Errata page as well as correct the issue in future versions of the book.

P2P.WROX.COM

For author and peer discussion, join the P2P forums at p2p.wrox.com. The forums are a Web-based system for you to post messages relating to Wrox books and related technologies and interact with other readers and technology users. The forums offer a subscription feature to e-mail you topics of interest of your choosing when new posts are made to the forums. Wrox authors, editors, other industry experts, and your fellow readers are present on these forums.

At p2p.wrox.com you will find a number of different forums that will help you not only as you read this book, but also as you develop your own applications. To join the forums, just follow these steps:

1. Go to p2p.wrox.com and click the Register link.

2. Read the terms of use and click Agree.

3. Complete the required information to join as well as any optional information you wish to provide and click Submit.

4. You will receive an e-mail with information describing how to verify your account and complete the joining process.

 You can read messages in the forums without joining P2P but in order to post your own messages, you must join.

Once you join, you can post new messages and respond to messages other users post. You can read messages at any time on the Web. If you would like to have new messages from a particular forum e-mailed to you, click the Subscribe to this Forum icon by the forum name in the forum listing.

For more information about how to use the Wrox P2P, be sure to read the P2P FAQs for answers to questions about how the forum software works as well as many common questions specific to P2P and Wrox books. To read the FAQs, click the FAQ link on any P2P page.

PART I
Getting Started

Introducing Flash Development for Mobile Devices

WHAT'S IN THIS CHAPTER?

➤ Discovering Adobe AIR for Android

➤ What you can do on Android devices

➤ What you cannot do on Android

➤ A look at the Application Security Model

Not long after my wife and I got married, we moved 500 miles away to a new city. We were still the same couple as before, but we had to get used to our new environment — living in a new apartment, working in a new metro area, and finding new friends.

Developing Flash/ActionScript (AS3) apps for Android and iOS devices is quite similar. You already know the tool and the language that you've worked with for web and desktop-based Adobe Integrated Runtime (AIR) environments. Yet, you find yourself in a completely different runtime environment, with different capabilities and constraints that you never have to consider when working with desktop computers.

This chapter introduces these new two mobile environments and highlights some of the things you need to consider as you get started developing Flash-based applications for Android and iOS devices.

EXPANDING TO THE MOBILE WORLD

Ever since its early days at Macromedia in the 1990s, Flash has been synonymous with interactive media, animations, and games that run embedded inside a Web page. And it has been Flash's ability and power to provide what HTML and JavaScript alone could not that has awarded the Flash plug-in a 99 percent installation rate among all Internet users.

Fast forward several years. Although Flash is still utilized predominately for browser-based purposes, the overall Flash landscape is becoming more diversified. Flash isn't just for interactive media and light apps; you can use it to deploy full-fledged mission-critical applications. In addition to Flash, its ActionScript "brother" Flex offers a more traditional application development environment that utilizes both AS3 and Flash run time.

Flash is no longer constrained to a browser window. With the release of AIR in 2007, Flash and Flex developers could, for the first time, create standalone, cross-platform, rich Internet applications (RIAs) for Windows, Mac OS X, and Linux platforms. These AIR desktop applications not only had the look and feel of native apps but could take advantage of native operating system capabilities, such as local file access, native menus and UI elements, and OS-specific events.

Although Flash's dominance on the desktop is unquestioned, its entry into the rapidly emerging mobile phone world has been far more problematic. Apple's refusal to support the Flash plug-in in the iPhone in its Mobile Safari browser left Flash Web developers out in the cold. In response, Adobe engineers came up with a different plan to get Flash-created content and applications onto iOS devices (iPhone, iPad, iPod touch): bypass the browser and go native. In other words, Adobe engineers figured out a way to package Flash apps as native iPhone apps — yes, the same apps that you can download and install from the App Store (see Figure 1-1). Adobe made Packager for iPhone available in Flash Professional CS5.

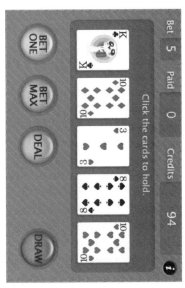

FIGURE 1-1

Beyond the iOS universe, Adobe also is expanding support for Flash onto other mobile platforms, particularly Android and BlackBerry. But, unlike the roadblocks that Adobe encountered with Apple, Adobe has been providing support for both Flash Player and AIR on these other mobile devices (as shown in Table 1-1). However, a strategic goal for Adobe has been to ensure that you will be able to take the same Flash project that you use for deploying on the iPhone and outputting it as an AIR app on Android or BlackBerry.

TABLE 1-1: Flash Platform Support

PLATFORM	BROWSER	NATIVE
Windows	Flash Player	AIR
Mac OS X	Flash Player	AIR
Linux	Flash Player	AIR
iOS	None	Packager for iPhone
Android	Flash Player	AIR
BlackBerry	Flash Player	AIR

DISCOVERING ADOBE AIR

Before you begin to tackle Flash-based mobile development, it's important to have some basic understanding of the runtime environment on which you will be developing applications.

Building for Android

Before you begin to develop Flash-based mobile apps, I wanted to "peek under the hood" for a moment and explain to you just exactly how Adobe can take a Flash file (.fla) and publish it as an .apk for Android or .ipa for iOS.

For Android apps, the process is not much different than AIR apps for the desktop. The AIR for Android run time provides an environment on which developers can build applications using Flash technologies and deliver it as a standalone application, outside of any browser. Users need to install the AIR for Android run time on their Android devices, and then Flash-based Android apps run on top of it.

AIR for Android embeds the cross-platform virtual machine Flash Player used to run media and apps created using Adobe Flash or Flash Builder. Inside of an AIR app, you have programmatic access to existing Flash Player API calls as well as some enhanced functionality for vector-based drawing, multimedia support, and a full networking stack.

AIR for Android also embeds SQLite, a database engine for enabling local database access. It is an extremely lightweight, open source, cross-platform SQL database engine that is embedded in many desktop and mobile products. Unlike most SQL databases, it does not require a separate server process and uses a standard file to store an entire database (tables, indexes, and so on). For more information on SQLite, go to www.sqlite.org.

When you publish a Flash file for Android, your .fla, .as source code, and other source files are transformed by the ActionScript compiler into a binary format called ActionScript Byte Code (ABC). The ABC is packaged inside a .swf file (see Figure 1-2). The .swf and supporting resource files are then packaged together as an Android package (.apk) ready for installation onto a device.

Compile Time (Standard)

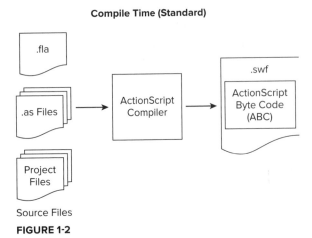

Source Files

FIGURE 1-2

At run time, the `.swf` file inside of the Android app is processed by the ActionScript Virtual Machine (AVM2), which is part of the AIR for Android run time. The AVM2 loads the ABC file into memory and decodes it. The bytecodes are then run through an interpreter and executed as native machine code (see Figure 1-3) by the AIR run time. This process of bytecode compilation by the AVM2 is specific to the Android platform.

Run Time (Standard)

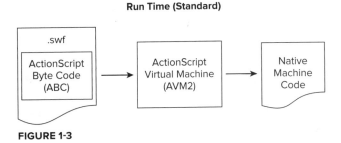

FIGURE 1-3

Building for iOS

So, while Android apps run on top of an AIR runtime environment that is installed separately, iOS apps wrap the runtime code inside of the app itself, making it self-contained. Not surprisingly, then, the process in which an iOS app is created, is quite distinct. Let me explain.

When you compile a Flash project for iPhone, the ABC code is compiled by the Low Level Machine Compiler (LLVM), which is an open source compiler infrastructure that is used to generate machine code for iOS. (Apple itself uses the LLVM). However, as shown in Figure 1-4, in its Packager for iPhone, Adobe provides an ActionScript front-end to the LLVM for handling Flash files.

While the AVM2 supports JIT for Web and AIR, LLVM uses Ahead-Of-Time (AOT) compilation to produce native ARM assembly code wrapped inside of an iPhone executable file. The `.ipa` also contains a `.swf` containing assets and a configuration file.

During the publishing process, the AIR Developer Tool (ADT) is used to add the .p12 certificate to the .ipa application file for developer authentication. The resulting .ipa is a native iPhone application ready for installation on your iPhone device.

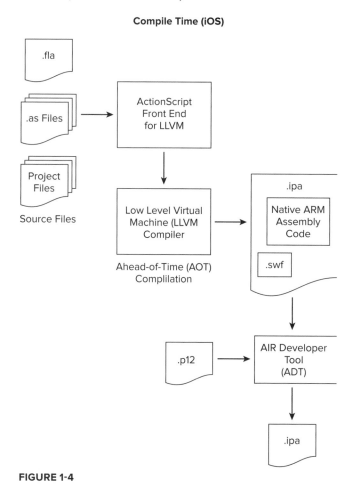

Compile Time (iOS)

FIGURE 1-4

WHAT YOU CAN AND CANNOT DO

Flash CS5 and Flash Builder allow you to create native Android and iOS apps, but it is important to understand from the get-go the capabilities and limitations of the types of functionality you develop.

Device Support

Support for Android and iOS APIs are similar, but at the time of writing, not identical. Table 1-2 summarizes the API capabilities of Flash apps running on Android and iOS.

TABLE 1-2: API Support

API	ANDROID	IOS
Touch/Gestures	X	X
Accelerometer	X	X
Geolocation Sensor	X	X
Camera	X	
Microphone	X	
StageWebView	X	
CameraRoll/Photo Library	X	Add to library only
File I/O	X	X
SQLite database	X	X
Ability to launch mobile services via URL protocol, such as Phone (`tel:`) and E-mail (`mailto:`) and SMS (`sms:`)	X	X

As you can see, some core mobile services are unsupported:

➤ Native UI controls

➤ Music player and library

➤ Bluetooth

➤ Contacts

➤ Calendar

➤ Preferences

The areas of strongest support center on multitouch and gesture events, Accelerometer, and persistent file and database storage. Both AIR for Android and Packager for iPhone are weaker than their native SDK counterparts in being able to integrate with other parts of the respective devices — both hardware and system services. Therefore, as you architect your apps, factor in those constraints.

Unsupported AS3 API Objects

When creating mobile applications, you have access to many parts of the core AS3 library and AIR API extensions. However, not all core and AIR functionality is supported on Android and iOS. The following is a list of AS3 API objects or members that are *not* supported:

➤ `Accessibility`

➤ `DNSResolver`

- ➤ DockIcon
- ➤ DRMManager
- ➤ EncryptedLocalStore
- ➤ HTMLLoader
- ➤ LocalConnection
- ➤ NativeApplication exit(), isSetAsDefaultApplication(), menu, and startAtLogin
- ➤ NativeMenu
- ➤ NativeProcess
- ➤ NativeWindow and NativeWindow.notifyUser()
- ➤ NetworkInfo
- ➤ PDF support
- ➤ PrintJob
- ➤ Socket support (DatagramSocket, SecureSocket, ServerSocket)
- ➤ Shader
- ➤ ShaderFilter
- ➤ Socket.bind()
- ➤ StorageVolumeInfo
- ➤ XMLSignatureValidator

What's more, although you can use Flash Builder to create AIR for Android apps, the Flex MXML framework is not officially supported on Android and incompatible with iOS.

UNDERSTANDING THE AIR FOR ANDROID SECURITY MODEL

AIR for Android carries over the same basic security model that Adobe created for the desktop version of AIR. In the traditional desktop environment, desktop apps get permission in terms of what they can do and cannot do from the OS and the available permissions of the currently logged in user. They receive this level of access because the users need to explicitly install the app — effectively telling their computer that they trust the app they are about to launch. As a result, native apps have access to read and write to the local file system and perform other typical desktop functions.

Web apps, however, are far more restrictive because of the potentially malicious nature of scripting. As a result, web apps limit all local file access, can only perform web-based actions inside the context of a browser, and restrict data access to a single domain.

The hybrid nature of an AIR for Android application puts it somewhere between the traditional desktop and restrictive web security models. On the one hand, you can create an Android application that runs on top of the normal Android OS security layer. Therefore, it is able to read and write from the local file system. However, because AIR utilizes web technologies that, if unchecked, could be hijacked by a malicious third party and used in harmful ways when accessing the local system, AIR has a security model to guard against that happening. Specifically, AIR for Android grants permissions to each source or data file in an AIR application based on their origin and places them into one of two kinds of sandboxes.

The application sandbox contains all content that is installed with the app inside of the home directory of an application. Only these resources have access to the AIR for Android API and its runtime environment.

Adobe AIR does allow you to link in other local and remote content not inside the root directory of the application, but it places this content in a non-application sandbox. Content inside the non-application sandbox is essentially handled from a security standpoint just like a traditional web app and is not granted access to the AIR APIs (see Figure 1-5).

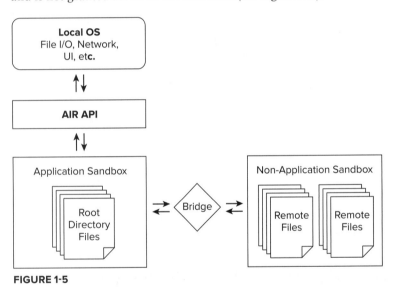

FIGURE 1-5

GETTING TO KNOW THE ANDROID SDK

Apart from using Flash CS5, Flash Builder, or the AIR command-line utilities, the only way to create Android applications is by working with the Android Software Developer Kit (SDK). The SDK is a set of APIs and development tools that developers use to create native Android apps. Although much of the Android SDK is not directly useful to Flash developers, you will still utilize some of its tools during your app development process. Therefore, you'll want to begin by downloading and installing the latest version at `http://developer.android.com` before continuing.

GETTING TO KNOW THE IOS SDK

Apart from Flash CS5, the only way to create iOS applications is by working with Apple's iOS Software Developer Kit (SDK). The SDK is a set of APIs and development tools that are used by Objective-C developers to create native iOS apps. While much of the iOS SDK is not useful to Flash developers, you can still utilize some of its profiling and diagnostic tools to debug your apps. Additionally, it is also a good idea to know what's in the SDK, particularly as you read Apple reference materials pertaining to iOS app development.

The core API frameworks include:

➤   Cocoa Touch framework is the core API used for developing iPhone apps. It includes support for multi-touch and gestures, accelerometer, and camera.

➤   The Media API provides support for video, audio, and core animation processes.

➤   Core Services are lower level services that provide networking, database, and thread support.

➤   OS X Kernel is the lowest level of services providing basic File I/O, TCP/IP, security, and power management.

iOS SDK apps are built using Xcode developer tools. Xcode consists of the following:

➤   Xcode IDE is the Objective-C based development environment.

➤   Interface Builder is used to create user interfaces in a visual environment and then link them into the Xcode project.

➤   Instruments is a diagnostic tool that collects disk, memory, and CPU data of an app in real time.

➤   Shark is a companion tool for profiling your app.

As Chapter 13 explains, you can use Shark and Instruments with your Flash-built apps.

SUMMARY

In this chapter, you were introduced to Android and iOS application development using Flash CS5 and Flash Builder. You reviewed the API support for both mobile operating systems and explored what you can and cannot do in your Flash app. After that, you read aspects of the general AIR API that are available to you as you develop for Android devices. Finally, you took a quick survey of the Android SDK and iOS SDK. Although you do not need to use many parts of it for Flash apps, it is helpful to know that it contains support tools that can make your life easier.

2

Setting Up Your Development Environment

WHAT'S IN THIS CHAPTER?

➤ Install the SDKs

➤ Install the Flash Extension

➤ Create a self-signed digital certificate

➤ Joining the iPhone Developer Program

Although you may be ready to begin coding right now, you'll need to do a couple of things before you can begin creating and publishing Android and iOS apps. There are some Software Development Kits (SDKs) to install and developer programs to join. What's more, to test and debug an application that you are developing, you must have the necessary certificates that you can use as part of the publishing process.

This chapter guides you through the process of getting all the necessary gear that you need to begin application development.

PREPARING FOR ANDROID DEVELOPMENT

If you're preparing to develop for Android, work through this section to set up your development environment.

Installing the AIR SDK

If you don't already have it installed, your first task is to install the Adobe Integrated Runtime (AIR) 2.5 SDK on top of your existing SDK installation. Exactly where depends on which tool you're using.

Before beginning, be sure to download the latest AIR 2.5 SDK from the Adobe website at `www.adobe` `.com/products/air/tools`.

Use the latest version of the AIR SDK, which at the time of writing is 2.5.

Flash CS5 Professional

If you use Flash CS5 to build AIR applications, you should first update Flash to the latest available version at `www.adobe.com/support/flash/downloads.html`.

Once you have the latest update, follow the instructions that follow:

1. Exit Flash if it is running.

2. Locate the Flash installation folder. For Windows, it is probably `c:\Program Files\Adobe\` `Adobe Flash CS5`, and on Mac OS X, it is `/Applications/Adobe Flash CS5`.

3. Within the installation folder, look for the `AIK2.5` folder. If you're running CS4, it will likely be the `AIK1.5` folder.

4. Rename the folder to **`AIK2.5-old`** or something like that. You'll only need it again if there's a configuration issue and you have to restore.

5. Create a new `AIK2.5` folder (or `AIK1.5` if you're using CS4).

6. Copy the uncompressed files from the AIR 2.5 SDK download into the new `AIK2.5` folder you just created.

7. Copy the `airglobal.swc` file within the `Adobe Flash CS5/AIK2.5/frameworks/` `libs/air` folder into the `Adobe Flash CS5/Common/Configuration/` `ActionScript 3.0/AIR2.5/` folder

Flash Professional is now configured to use the AIR 2.5 SDK.

Flex Builder and Flex SDK

If you're creating Android apps outside of Flash Professional using Flash Builder, Flex Builder, or just the Flex SDK, you'll want to overlay the AIR 2.5 SDK onto the Flex SDK.

1. Exit Flash Builder or Flex Builder if it is running.

2. Locate the Flex SDK folder that you're using with your tool. For Flash Builder, it is probably `c:\Program Files\Adobe\Adobe Flash Builder 4\sdks\3.5.0` or `c:\Program Files\` `Adobe\Adobe Flash Builder 4\sdks\4.0.0`. For Flex Builder, it is usually `c:\Program` `Files\Adobe\Flex Builder 3\sdks\3.2.0`.

3. Back up the current SDK folder under a new name.

4. Copy the uncompressed files from the AIR 2.5 SDK download on top of the original Flex SDK, overriding any files with the same name.

Your Flex SDK is now ready to compile Android apps using the command-line tool.

Creating a Code-Signing Certificate

Before you can publish an AIR for Android app, you need to have the application signed by a code-signing certificate. There are two types of certificates:

➤ **Commercial code-sign certificates** — A CA, such as ChosenSecurity, GlobalSign, Thawte, or VeriSign, purchases these certificates. The CA serves as a trusted third party that authenticates the identity of the developer. A commercial certificate gives you the greatest degree of "trust" and authenticity for users installing your app.

The cost of commercial certificates varies significantly ($200–500), so be sure to shop around. If you're an individual developer, GlobalSign has a special individual certificate for $99 annually, which is much more reasonable if you are just getting started.

➤ **Self-signed certificates** — These are make-it-yourself certificates that you can generate with Flash CS5, Flash Builder, or the AIR SDK. Self-signed certificates provide a minimal degree of trust for users, because you have no independent confirmation of your authenticity. Self-signed certificates are intended mainly for internal use when debugging and testing your app.

You don't need to create a new certificate for each AIR for Android application. You can use one certificate for multiple apps. What's more, if you have already created a .p12 certificate for AIR desktop apps, you're all set. You can use it for Android apps as well.

Creating a Certificate in Flash CS5

If you are using Flash CS5, the easiest way to create a self-signed certificate inside the integrated development environment (IDE) is to do the following:

1. Choose File ➪ New.

2. Click the Templates tab.

3. From the Category list, choose AIR for Android.

4. Click the OK button.

5. In the Properties panel, click the Edit button next to the AIR Android Settings.

   The Application & Installer dialog box is displayed.

6. Click the Deployment tab.

   Figure 2-1 shows the Deployment tab.

7. Click the Create button next to the Certificate box.

   The Create Self-Signed Digital Certificate dialog box is displayed (see Figure 2-2).

8. Fill in the boxes with the appropriate information.

   The Type drop-down list specifies the level of security that the certificate carries: 1024-RSA uses a 1024-bit key, whereas 2048-RSA uses a 2048-bit key (more secure).

9. Enter the filename for your certificate in the Save As box.

10. Click OK to create the `.p12` file in the location specified.

FIGURE 2-1

FIGURE 2-2

This `.p12` file will be the certificate displayed in the Deployment tab. Click Cancel unless you are planning to publish the current file.

Creating a Certificate from the Command Line

You can also create a self-signed certificate from the command line using the AIR Developer Tool (ADT) utility, which comes with the AIR SDK. The syntax is as follows:

```
adt -certificate -cn commonName keyType certificateFile password
```

For example:

```
adt -certificate -cn cert1 1024-RSA mycert.p12 2010AN12as
```

This command creates a certificate with a common name of `cert1`, a `1024-RSA` key type, a filename of `mycert.p12`, and a password of `2010AN12as`.

The `mycert.p12` file is created in the directory where you ran the command.

Installing the Flash CS5 Extension for AIR 2.5

Before you can use Flash CS5 to publish Android apps, you need to install the Adobe Flash Professional CS5 Extension for AIR 2.5:

1. Exit Flash CS5 if it is running.

2. Download the Adobe Flash Professional CS5 Extension for the AIR 2.5 extension from `http://labs.adobe.com/technologies/flashpro_extensionforair/`. The file will have a `.zxp` extension.

3. Double-click the `.zxp` file to launch the Adobe Extension Manager (see Figure 2-3).

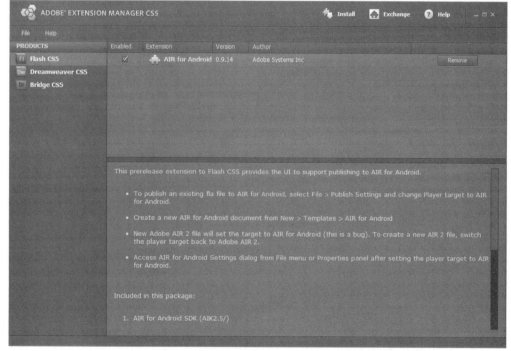

FIGURE 2-3

Make sure you're running the Extension Manager as Administrator.

4. Restart Flash CS5.

Installing the Android SDK

Although you do not need the Android SDK to create compiled AIR for Android apps, you do need it to install and debug your apps on your Android device or desktop emulator.

1. Download the Android SDK from `developer.android.com/sdk`.

Be sure to read the Quick Start notes on the page before continuing. It provides the latest installation notes and system requirements.

2. Uncompress the `.zip` file into `C:\Program Files\Android-SDK` or wherever you want to install it.

3. Add the `tools` subdirectory to your system path. See the section "Adding the Android SDK to Your System Path" for details.

4. Double-click the `SDK Setup.exe` in the Android SDK directory.

5. Select the packages you want to install.

For AIR for Android, make sure to download SDK Platform Android 2.2, API8 and higher.

When your downloads are complete, the Android SDK and AVD Manager are displayed, as shown in Figure 2-4.

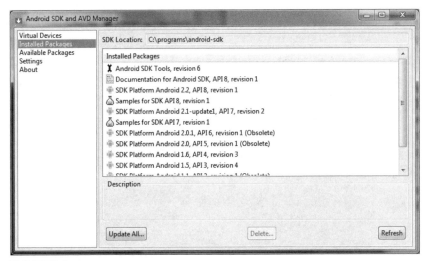

FIGURE 2-4

6. To connect your Android device to a Windows machine, download the USB Driver for Windows at `http://developer.android.com/sdk/win-usb.html`. Be sure to follow the instructions on the website.

7. On your Android device, enable USB debugging in the Settings app under Applications ⇨ Development.

You'll want to be aware of various tools that are included with the Android SDK. Following are three of the ones you'll use most often:

➤ Android Debug Bridge (`tools/adb.exe`) is used for installing AIR for Android apps and Android SDK to devices and the emulator.

➤ Android SDK and AVD Manager (`SDK Setup.exe`) for installing and configuring the Android SDK. You can also set up and run Android emulators through this manager.

➤ Dalvik Debug Monitor (`tools/ddms.bat`) provides log and other debug information about a connected Android device. (See Figure 2-5.)

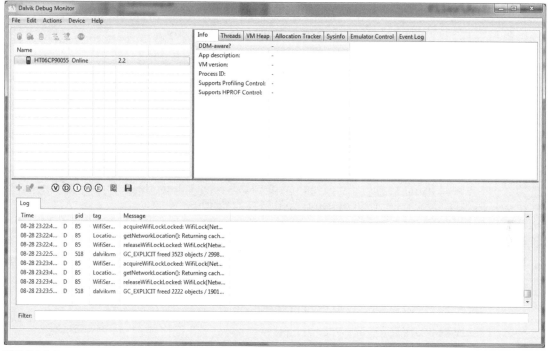

FIGURE 2-5

Before continuing, I recommend testing to make sure your Android device is recognized when you connect it using USB. To do so, type the following at the command prompt:

```
adb devices
```

If your device is recognized, you get a response like this:

```
List of devices attached
HT06CP910453     device
```

If your connected device is not recognized, make sure USB debugging is enabled on your device.

Adding the Android SDK to Your System Path

You'll need to be sure to add the Android SDK folder to your system path.

Setting the Environment Path in Windows

1. Press the Windows key and the Pause/Break key at the same time.

If you're running Windows 7 or Vista, the System section of the Control Panel is displayed.

If you're running Windows XP, the System Properties dialog box is displayed. Skip ahead to step 3.

2. Click the Advanced System Settings link.

The System Properties dialog box is displayed.

3. Click the Advanced tab in the System Properties dialog box.

4. Click the Environment Variables button.

5. Edit the system variable named `Path`.

6. At the far right end of the existing path value, type a semicolon (`;`) and then a path for the `tools` subdirectory of the Android SDK folder.

7. Test the new path by opening a new Console window and typing **adb** at the command prompt.

You should see a listing of the various options available when calling the `adb` utility. If not, check to make sure you added the correct directory to the system path.

Setting the System Path in Mac OS X

If you're installing the Android SDK on the Mac, follow these steps to add it to your system path:

1. Open the Terminal.

By default, you will be in your home directory.

2. Enter **ls -la** at the command prompt.

The terminal displays a list of all files in your home directory.

3. Check to see if a file called `.profile` exists.

If so, go on to step 5. Otherwise, go to step 4.

4. If needed, create the `.profile` file by typing **touch .profile** at the command prompt.

5. Type **open -a TextEdit .profile** at the command prompt.

6. Add your Android SDK tools subdirectory to the `export PATH=$PATH:` line.

Here's how mine looks:

```
export PATH=$PATH:/Users/rich/android-sdk/tools
```

Or, if you already have an `export PATH` line, add the Android SDK tools subdirectory to the far right, separate it with a semicolon (`;`).

For example:

```
export PATH=$PATH:/usr/local/bin;/Users/rich/android-sdk/tools
```

7. Save the file.

8. Quit the Terminal.

9. Restart your computer.

10. Open the Terminal.

11. Type . **.profile** at the command prompt to load the new settings.

12. Confirm the path by typing **echo $PATH** at the command prompt.

You should see the Android SDK tools path in the output line.

13. Test the installation by typing **adb** at the command prompt.

You should see a listing of the various options available when calling the adb utility. If not, check to make sure you added the correct directory to the system path.

Creating an Android Virtual Device

After you have the Android SDK installed, you can create and run an emulator of an Android device on your desktop. The emulator, or Android Virtual Device (AVD), can be invaluable if you don't have access to an Android device or you want to test your app on various screen resolutions or device configurations.

To create an AVD, follow these steps:

1. Launch the Android SDK and AVD Manager (SDK Setup.exe for Windows), which is located in your Android SDK directory. (See Figure 2-4.)

2. Click the Virtual Devices item on the left side.

3. Click the New button to display the Create New Android Virtual Device (AVD) dialog box (see Figure 2-6).

4. Enter the name of your device in the Name box.

5. Select a target Android version from the Target list. You'll want to select Android 2.2 - API Level 8 (or higher).

6. Specify the size of the SD Card, such as 1024MB.

7. Specify the screen size in the Skin area. I specify 480 × 800.

8. Leave the Hardware section as is for now.

9. Click the Create AVD button.

FIGURE 2-6

The AVD is now displayed in the Virtual Devices list. Click the Start button to launch the emulator. The device goes through a boot-up process and becomes available in a couple of minutes.

Installing the AIR Runtime onto Your Device

Before you can install and run AIR for Android apps on your device or emulator, you need to install the AIR runtime onto it.

The easiest way to do install it is to download and install it from the Android Market. You can find it by searching for "Adobe AIR". Once you find it, simply follow instructions on screen to install.

Comparing the Development Environment Options

Adobe provides several options for Flash, ActionScript 3 (AS3), and Flex developers to create AIR for Android apps. Here's a brief look at your options.

Flash CS5

Adobe's standard way of creating AIR for Android apps is by using Flash CS5 Professional. After you have the Android extension installed, you can do any of these:

➤ Create a new Android-based .fla based on an AIR for Android template.

➤ Configure AIR for Android settings from a dialog box.

➤ Publish Android apps and create the .apk file.

➤ Automatically install and run the app if you have an Android device connected.

Flash Builder + Flash CS5

Flash Builder developers who also have Flash CS5 can create Android apps using a combination of the two tools. Create the .fla inside of Flash, but use Flash Builder as the AS3 code editor and IDE.

If you have Flash Builder installed, when you edit the document class, Flash CS5 asks you if you want to edit the file in Flash Professional or Flash Builder (see Figure 2-7). If you choose Flash Builder, its IDE is launched using a workspace you create for this purpose. You can then use the full Flash Builder IDE, moving back and forth between Flash as needed. For larger AS3 apps, this is my preferred development option.

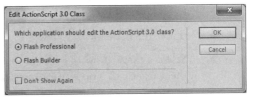

FIGURE 2-7

Flash Builder, Flex Builder, or Flex SDK

Because the Flex SDK command-line tools can compile .apk files, you don't have to have Flash CS5 Professional to create Android apps. You can create AS3-based apps using Flash Builder, Flex Builder, or your own IDE with the Flex SDK. The downside is that you have to do everything yourself:

➤ You have to structure your own AS3-only app in an environment oriented toward MXML architecture.

➤ You have to compile .apk files using command-line tools.

➤ You install apps to your Android device from the command line using Android SDK tools.

Using MXML in Android Apps

As this book goes to press, Adobe is offering beta support for Flex framework and MXML in AIR for Android apps. So, if you plan to use MXML to develop Android apps, visit the Adobe website and look for releases of Flash Builder 4.5 and Flex SDK 4.5.

The issue with earlier versions of the Flex IDEs (Flash Builder 4.0 and Flex Builder 3.x) and 4.0 and earlier SDKs is that their components were not optimized or designed for a multitouch environment.

PREPARING FOR IOS DEVELOPMENT

While your AS3 code might look quite similar to Android when creating an iOS app, the process in which you prepare for installing into the iPhone or other iOS device is quite different.

This section guides you through the process of getting all the necessary certificates you need to begin application development. Before continuing, make sure you have the latest version of iTunes installed on your development machine. You use iTunes to install the app on your iPhone as well as to get your phone's device ID, which generates a developer certificate.

Joining the iPhone Developer Program

Before you can actually publish and install an application onto your iPhone for testing, you need to join the Apple Developer Program. (Yes, you need to pay for the program before you can even test a Hello World application.) There are two types of programs; the one you choose to use depends on your situation. At the time this book went to press, the Standard Program was running $99 annually, whereas the Enterprise Program was $299 (for developers at companies with more than 500 employees).

Unfortunately, many of the benefits of using the Apple Developer Program are specifically for the Objective-C developer; thus, they are largely useless to you as a Flash/AS developer. However, the Developer Program gives you the keys to the kingdom in the form of the iPhone developer certificate, which enables you to install and test on your iPhone as well as to submit your application to the App Store.

To join the Apple Developer Program, follow these steps:

1. Go to `http://developer.apple.com/iphone/program`.

   This is your starting point for registering and purchasing the program.

2. Click the Enroll Now button to begin.

3. Complete the steps of enrollment that follow, and purchase the Developer Program of your choice.

   After you purchase the Developer Program, Apple has to approve you before awarding your developer certificate. The usual turnaround time is within a couple of hours, although it might take a day or two. You receive an e-mail, as shown in Figure 2-8, once your application has been approved.

FIGURE 2-8

4. Click the activation link in the e-mail you receive from Apple, and then follow the on-screen instructions to complete the enrollment process.

Getting an iPhone Developer Certificate

With Apple's approval in hand, you've joined the club and are ready to log in to the Program Portal and download your developer certificate. Your iPhone app must be signed by a valid digital certificate before it can run on an iPhone or iPod touch. This certificate links your developer identity to your confirmed contact information that you provided during the registration process; it is crucial to the trust process involved when downloading and installing an application from a previously unknown source.

The developer certificate is used during testing and debugging and has an expiration date associated with it. You use a different certificate when submitting your app to the App Store.

To obtain a developer certificate, you need to generate a Certificate Signing Request (CSR) either from your Mac or Windows computer.

Generating a CSR Using Mac OS X

To generate a CSR using your Mac:

1. Launch the Keychain Access utility from Applications/Utilities.

2. Choose Keychain Access ➪ Preferences.

3. In the Certificates pane, set the Online Certificate Status Protocol and Certificate Revocation List to Off.

4. Close the Preferences dialog box.

5. Choose Keychain Access ➪ Certificate Assistant ➪ Request a Certificate from a Certificate Authority.

The Certificate Assistant is displayed (see Figure 2-9).

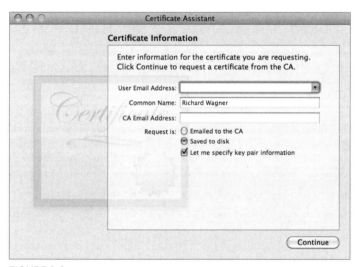

FIGURE 2-9

6. Enter your e-mail address in the space provided.

 The e-mail address you enter here must be the same one you previously used to register with the iPhone Developer Program.

7. In the Common Name field, enter a unique name (usually your own name) that you'll use later to identify as your private key in the Keychain Access utility.

8. Select the Saved to Disk radio option.

9. Check the Let Me Specify Key Pair Information check box.

10. Click Continue.

11. Save your `.certSigningRequest` file on your desktop or in another appropriate location.

12. In the Key Pair Information panel, select 2048 bits in the Key Size combo box.

13. Select RSA for the Algorithm.

14. Click Continue to generate the certificate request.

Skip down to "Submitting Your CSR" to upload the certificate request to Apple.

Generating a CSR Using Windows

If you don't have access to a Mac, use the following steps to generate a CSR using your Windows computer:

1. If you don't have OpenSSL installed, download the latest binaries from `www.openssl.org/related/binaries.html`.

2. Open a Command window (by running `cmd.exe`) and change to the OpenSSL `bin` subdirectory.

3. Before creating a CSR, you need to generate a private key that associates with the CSR. To do so, enter the following command at the prompt:

```
openssl genrsa -out devkey.key 2048
```

The `devkey.key` is created in the directory where it is run. You use this file when creating the CSR.

 You can also specify the `devkey.key` *path in the command line.*

4. Generate the CSR by entering the following at a command prompt (in your OpenSSL `bin` subdirectory), substituting your own information in the parameters:

```
openssl req -new -key devkey.key -out
CertificateSigningRequest.certSigningRequest -subj
"/emailAddress=myEmailAddress@company.com, CN=Richard Wagner, C=US"
```

 The e-mail address you use must be the same one you previously used to register with the iPhone Developer Program.

Your certificate request is now ready to be submitted to Apple.

Submitting Your CSR

After you have created a CSR, you need to submit the request to Apple and have it approved. Once it is approved, you receive the developer certificate.

To submit your CSR, follow these steps:

1. Go to the Program Portal section of the iPhone Developer Program website.

The Program Portal (see Figure 2-10) is the main area you'll work with in the iPhone Developer Program for testing your apps before submittal to the App Store. You can manage team members, certificates, devices, and provisioning profiles.

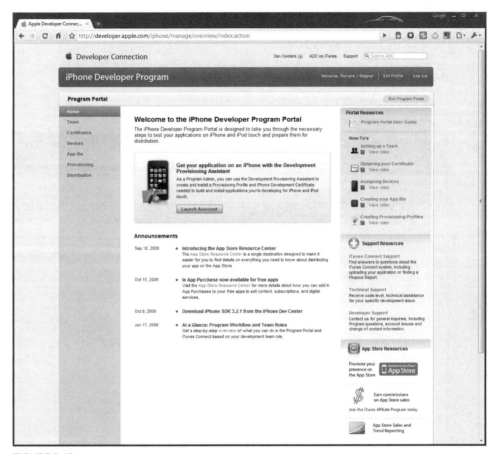

FIGURE 2-10

2. Click the Certificates link.

3. Click the Request Certificate button.

4. Click the Choose File button on the Create iPhone Development Certificate page, and choose the certificate file from your computer.

5. Click the Submit button.

After your certificate request is submitted, you receive the approval (or disapproval) via e-mail. If the request is approved in the e-mail, you can download your certificate.

Retrieving the Developer Certificate

When you receive an acceptance e-mail, you can go to the Program Portal to download the certificate. The developer certificate file (which is named `developer_identity.cer`) is downloaded from Apple's Program Portal. However, before you can use it with your Flash-based app, you need to convert it from the `.cer` format to a `.p12` certificate file. First, download the `.cer` file:

1. Go to the Program Portal section of the iPhone Developer Program website.

2. Click the Certificates link to display the Current Development Certificates list.

As shown in Figure 2-11, you see a certificate in your name (or the name you signed up for the developer program with).

3. Click the Download button to retrieve the `developer_identity.cer` file.

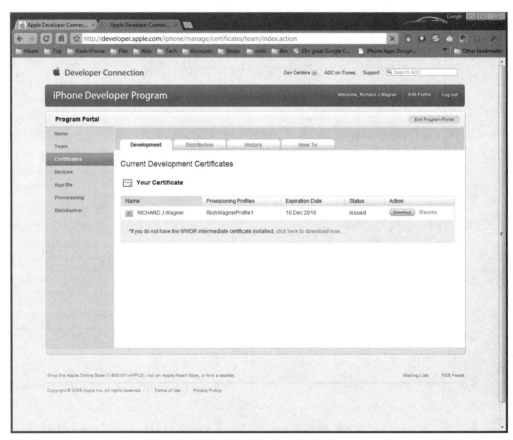

FIGURE 2-11

Next, you need to convert the file to `.p12` certificate format so you can sign it in CS5. You can convert the file using one of two methods, depending on whether you're running Mac or Windows. (If you have both systems, I recommend the Mac conversion process.)

Converting the Certificate on Mac OS X

If you are running Mac OS X, you can convert the certificate to `.p12` format using the Keychain Access application. Here's how:

1. Double-click the `developer_identity.cer` file to launch the Keychain Access utility (see Figure 2-12).

FIGURE 2-12

2. Select the Keys category from the left pane. You'll see a public and private key listed.

3. Right-click the private key and click the Export item from the pop-up menu.

4. Save the certificate in the Personal Information Exchange (`p.12`) format.

Your developer certificate is now ready to go. You'll need this when you publish your iPhone apps in Flash CS5, so copy the file to a safe place.

Converting the Certificate on Windows

If you only have access to a Windows computer, you need to use OpenSSL to convert the certificate to `.p12` format. To do so, follow these steps:

1. Copy the `developer_identity.cer` file you download from the Program Portal to the OpenSSL `bin` subdirectory on your computer.

2. Open a Command window (running `cmd.exe`) and change to the OpenSSL `bin` subdirectory.

3. Enter the following at the command prompt:

```
openssl x509 -in developer_identity.cer -inform DER -out developer_identity.pem
-outform PEM
```

A .pem file is created. You'll use this file in combination with the .key file you created earlier to create the .p12 file.

4. If the .key file is not in the OpenSSL bin subdirectory, copy it in now.

5. Enter the following command to generate the .p12 file:

```
openssl pkcs12 -export -inkey devkey.key -in developer_identity.pem
-out developer_identity.p12
```

Modify the filenames used as parameters if needed.

Your .p12 certificate is now ready to go. You'll need this when you publish your iPhone apps in Flash CS5, so copy the file to a safe place.

Adding a Device

Your next step is to register one or more devices that you intend to use during the development process. You can enter up to 100 devices per year. To add a device:

1. Connect your iPhone or iPod touch to your desktop computer and open iTunes.

2. Display the Summary page for your iPhone.

3. Click the serial number displayed at the top to display the UDID (unique device identifier) identifier (see Figure 2-13).

FIGURE 2-13

4. Copy the UDID number to the Clipboard.

5. Go to the Program Portal section of the iPhone Developer Program website.

6. Click the Devices link, and then click the Add Device button.

7. Enter a name you want to give the device, and then paste the UDID into the Device ID box (see Figure 2-14).

8. Click Submit to add your device.

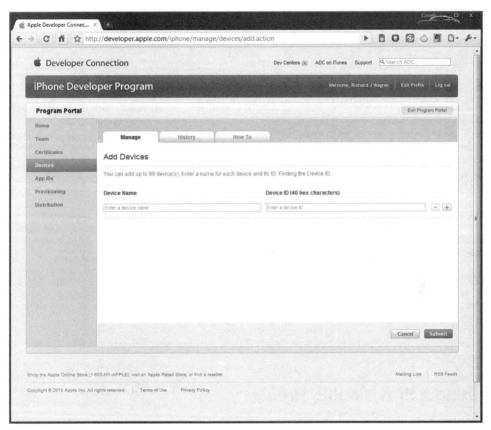

FIGURE 2-14

Creating an App ID

Although I have not even started covering how to create a Flash-based iPhone app, go ahead and create an App ID anyway. It's needed to create a provisioning profile, which is discussed in the next section. An App ID is a unique identifier for your application that consists of two parts:

➤ **Bundle Seed ID** — is a 10-character prefix that Apple generates.

➤ **Bundle Identifier** — is a reverse-domain style string that you decide upon. It can contain standard alphanumeric characters (A–z, 0–9), periods, and hyphens.

For example, a typical App ID might look something like the following:

```
A1B2C3D4E5.com.richwagner.myapp
```

Because your Bundle Identifier uniquely identifies a particular app, you can use the string only once. This is known as an Explicit App ID.

In addition to the standard App ID, you can create a Wildcard App ID if you want to use the same App ID for all applications. A Wildcard App ID uses the familiar asterisk as the Bundle Identifier or the last part of it. For example:

```
A1B2C3D4E5.*
```

Or:

```
A1B2C3D4E5.com.richwagner.*
```

A Wildcard App ID is ideal for getting started, enabling you to work with many sample apps without assigning a unique App ID to each.

To create a Wildcard App ID for use in testing:

1. Go to the Program Portal section of the iPhone Developer Program website.

2. Click the App IDs link to display the Create App ID page (see Figure 2-15).

3. In the Description box, enter a descriptive name for the App ID. Because I am creating a Wildcard App ID, I am using `BookSamples`.

4. In the Bundle Seed ID combo box, select Generate New (the default item).

5. In the Bundle Identifier box, enter an * if you are creating a Wildcard App ID or a reverse-domain name style string if you are creating an Explicit App ID.

You need to have an Explicit App ID to have In App Purchases and Push Notification services. Currently, Flash CS5 does not currently support these, but keep in mind you will need one when support is added in the future.

Creating a Provisioning Profile

After you have obtained a developer certificate, registered your device, and created an App ID, you're ready for the final credential you need to run an app on a device: a provisioning profile. A provisioning file binds a developer certificate, an application, and one or more devices. You need to have a provisioning profile installed on each iPhone device that runs your app, or it will not install successfully.

There are three types of provisioning profiles: a *development provisioning profile* is used for testing on your own iPhone; an *ad-hoc provisioning profile* is used for more general beta testing on multiple devices outside of the App Store; and a *distribution provisioning file* is used for submitting to the App Store. You can create new provisioning profiles for an application as you move through the development life cycle.

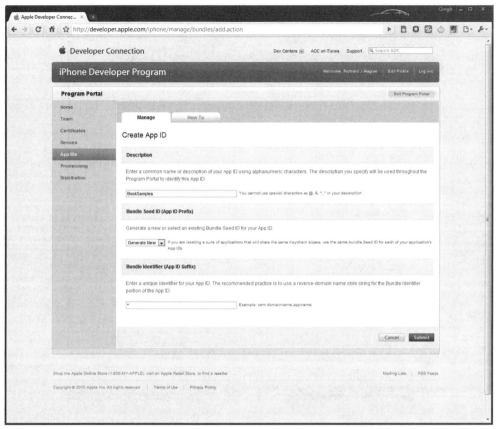

FIGURE 2-15

To create a development provisioning file:

1. Go to the Program Portal section of the iPhone Developer Program website.

2. Click the Provisioning link.

3. Click the New Profile button to display the page shown in Figure 2-16.

4. Enter the name of the profile. In my case, I enter `BookSamplesProfile`.

5. The name of your developer certificate appears next to the Certificates label. Click the check box to assign your developer certificate to this profile.

6. Select the App ID you created in the App ID combo box.

7. Click the check box next to the device you previously registered.

8. Click the Submit button to create the provisioning profile.

Figure 2-17 shows the list of provisioning profiles in my Program Portal.

9. Click the Download button beside the provisioning profile you just created to download the `.mobileprovision` file to your desktop computer.

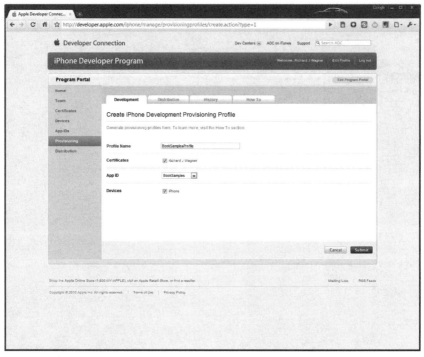

FIGURE 2-16

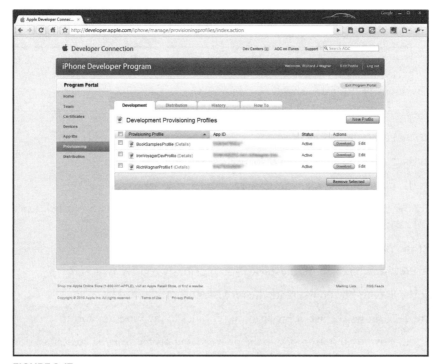

FIGURE 2-17

Installing the Provisioning Profile

You need to install a provisioning profile on your desktop computer and iPhone. To do so, you can use either iTunes or the iPhone Configuration Utility.

Install Using iTunes

To install using iTunes, you can drag the `.mobileprovision` file on top of your iTunes window. (Alternatively, you can use the Add to Library command from the File menu.) iTunes adds the provisioning profile to your library.

When you synch your iPhone to iTunes, the development provisioning profile is added onto your iPhone. You can check to make sure it is on your iPhone by going to the Settings app on your iPhone and choosing General ⇨ Profiles. As Figure 2-18 shows, the profile is displayed on the list.

If you select the profile from the list, you see its verification information and its expiration date (see Figure 2-19). You can also remove the profile from your iPhone if and when you are finished using it.

FIGURE 2-18

FIGURE 2-19

Install Using iPhone Configuration Utility

You can also install the provisioning profile using the iPhone Configuration Utility (see Figure 2-20). This free utility is available for both Mac and Windows. To download, go to `www.apple.com/support/iphone/enterprise`.

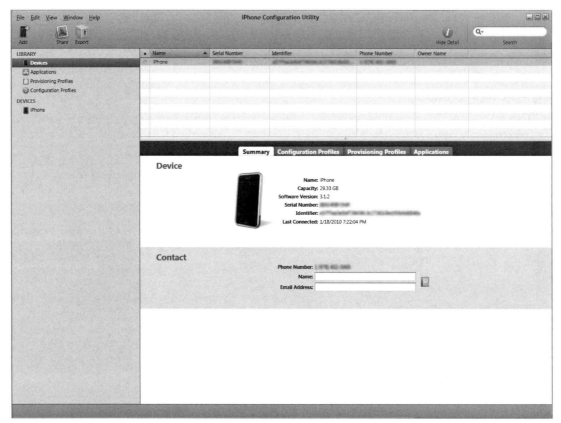

FIGURE 2-20

You can use this utility for a variety of configurations, but for your immediate purposes, you only need to concern yourself with the Provisioning Profiles section of the app. To install:

1. Drag the `.mobileprovision` file on top of the iPhone Configuration Utility window.

    If you click the Provisioning Profiles item in the Library tree, you see the file displayed in the list. (Note that provisioning profiles added via iTunes are *not* displayed in the list.)

2. If your device is not already connected, plug your iPhone into your computer.

3. Select your iPhone from the Devices tree on the left-side pane.

4. Click the Provisioning Profiles tab.

    A list of provisioning profiles associated with your device is shown (see Figure 2-21).

5. Click the Install button next to the provisioning profile you created to install the profile onto your device.

As I mentioned in the previous section, you can check to ensure that your profile was added to your iPhone by choosing Settings ➪ General ➪ Profiles.

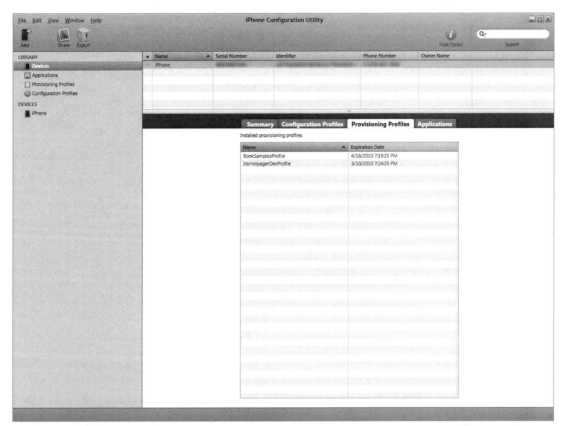

FIGURE 2-21

SUMMARY

In this chapter, you discovered all the preliminary steps before beginning Android development. You learned the steps for installation of the AIR SDK, AIR Runtime, and Android SDKs. You also learned how to create a self-signed .p12 certificate, which Flash CS5 can use when it compiles Android apps. Finally, you discovered the various ways to use Flash, Flash Builder, and Flex Builder to create apps.

You also discovered all of the preliminary steps you need to do before you can begin installing apps you develop with Flash CS5 onto your iPhone. I walked you through the steps needed to join the iPhone Developer Program and acquire an iPhone Developer Certificate. I then showed you how to convert that certificate into a .p12 certificate which can then be used by Flash CS5 when it compiles iPhone apps. Finally, I showed you how to create and install a provisioning file using iTunes and the iPhone Configuration Utility.

3

Building and Installing VanillaApp

WHAT'S IN THIS CHAPTER?

➤ Creating your first Android app

➤ Creating your first iOS app

➤ Responding to basic touch events

➤ Installing the app onto your device

Okay, enough with the intros, it's time to build your first mobile application. This chapter walks you through the start-to-finish process of building a basic HelloWorld-style application using Flash CS5 for both Android and iOS. To avoid the typical naming cliché, I'm naming this simple little app `VanillaApp`. It displays an image that the user can pan and zoom.

I walk you through the process of building and installing the app for both Android and iOS devices in separate sections. Follow along on the mobile OS you are most interested in. If you plan on creating both, be sure to create separate projects to avoid confusion.

VANILLAAPP FOR ANDROID

The actual workings of the Android application are minimal, but this chapter shows you all the steps required to create and install an Android app using Flash CS5.

To create `VanillaApp`, you perform the following steps:

1. Create a project.

2. Create an `.fla` file.

3. Create an ActionScript document class.

4. Write the application code.

5. Add a splash screen.

6. Create the application icons.

7. Define the Android settings.

8. Publish the file.

9. Install the app on an Android.

Before you begin, I recommend changing the Flash CS5 workspace to Developer by selecting Developer from the Workspace toolbar.

Creating a Project

Begin by creating a new Flash project. Working within a project is not essential, particularly with a small app such as this one. However, I recommend it as standard practice because it enables you to manage your files more easily.

1. From the Welcome screen, click the Flash Project under the Create New list. (Or, choose File ➪ New from the menu and select Flash Project from the list.)

The Project panel displays.

2. Click the Projects combo box and select the New Project item from the list.

The Create New Project dialog is displayed, as shown in Figure 3-1.

3. Enter **VanillaApp** in the Project name field.

4. Specify a folder in the Root folder field. I am using d:\android-dev\VanillaApp.

5. Keep ActionScript 3.0 as the default ActionScript version.

6. Click Create Project. The new blank VanillaApp project is created and ready for use.

FIGURE 3-1

With your Flash project set, you can begin to add content to it.

Creating a Flash Document for AIR for Android

When you create a Flash document (.fla) file, you'll want to create it to have the publishing settings configured for Android deployment. To do so, follow these steps:

1. From the Welcome screen, click AIR for Android under the Create From Template list. (Or, choose File ➪ New from the menu and select AIR for Android from the Templates list.)

The untitled.fla is created and displayed in the Flash window.

2. Using File ➪ Save, save the document as **VanillaApp.fla** in your project's root directory.

When the Project panel refreshes, the .fla extension shows up.

Figure 3-2 shows the blank document inside the Flash environment.

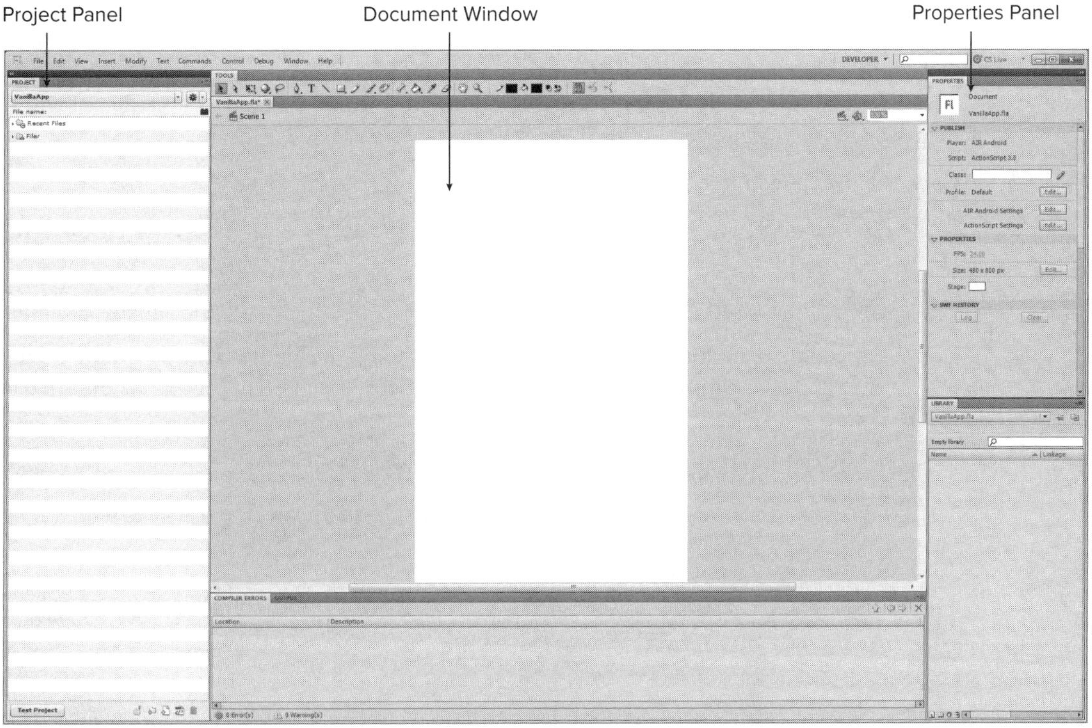

Project Panel   Document Window   Properties Panel

FIGURE 3-2

Because this is an ActionScript project, you won't be doing anything more to the `.fla` document or its timeline. But you'll want to keep it open in the Flash CS5 editor to give you access to the commands you need through the Properties panel.

Creating an ActionScript Document Class

Because `VanillaApp` is an ActionScript project, your next step is to create an ActionScript document class. In Flash, the *document class* serves as the command and control center for the application. The document class is also the first code executed when the app is launched. (If you're a Flex developer, think of the document class as equivalent to a Flex project's primary `.mxml` file, the one that contains `mx:Application` or `mx:WindowedApplication`).

To create a document class, follow these steps:

1. Select the stage of the `VanillaApp.fla` document.

2. Press Ctrl+F3 (Windows) or Cmd+F3 (Mac OS X) to activate your Properties panel (if it is not already visible).

3. In the Properties panel, type the name of the class in the Document edit box.

For this example, I enter `VanillaApp`. Although the document class can be any name you want, it's often helpful to use the same name as the `.fla` file or something similar, such as `VanillaAppClass`.

No matter what name you decide to use, keep in mind an important ActionScript convention. Class names should be *camel case* — compound words joined without spaces with each word's initial letter capitalized, such as `MyClass` or `MainAppClass`.

4. Click the pencil icon to edit the class definition.

5. In the Edit ActionScript 3.0 Class dialog box, select the application whose class you want to edit.

➤ Selecting Flash Professional opens the editor inside the existing Flash environment.

➤ Selecting Flash Builder allows you to open the Flash Builder IDE. If you are a Flex developer or simply want a powerful editor, you'll definitely prefer this option for larger projects.

Because this is a small app, choose Flash Professional and click OK.

The shell of the `VanillaApp` class is created and displayed in the document window. (See Figure 3-3.)

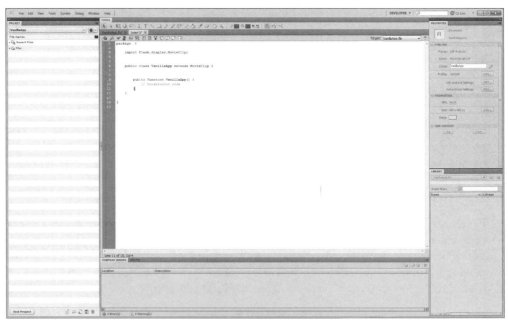

FIGURE 3-3

6. Choose File ➪ Save to save the file as `VanillaApp.as`.

Make sure you save it in the same directory as the `.fla` document.

Coding the Document Class

When Flash creates the document class, it provides the shell class structure. An example of the shell class structure is shown here:

```
package  {

        import flash.display.MovieClip;
                          public class VanillaApp extends MovieClip
        {


       public function VanillaApp() {
              // constructor code
              }
.....}

       }
```

Code snippet VanillaApp.as

The `VanillaApp` class is contained inside the default package and is a subclass of `MovieClip`. A document class needs to extend `MovieClip` or `Sprite`. Use `MovieClip` if you need to do anything involving the timeline, such as animations. If you need an ordinary base class, you can use `Sprite`, which requires less memory overhead.

Define Import Statements

For every ActionScript class you reference in your code, you need to import a reference to the class name. For this example, you'll want to add the following import statements above the class definition:

```
import flash.display.Bitmap;
import flash.display.MovieClip;
import flash.display.Sprite;
import flash.events.TouchEvent;
import flash.events.TransformGestureEvent;
import flash.geom.Matrix;
import flash.text.TextField;
import flash.text.TextFormat;
import flash.ui.Multitouch;
import flash.ui.MultitouchInputMode;
```

Code snippet VanillaApp.as

In normal practice, you won't know all of these references upfront and add them incrementally as you develop the class. What's more, a good short-cut is to press Ctrl+Space after you type in an ActionScript type and Flash automatically adds the import statement for you.

Define Class Properties

Your first step is to define two class properties and four class constants that you will be using in the document class. The most significant of these definitions is a reference to an external file named `Mini.jpg`. (You can find this graphic on the book's website at `wrox.com`.) Using the `[Embed]` metadata declarative, you can define a class reference as follows after the opening `VanillaApp` class definition and before the constructor:

```
[Embed(source="Mini.jpg")]
private var MiniImage:Class;
```

The compiler uses the `[Embed]` tag to embed the file named `Mini.jpg` into the app and associate it with the `MiniImage` variable.

Note that the `[Embed]` metadata tag requires the Flex SDK. As a result, when you first publish the app, Flash CS5 prompts you to the Flex SDK path to the Library path of your project.

If you have the Flex SDK (or Flash Builder) already installed on your computer, simply provide your existing Flex SDK directory. Or, if you don't have the Flex SDK, it's a free download at `http://opensource.adobe.com/wiki/display/flexsdk/Downloads`.

In addition, you define the following property and constants:

Available for download on Wrox.com

```
// TextField
private var tfInfo:TextField;

// Constants
private const VIEWPORT_WIDTH:int = 480;
private const VIEWPORT_HEIGHT:int = 800;
private const IMG_WIDTH:uint = 1000;
private const IMG_HEIGHT:uint = 760;
```

Code snippet VanillaApp.as

The `tfInfo` property is the `TextField` I'll be using in the app. The constants are height and width values for the Android viewport and the image.

Write the Constructor

The constructor of a class is a special type of function that is called at the time an object based on the class is constructed. For `VanillaApp`, you create the following display objects in the constructor:

➤ `TextField` to provide information text

➤ `Bitmap` to display the external image file

➤ `Sprite` that contains the bitmap

The `TextField` receives its formatting rules from the `TextFormat` class. Begin by creating the `TextFormat` instance and providing formatting assignments as follows:

Available for download on Wrox.com

```
// Format TextField
var tf:TextFormat = new TextFormat();
tf.color = 0xffffff;
tf.font = "Helvetica";
tf.bold = true;
tf.size = 14;
```

Code snippet VanillaApp.as

When you create the `TextField`, you assign `tf` as its `defaultTextFormat`. You also specify basic width, dimensions, and starter text:

```
// Create TextField
tfInfo = new TextField();
tfInfo.width = 310;
tfInfo.defaultTextFormat = tf;
tfInfo.x = 2;
tfInfo.y = 20;
tfInfo.selectable = false;
tfInfo.text = "Welcome to VanillaApp. Zoom or pan to begin.";
```

Code snippet VanillaApp.as

Next, you add the `tfInfo` instance to the stage using the `addChild()` method of the parent class, `VanillaApp`:

```
addChild(tfInfo);
```

Although you already defined the image class that references the external image, you need to instantiate an instance of it by performing the following:

```
var bitmap:Bitmap = new MiniImage();
```

Because the app allows panning and zooming of the image, you want to avoid choppy image movements by using smoothing:

```
bitmap.smoothing = true;
```

Because you will be zooming in and panning around the image, you need a `Sprite` instance as a container (the viewport) for the image, which is responsible for dispatching these events. You create it as a local variable named `sprite`, add `bitmap` variable as its child, and add it to the stage:

```
// Create sprite container for image
var sprite:Sprite = new Sprite();
sprite.addChild(bitmap);
addChild(sprite);
```

Inside the constructor, you set up the dimensions, positioning, and scaling of the sprite and bitmap:

```
// Scaling and positioning
var fx:Number = VIEWPORT_WIDTH / IMG_WIDTH;
sprite.scaleX = fx;
sprite.scaleY = fx;
sprite.x = VIEWPORT_WIDTH / 2;
sprite.y = VIEWPORT_HEIGHT / 2;
bitmap.x = (IMG_WIDTH - (IMG_WIDTH / 2)) * -1;
bitmap.y = (IMG_HEIGHT - (IMG_HEIGHT / 2)) *-1;
```

In this code, `sprite` is scaled based on the relative width of the viewport and image and is positioned. The `bitmap` variable is then positioned inside `sprite` so that it is displayed in the middle of the viewport.

The final task you need to perform in the constructor is setting up the application for responding to multitouch events. You begin by specifying the `Multitouch.inputMode`:

```
Multitouch.inputMode = MultitouchInputMode.GESTURE;
```

This property specifies the type of touch and gesture events that you want to process. By specifying `MultitouchInputMode.GESTURE` (the default, by the way), you are telling the app to dispatch touch events with multiple points of contact, which is what you need to work with zooming and panning.

You must then assign listeners to the zoom and pan multitouch events that are dispatched by `sprite`:

```
// Assign event handlers
sprite.addEventListener(TransformGestureEvent.GESTURE_ZOOM, zoomHandler);
sprite.addEventListener(TransformGestureEvent.GESTURE_PAN, panHandler);
```

You can see the full constructor code in Listing 3-1.

Defining Event Handlers

You need to define event handlers to respond to the zoom and pan events. The `zoomHandler()` method handles zoom events:

**Available for
download on
Wrox.com**

```
private function zoomHandler(event:TransformGestureEvent):void
{
    tfInfo.text = "Zoom event";

    var sprite:Sprite = event.target as Sprite;
    sprite.scaleX *= event.scaleX;
    sprite.scaleY *= event.scaleY;
}
```

Code snippet VanillaApp.as

In this code, the `tfInfo` text is updated. The `Sprite` instance is then scaled by multiplying the existing scale by the new scale values provided by the event.

The `panHandler()` method handles pan events:

**Available for
download on
Wrox.com**

```
private function panHandler(event:TransformGestureEvent):void
{
    tfInfo.text = "Pan event";

    var sprite:Sprite = event.target as Sprite;
    sprite.x += event.offsetX;
    sprite.y += event.offsetY;

}
```

Code snippet VanillaApp.as

This code changes the x, y position of the `Sprite` by adding its current position with the `offsetX` and `offsetY` properties of the event.

Go ahead and save changes to the `VanillaApp.as` file.

The full code for the document class is provided in Listing 3-1.

LISTING 3-1: VanillaApp.as

```actionscript
package
{
    import flash.display.Bitmap;
    import flash.display.MovieClip;
    import flash.display.Sprite;
    import flash.events.TouchEvent;
    import flash.events.TransformGestureEvent;
    import flash.geom.Matrix;
    import flash.text.TextField;
    import flash.text.TextFormat;
    import flash.ui.Multitouch;
    import flash.ui.MultitouchInputMode;

    /**
     * Document class for VanillaApp application.
     * Sample application
     *
     * @author Rich Wagner
     *
     */
    public class VanillaApp extends MovieClip
    {

        // External image
        [Embed(source="Mini.jpg")]
        private var MiniImage:Class;

        // TextField
        private var tfInfo:TextField;

        // Constants
        private const VIEWPORT_WIDTH:int = 480;
        private const VIEWPORT_HEIGHT:int = 800;
        private const IMG_WIDTH:uint = 1000;
        private const IMG_HEIGHT:uint = 760;

        /**
         * Constructor
         *
         */
        public function VanillaApp()
        {
            super();

            // Format TextField
            var tf:TextFormat = new TextFormat();
            tf.color = 0xffffff;
            tf.font = "Helvetica";
            tf.bold = true;
```

continues

LISTING 3-1 *(continued)*

```
        tf.size = 20;

        // Create TextField
        tfInfo = new TextField();
        tfInfo.width = 470;
        tfInfo.defaultTextFormat = tf;
        tfInfo.x = 2;
        tfInfo.y = 20;
        tfInfo.selectable = false;
        tfInfo.text = "Welcome to VanillaApp. Zoom or pan to begin.";
        addChild(tfInfo);

        // Create bitmap
        var bitmap:Bitmap = new MiniImage();
        bitmap.smoothing = true;

        // Create sprite container for image
        var sprite:Sprite = new Sprite();
        sprite.addChild(bitmap);

        // Scaling and positioning
        var fx:Number = VIEWPORT_WIDTH / IMG_WIDTH;
        sprite.scaleX = fx;
        sprite.scaleY = fx;
        sprite.x = VIEWPORT_WIDTH / 2;
        sprite.y = VIEWPORT_HEIGHT / 2;
        bitmap.x = (IMG_WIDTH - (IMG_WIDTH / 2)) * -1;
        bitmap.y = (IMG_HEIGHT - (IMG_HEIGHT / 2)) *-1;

        addChild(sprite);

        // Set input mode
        Multitouch.inputMode = MultitouchInputMode.GESTURE;

        // Assign event handlers
        sprite.addEventListener(TransformGestureEvent.GESTURE_ZOOM,
zoomHandler);
        sprite.addEventListener(TransformGestureEvent.GESTURE_PAN, panHandler);
        //sprite.addEventListener(TouchEvent.TOUCH_TAP, touchTapHandler);

    }

    /**
     * Handler for Zoom events
     *
     * @param event
     *
     */
    private function zoomHandler(event:TransformGestureEvent):void
    {
        tfInfo.text = "Zoom event";

        var sprite:Sprite = event.target as Sprite;
```

```
        sprite.scaleX *= event.scaleX;
        sprite.scaleY *= event.scaleY;
    }

    /**
     * Handler for Pan events
     *
     * @param event
     *
     */
    private function panHandler(event:TransformGestureEvent):void
    {
        tfInfo.text = "Pan event";

        var sprite:Sprite = event.target as Sprite;
        sprite.x += event.offsetX;
        sprite.y += event.offsetY;

    }
  }
}
```

Adding Icons

As you'd expect, every Android application is represented on the Android device itself with an icon. An icon set for an app follows these rules and conventions:

- ➤ Images are in PNG format.

- ➤ The icon set is a set of image files of three different sizes: 36×36, 48×48, and 72×72. The 36×36 image is displayed on low-density displays, the 48×48 on medium-density devices, and the 72×72 icon is used for high-density devices.

- ➤ Icon images are usually placed in an `icons` or `assets` subdirectory of the project.

- ➤ Image files are specified as icons in the Android Settings dialog box (or in the application descriptor XML file).

For `VanillaApp`, I mocked up a quick set of icons using Photoshop. I then saved the same PNG image in three different sizes using the following names: `36x36.png`, `48x48.png`, and `72x72.png`.

If you don't define a set of icons, Flash CS5 supplies a default icon set automatically.

Now that all your images are created and in the right place, you need to assign them to your Android applications by adding them to the Android OS Settings.

Defining Android Settings

Your final step before compiling is to configure the Android-related settings for the application. To do so, you need to have the `.fla` document active in the Flash CS5 IDE, so click the tab corresponding to that file. Next, in the Properties panel, click the Edit button next to Android OS Settings (or choose File ➪ Android OS Settings from the menu). The Android Settings dialog box is displayed, as shown in Figure 3-4.

There are several configuration settings to make across the three tabs of the dialog box.

You can also make these settings manually by editing the application descriptor XML file (named `VanillaApp-app.xml` for the sample app). See Appendix A for more details on the application descriptor file.

General Settings

Edit the settings in the General tab (see Figure 3-4) as described here:

➤ **Output File** — Gives you the option to specify the location of the compiled `.apk` file. If you don't specify, the `.apk` is created in the root project directory. My personal preference is to place it in a `build` subdirectory.

➤ **App Name** — Enter the name of your app; Flash supplies a suggested name in the box already. This is the name that Android displays.

➤ **App ID** — Provide the App ID that you want to use to uniquely identify your application.

➤ **Version** — Enter the version number of your app. Flash automatically supplies `1.0` for you. The format should adhere to the *xx[.xx[.xx]]* format, where *x* is a digit 0–9. Subversions inside the brackets are optional.

➤ **Version label** — Optionally add a label to your version, such as `Alpha` or `Beta`.

➤ **Aspect Ratio** — Indicates the aspect ratio (portrait or landscape) of the app on startup.

`VanillaApp` is designed as a portrait app, so leave the default portrait as is.

➤ **Full Screen** — Indicates whether to launch the app in full screen or whether to show the Android status bar at the top of the screen. I left this unchecked.

➤ **Auto Orientation** — Specifies whether your app automatically reorients the aspect ratio when the user shifts the Android device into landscape or portrait mode.

If `VanillaApp` were more sophisticated, I'd implement orientation. However, at this point, I will simply leave it unchecked. Therefore, no reorientation is made when a user shifts the Android device to landscape mode.

➤ **Included Files** — Use this location to add any additional resource files that your app needs to include inside the `.apk` file. Your project's `.swf` and application descriptor file (*myapp*-app `.xml`) are automatically added to the Included Files list. You don't need **to** include the `mini.jpg` image because it is embedded into the application at compile time.

Deployment Settings

When you click the Deployment tab (see Figure 3-5), you see the following settings displayed:

➤ **Certificate** — Enter the location of the `.p12` certificate file that you created in Chapter 2.

➤ **Password** — Supply the password for the `.p12` file here. I recommend clicking the Remember Password for This Session check box to save you from re-entering the password multiple times during a debugging session.

FIGURE 3-4

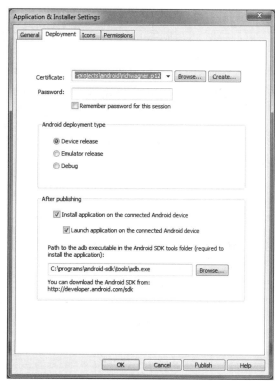

FIGURE 3-5

➤ **Android Deployment Type** — Used to indicate the type of deployment to make:

➤ **Device release** — Use if you want to create a release-ready version or want to preview what the release version will look like. I'm selecting this option for `VanilaApp` at this time.

➤ **Emulator release** — Use if you want to create a version for the desktop Android emulator.

➤ **Debug** — Use if you want to debug your app. When this option is selected, Flash debugger can receive `trace()` commands from the app.

➤ **Install Application on the Connected Android Device** — Check this box to have Flash automatically install the application after compilation.

➤ **Launch Application on the Connected Android Device** — Check this box to have automatically launch the application to begin testing.

➤ **Path to adb.exe** — Enter the path of the `adb.exe`, which is located in the tools subdirectory in your Android SDK directory. This is required to install the app onto the device.

Icons Settings

The Icons tab (see Figure 3-6) allows you to specify which icons to use in your app. Select the appropriate size icon at the top, and then provide the location of the corresponding `.png` file in the middle text box.

Permissions

The final tab (see Figure 3-7) is used to specify certain permissions that you need your app to request to make for accessing certain parts of the Android device, such as the Camera or Geolocator. The user will then need to grant your app permission during the installation process.

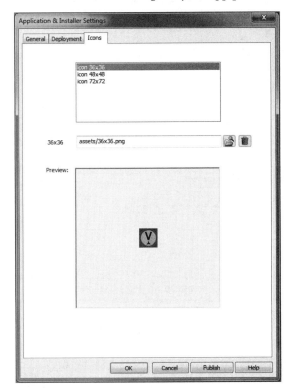

FIGURE 3-6

FIGURE 3-7

For this app, you don't need to ask for special permission, so you can leave them all unchecked.

Click OK to save your changes.

Previewing the App inside Flash

Before publishing and installing your app on your Android, you can preview it inside Flash CS5 by using the familiar Control ⇨ Test Movie or Debug ⇨ Debug Movie commands. Flash enables you to test or debug the app in the AIR Debug Launcher (Mobile) window.

However, don't confuse this preview capability with an Android simulator. Unless your development machine supports multitouch input, you can't simulate Android-specific events or capabilities. Therefore, exactly how useful the mobile AIR Debug Launcher is depends on the nature of your app. In the case of VanillaApp (see Figure 3-8), the preview provides a good way to check for obvious errors, but it does not allow you to test the zoom and pan multitouch event handling. You have to wait and test that on the Android device or in the Android emulator (discussed in Chapter 13).

Publishing and Installing the Application

You are now ready to publish and compile the Flash project into an .apk file that you can use on the Android. (If you'd like to know more about the compilation process, check out Chapter 1.) To do so, choose File ⇨ Publish from the menu (or click the Publish button if you are inside the Android Settings dialog box)

The compilation process takes a few moments to complete. When you're done, an .apk file is created in the outgoing location that you specified in the Android Settings dialog box. If you checked the Install and Launch on Device options, your app launches on your Android device.

Running the App on an Android Device

You're now ready to test the app on the device itself. The app is shown in Figure 3-9.

FIGURE 3-8

FIGURE 3-9

You can perform zoom and pan operations using your fingers, as shown in Figures 3-10 and 3-11.

FIGURE 3-10

FIGURE 3-11

You can also exit out of the app itself and go to the main screen to view the app icon in the application listings (see Figure 3-12).

VANILLAAPP FOR IOS

In this section, I'll walk you through the process of building a basic HelloWorld-style application for iOS. It's quite similar to the Android version, but is customized for the iPhone.

To create VanillaApp for iOS, you perform the following steps:

1. Create a project.
2. Create a `.fla` file.

3. Create an `ActionScript` document class.

4. Write the application code.

5. Add a splash screen.

6. Create application icons.

7. Define iPhone settings.

8. Publish the file.

9. Install the app on an iPhone.

VanillaApp is displayed among all your other apps.

FIGURE 3-12

Creating a Project

Begin by creating a new Flash project. Working within a project is not essential, particularly with a small app such as this one. However, I recommend it as standard practice because it enables you to more easily manage your files.

1. From the Welcome screen, click the Flash Project under the Create New list. (Or, choose File ⇨ New from the menu and select Flash Project from the list.)

   The Project panel is displayed.

2. Click the Projects combo box and select the New Project item from the list.

   The Create New Project dialog is displayed, as shown in Figure 3-13.

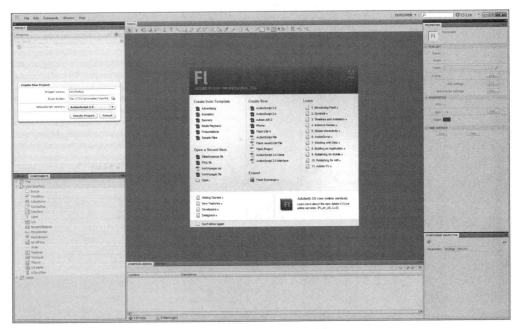

FIGURE 3-13

3. Enter **VanillaApp** in the Project name field.

4. Specify a folder in the Root folder field. I am using d:\iphonedev\VanillaApp.

5. Keep ActionScript 3.0 as the default ActionScript version.

6. Click Create Project.

The new blank VanillaApp project is created and ready for use, as shown in Figure 3-14.

With your Flash project set, you can now begin to add content to it.

FIGURE 3-14

Creating an iPhone-Based Flash Document

When you create a Flash document (.fla) file, you'll want to create it to have the publishing settings configured for iPhone deployment. To do so:

1. From the Welcome screen, click iPhone under the Create New list. (Or, choose File ⇨ New from the menu and select Flash Project from the list.)

The untitled.fla is created and displayed in the Flash window.

2. Using File ⇨ Save, save the document as VanillaApp.fla into your project's root directory.

When the Project panel refreshes, the .fla will show up.

Since this is an ActionScript project, you won't be doing anything more to the .fla document or its timeline. But you'll want to keep it open in the Flash CS5 editor to give you access to the commands you'll need through the Properties panel.

Creating an ActionScript Document Class

Because VanillaApp is an ActionScript project, your next step is to create an ActionScript document class. In Flash, the *document class* serves as the command and control center for the application. The document class is also the first code executed when the app is launched. (If you're a Flex developer, think of the document class as equivalent to a Flex project's primary .mxml file, the one that contains mx:Application or mx:WindowedApplication).

To create a document class, you perform these actions:

1. Select the stage of the VanillaApp.fla document.

2. Press Ctrl+F3 (Windows) or Cmd+F3 (Mac OS X) to activate your Properties panel (if it is not already visible).

3. In the Properties panel, type the name of the class in the Document edit box.

   For this example, enter **VanillaApp**. Although the document class can be any name you wish, it's often helpful to use the same name as the .fla file or something similar, such as VanillaAppClass.

> *Whatever you decide to name it, keep in mind that by convention* ActionScript *class names should be camel case.*

4. Click the pencil icon to edit the class definition.

5. In the Edit ActionScript 3.0 Class dialog box, select the application in which you wish to edit the class.

   ➤ Selecting Flash Professional opens up the editor inside of the existing Flash environment.

   ➤ Selecting Flash Builder allows you to open up the Flash Builder IDE. If you are a Flex developer or simply want a powerful editor, you'll definitely prefer this option for larger projects.

   Since this is a small app, choose Flash Professional and click OK.

   The shell of the VanillaApp class is created and displayed in the document window as shown in Figure 3-15.

6. Choose File ⇨ Save to save the file as **VanillaApp.as**.

   Make sure you save it in the same directory as the .fla document.

Coding the Document Class

When Flash creates the document class, it provides the shell class structure, such as the code shown here:

```
package   {

    import flash.display.MovieClip;


    public class VanillaApp extends MovieClip
```

```
        {


            public function VanillaApp() {
                // constructor code
            }
        }


    }
```

Code snippet VanillaApp.as

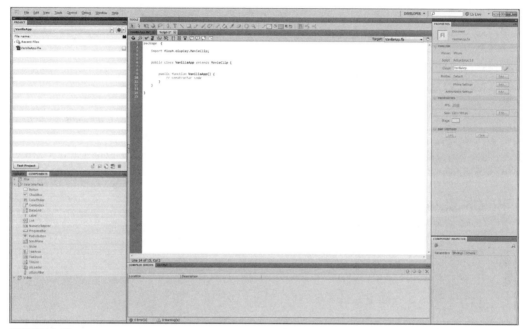

FIGURE 3-15

The `VanillaApp` class is contained inside of the default package and is a subclass of `MovieClip`. A document class needs to either extend `MovieClip` or `Sprite`. Use `MovieClip` if you need to do anything involving the timeline, such as animations. Or, if you just need an ordinary base class, you can use `Sprite`, which requires less memory overhead.

Define Class Properties

Your first step is to define two class properties and four class constants that you'll be using in the document class. The most significant is a reference to an external file named `Mini.jpg`. Using the `[Embed]` metadata declarative, you can define a class reference as follows:

```
[Embed(source="Mini.jpg")]
private var MiniImage:Class;
```

Code snippet VanillaApp.as

The [Embed] tag is used by the compiler to embed the file named Mini.jpg into the app and associate it with the MiniImage variable.

Note that the [Embed] metadata tag requires the Flex SDK. As a result, when you first publish the app, Flash CS5 prompts you to the Flex SDK path to the library path of your project.

If you have Flex installed on your computer, simply provide your existing Flex SDK directory. Or, if you don't have the Flex SDK, it's a free download at http://opensource.adobe.com/wiki/display/flexsdk/Downloads.

In addition, you must define the following property and constants:

Available for
download on
Wrox.com

```
// TextField
private var tfInfo:TextField;

// Constants
private const VIEWPORT_WIDTH:int = 320;
private const VIEWPORT_HEIGHT:int = 480;
private const IMG_WIDTH:uint = 1000;
private const IMG_HEIGHT:uint = 760;
```

Code snippet VanillaApp.as

The txInfo property is the TextField you use in the app. The constants are height and width values for the iPhone viewport and the image.

Write the Constructor

For VanillaApp, you create the following display objects in the constructor:

➤ TextField to provide information text

➤ Bitmap to display the external image file

➤ Sprite that contains the bitmap

The TextField receives its formatting rules from the TextFormat class. So, begin by creating the TextFormat instance and providing formatting assignments:

Available for
download on
Wrox.com

```
// Format text field
var tf:TextFormat = new TextFormat();
tf.color = 0xffffff;
tf.font = "Helvetica";
tf.bold = true;
tf.size = 14;
```

Code snippet VanillaApp.as

When you create the TextField, assign tf as its defaultTextFormat. Also specify basic width, dimensions, and starter text:

Available for
download on
Wrox.com

```
// Create textfield
tfInfo = new TextField();
tfInfo.width = 310;
tfInfo.defaultTextFormat = tf;
```

```
tfInfo.x = 2;
tfInfo.y = 20;
tfInfo.selectable = false;
tfInfo.text = "Welcome to VanillaApp. Zoom or pan to begin.";
```

Code snippet VanillaApp.as

Add the `tfInfo` instance to the stage using `addChild()`:

```
addChild(tfInfo);
```

Although you already defined the image class that references the external image, you need to instantiate an instance of it by performing the following:

```
var bitmap:Bitmap = new MiniImage();
```

Code snippet VanillaApp.as

Because the app will allow panning and zooming of the image, you prevent choppy image movements by using smoothing:

```
bitmap.smoothing = true;
```

Code snippet VanillaApp.as

A `Sprite` instance is used as a container for the image, which will be responsible for dispatching the zoom and pan events. You create it as a local variable named `sprite`, add `bitmap` variable as its child, and add it to the stage:

```
// Create sprite container for image
var sprite:Sprite = new Sprite();
sprite.addChild(bitmap);
addChild(sprite)
```

Code note VanillaApp.as

Inside of the constructor, you set up the dimensions, positioning, and scaling of sprite and bitmap:

```
// Scaling and positioning
var fx:Number = VIEWPORT_WIDTH / IMG_WIDTH;
sprite.scaleX = fx;
sprite.scaleY = fx;
sprite.x = VIEWPORT_WIDTH / 2;
sprite.y = VIEWPORT_HEIGHT / 2;
bitmap.x = (IMG_WIDTH - (IMG_WIDTH / 2)) * -1;
bitmap.y = (IMG_HEIGHT - (IMG_HEIGHT / 2)) *-1;
```

Coed snippet VanillaApp.as

In this code, `sprite` is scaled based on the relative width of the viewport and image and is positioned. The `bitmap` variable is then positioned inside of `sprite` so that it is displayed in the middle of the viewport.

The final task you need to perform in the constructor is to set up the application for responding to multitouch events. You begin by specifying the `Multitouch.inputMode`:

```
Multitouch.inputMode = MultitouchInputMode.GESTURE;
```

Code snippet VanillaApp.as

This property is used to specify the type of touch and gesture events that you want to process. By specifying `MultitouchInputMode.GESTURE` (the default, by the way), you tell the app to dispatch touch events with multiple points of contact, which is what is needed to work with zooming and panning.

You then assign listeners to the zoom and pan multitouch events that are dispatched by `sprite`:

```
// Assign event handlers
sprite.addEventListener(TransformGestureEvent.GESTURE_ZOOM, zoomHandler);
sprite.addEventListener(TransformGestureEvent.GESTURE_PAN, panHandler);
```

Code snippet VanillaApp.as

You can see the full constructor code in Listing 3-2.

Defining Event Handlers

You need to define event handlers to respond to the zoom and pan events. The `zoomHandler()` method is used to handle zoom events:

```
private function zoomHandler(event:TransformGestureEvent):void
{
    tfInfo.text = "Zoom event";

    var sprite:Sprite = event.target as Sprite;
    sprite.scaleX *= event.scaleX;
    sprite.scaleY *= event.scaleY;
}
```

Code snippet VanillaApp.as

In this code, the `tfInfo` text is updated. The `Sprite` instance is then scaled by multiplying the existing scale by the new scale values provided by the event.

The `panHandler()` method is used to handle pan events:

```
private function panHandler(event:TransformGestureEvent):void
{
    tfInfo.text = "Pan event";

    var sprite:Sprite = event.target as Sprite;
    sprite.x += event.offsetX;
    sprite.y += event.offsetY;

}
```

Code snippet VanillaApp.as

This code changes the x, y position of the Sprite by adding its current position with the offsetX and offsetY properties of the event.

Go ahead and save changes to the VanillaApp.as file.

The full code for the document class is provided in Listing 3-2.

LISTING 3-2: VanillaApp.as

```
package
{
    import flash.display.Bitmap;
    import flash.display.MovieClip;
    import flash.display.Sprite;
    import flash.events.TouchEvent;
    import flash.events.TransformGestureEvent;
    import flash.geom.Matrix;
    import flash.text.TextField;
    import flash.text.TextFormat;
    import flash.ui.Multitouch;
    import flash.ui.MultitouchInputMode;

    /**
     * Document class for VanillaApp application.
     * Sample application
     *
     * @author Rich Wagner
     *
     */
    public class VanillaApp extends MovieClip
    {

        // External image
        [Embed(source="Mini.jpg")]
        private var MiniImage:Class;

        // TextField
        private var tfInfo:TextField;

        // Constants
        private const VIEWPORT_WIDTH:int = 320;
        private const VIEWPORT_HEIGHT:int = 480;
        private const IMG_WIDTH:uint = 1000;
        private const IMG_HEIGHT:uint = 760;

        /**
         * Constructor
         *
         */
        public function VanillaApp()
        {
```

continues

LISTING 3-2 *(continued)*

```
super();

                // Format text field
                var tf:TextFormat = new TextFormat();
                tf.color = 0xffffff;
                tf.font = "Helvetica";
                tf.bold = true;
                tf.size = 14;

                // Create textfield
                tfInfo = new TextField();
                tfInfo.width = 310;
                tfInfo.defaultTextFormat = tf;
                tfInfo.x = 2;
                tfInfo.y = 20;
                tfInfo.selectable = false;
                tfInfo.text = "Welcome to VanillaApp. Zoom or pan to begin.";
                addChild(tfInfo);

                // Create bitmap
                var bitmap:Bitmap = new MiniImage();
                bitmap.smoothing = true;

                // Create sprite container for image
                var sprite:Sprite = new Sprite();
                sprite.addChild(bitmap);

                // Scaling and positioning
                var fx:Number = VIEWPORT_WIDTH / IMG_WIDTH;
                sprite.scaleX = fx;
                sprite.scaleY = fx;
                sprite.x = VIEWPORT_WIDTH / 2;
                sprite.y = VIEWPORT_HEIGHT / 2;
                bitmap.x = (IMG_WIDTH - (IMG_WIDTH / 2)) * -1;
                bitmap.y = (IMG_HEIGHT - (IMG_HEIGHT / 2)) *-1;

                addChild(sprite);

                // Set input mode
                Multitouch.inputMode = MultitouchInputMode.GESTURE;

                // Assign event handlers
                sprite.addEventListener(TransformGestureEvent.GESTURE_ZOOM,
                    zoomHandler);
                sprite.addEventListener(TransformGestureEvent.GESTURE_PAN, panHandler);
                //sprite.addEventListener(TouchEvent.TOUCH_TAP, touchTapHandler);

        }

        /**
         * Handler for Zoom events
         *
```

```
     * @param event
     *
     */
    private function zoomHandler(event:TransformGestureEvent):void
    {
        tfInfo.text = "Zoom event";

        var sprite:Sprite = event.target as Sprite;
        sprite.scaleX *= event.scaleX;
        sprite.scaleY *= event.scaleY;
    }

    /**
     * Handler for Pan events
     *
     * @param event
     *
     */
    private function panHandler(event:TransformGestureEvent):void
    {
        tfInfo.text = "Pan event";

        var sprite:Sprite = event.target as Sprite;
        sprite.x += event.offsetX;
        sprite.y += event.offsetY;

    }
  }
}
```

Creating a Splash Screen

A standard component of an iPhone application is an opening splash screen that the app displays during the loading process. There are some basic conventions for the initial image you plan to use:

➤ The image must be 320px by 480px. The orientation of the splash screen should match the default orientation of your app.

➤ The image must be in PNG format during development/testing and in JPG format when you submit your app to the App Store.

➤ The image must be named Default.png (testing) and Default.jpg (App Store submission). Note that the filename is case sensitive.

➤ The image must be located in the root project directory (the same folder in which the .fla is located).

➤ The image must be added as an include file for the project.

If you have a Default.png file in the project directory, then it is displayed automatically during loading. Unlike AIR apps, you don't need to explicitly code the splash screen display. That's all taken care of for you.

You can choose any image you want: a blank image, a screen-shot of your running app, or a customized logo and graphic you create yourself. For `VanillaApp`, I created a simple splash screen in Photoshop (see Figure 3-16).

After you add the `Default.png` to the project directory, you need to add this file to the Included File list in the iPhone Settings dialog box. See the "Defining iPhone Settings" section later in this chapter for more details.

Adding Icons

Every iPhone application is represented in iTunes and on the iPhone itself with an icon. An icon set for an app follows these conventions:

FIGURE 3-16

> ➤ Images are in PNG format.

> ➤ The icon set is a set of image files of three different sizes: 29×29, 56×56, and 512×512. The 29×29 image is displayed on the iPhone, the 56×56 image is used by iTunes, and the 512×512 icon is used for testing only.

> ➤ When you submit the app to the App Store, the 512×512 image is provided separately as a JPG file (not PNG).

> ➤ Glassy glare effects are automatically added by the iPhone OS when it prerenders it, so keep the source image flat for best effect.

> ➤ Icon images are usually placed in an `icons` or `assets` subdirectory of the project.

> ➤ Image files are specified as icons in the iPhone Settings dialog box.

For `VanillaApp`, I mocked up a quick set of icons using Photoshop. I then saved the same PNG image in the three different sizes using the following names: 29×29.png, 56×56.png, and 512×512 .png. The set is shown in Figure 3-17.

If you don't define a set of icons, Flash CS5 supplies a default icon set.

You need to assign the files you created in the iPhone Settings dialog box. See the "Defining iPhone Settings" next for more details.

Defining iPhone Settings

Your final step before compiling is to configure the iPhone-related settings for the application. To do so, you'll need to have the `.fla` document active in the Flash CS5 IDE. Next, in the Properties panel, click the Edit button next to iPhone Settings (or choose File ➪ iPhone Settings from the menu). The iPhone Settings dialog box is displayed, as shown in Figure 3-18.

FIGURE 3-17

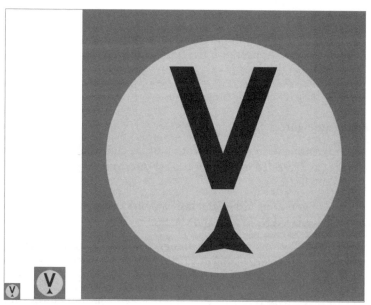

FIGURE 3-18

You can make several configuration settings on the dialog's box's three tabs.

These settings can also be made manually by editing the application descriptor xml file (named VanillaApp-app.xml for the sample app). See Appendix B for more details on the application descriptor file.

General Settings

Edit the settings in the General tab (see Figure 3-18) as shown here:

➤ **Output File** — Allows you to optionally specify the location of the compiled .ipa file. If you don't specify otherwise, the .ipa is created in the root project directory. My personal preference is to place it in a build subdirectory.

➤ **App Name** — Enter the name of your app, although Flash supplies the suggested name in the box already. This is the name displayed by iPhone and iTunes.

➤ **Version** — Enter the version number of your app. Flash automatically supplies 1.0 for you. The format should adhere to the *xx[.xx[.xx]]* format where *x* is a digit 0-9. Subversions inside of the brackets are optional.

➤ **Aspect Ratio** — Indicates the aspect ratio (portrait or landscape) of the app on startup.

VanillaApp is designed as a portrait app, so leave the default portrait as is.

➤ **Full Screen** — Indicates whether to launch the app in full screen or whether to show the iPhone status bar at the top of the screen. I left this unchecked.

➤ **Auto Orientation** — Specifies whether to have your app automatically reorient the aspect ratio when the user shifts the iPhone device into landscape or portrait mode.

If VanillaApp were more sophisticated, I'd implement orientation. However, at this point, I will simply leave it unchecked. Therefore, no reorientation is made when a user shifts the iPhone device to landscape mode.

➤ **Rendering** — Select the way in which display objects are rendered:

➤ If you choose CPU, the CPU is used for this task, and no hardware acceleration is utilized.

➤ If you choose GPU, the iPhone uses the GPU for rendering bitmaps.

➤ If you choose Auto, Flash examines your app and uses the best rendering mode for your app.

Given the nature of this app, I am selecting GPU. (Try compiling the app with both and you'll definitely notice the difference that hardware acceleration can make with bitmap rendering.) See Chapter 5 for more information on CPU vs. GPU rendering.

➤ **Included Files** — Use this location to add any resource files that your app needs to include inside of the .ipa file. Your project's .swf and application descriptor file (myapp-app.xml) are automatically added to the Included Files list.

If you have a `Default.png` file to be used as the opening splash screen, be sure to add the file here. If you don't, the initial image is ignored.

Deployment Settings

When you click the Deployment tab (shown in Figure 3-19), the following settings are displayed:

➤ **iPhone Digital Certificate** — Enter the location of the `.p12` file that you created back in Chapter 2.

➤ **Password** — Supply the password for the `.p12` file here. I recommend clicking the Remember password for this session check box to save you from re-entering the password multiple times during a debugging session.

➤ **Provisioning Profile** — Enter the location of the `.mobileprovision` file that you downloaded from the iPhone Dev Center back in Chapter 2.

➤ **App ID** — Provide the App ID that you wish to use to uniquely identify your application.

If you specified a wildcard ID back in Chapter 2, then add the Bundle Seed ID (the alphanumeric string before the `.*`) followed by your app name. For example, my App ID for `VanillaApp` is `5XS34A1JDN.VanillaApp`.

FIGURE 3-19

If your provisioning file is tied to a specific App ID, Flash automatically adds this ID into this box and won't allow you to modify it.

➤ **iPhone Deployment Type** — Used to indicate the type of deployment you wish to make:

➤ Use Quick Publishing for Device Testing for quick and easy testing purposes. Select this option for `VanilaApp` at this time.

➤ Use Quick Publishing for Device Debugging to debug your app. When this option is selected, Flash debugger can receive `trace()` commands from the app.

➤ Use Deployment - Ad Hoc to create an application for non-App Store deployment.

➤ Use Deployment - Apple App Store to prepare an `.ipa` for submittal to the App Store.

Icons Settings

The final Icons tab (shown in Figure 3-20) allows you to specify the icons to use in your app. Select the appropriate size icon at the top and then provide the location of the corresponding `.png` file in the middle text box.

Click OK to save your changes.

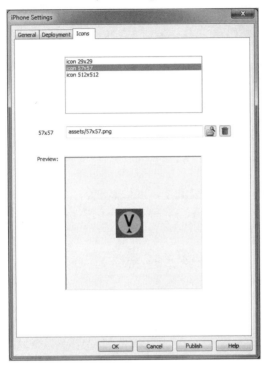

FIGURE 3-20

FIGURE 3-21

Previewing the App inside Flash

Before publishing and installing your app on your iPhone, you can preview it inside of Flash CS5 by using the familiar Control ➪ Test Movie or Debug ➪ Debug Movie commands. Flash enables you to test or debug the app in the AIR Debug Launcher (Mobile) window.

However, don't confuse this preview capability with an iPhone simulator. You can't simulate iPhone-specific events or capabilities. Therefore, exactly how useful the mobile AIR Debug Launcher is depends on the nature of your app. In the case of VanillaApp (see Figure 3-21), the preview provides a good way to check for obvious errors, but it does not allow you to test zoom and pan multitouch event handling. You have to wait and test that on the iPhone itself.

Publishing the Application

You are now ready to publish and compile the Flash project into an .ipa file ready for use on the iPhone. (If you'd like to know more about the compilation process, check out Chapter 1.) To do so, choose File ➪ Publish from the menu (or click the Publish button if you are inside of the iPhone Settings dialog box).

The compilation process will take several minutes to complete. When done, an .ipa file is created in the outgoing location that you specified in the iPhone Settings dialog box.

Installing the App on an iPhone

Your final step is to take the `.ipa` file and install it onto the iPhone. To do so, perform the following steps:

1. Drag and drop the `.ipa` file onto your iTunes window.

iTunes will accept the drop operation only if you drag the file over the Library tree or onto the Applications view if that is active. Figure 3-22 shows `VanillaApp` displayed in among other apps.

VanillaApp icon

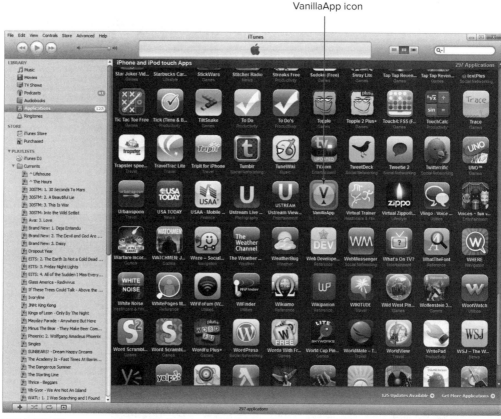

FIGURE 3-22

2. With your iPhone connected to your computer, select the Applications tab of your iPhone configuration window in iTunes (see Figure 3-23).

3. If it is not already selected, check the Sync Applications check box.

4. Find `VanillaApp` in the applications list and make sure its Sync check box is selected.

5. Click the Sync button. Your newly added app will be copied over to your iPhone

The `VanillaApp` icon will be displayed at the next available slot on the iPhone home screen, as shown in Figure 3-24.

You can now launch `VanillaApp` (see Figures 3-25 and 3-26) and perform zoom and pan operations using your fingers (as shown in Figures 3-27 and 3-28).

FIGURE 3-23

FIGURE 3-24

FIGURE 3-25

FIGURE 3-26

FIGURE 3-27

FIGURE 3-28

SUMMARY

In this chapter, you read about how to build and deploy your first mobile app using Flash Professional. I began by showing you how to create a Flash document for Android or iPhone and create an AS3 document class for the app. I then walked through the basics of coding the document class to provide some basic functionality. Finally, you discovered how to publish and install the apps onto both devices.

PART II
Touch and User Interaction

Rethinking ActionScript Programming

Flash and Flex developers have been working with ActionScript for years now and have created a storehouse of ActionScript 3 (AS3) programming techniques and open-source code libraries. However, when it comes to developing applications for Android and iOS mobile devices, it helps to borrow the old 90s Apple slogan: *Think Different.* When you develop for the Web or desktop environments, you don't have to be overly concerned about CPU resources or memory constraints.

That's not so with smaller mobile devices. Although the latest iPhone and Android offerings feature faster and faster processors and greater amounts of RAM, their capacities remain small compared to desktop varieties. As a result, to create an app that performs well, you need to think different when it comes to your programming techniques and application architecture.

This chapter walks you through key issues to think about as you develop your apps.

CONSERVING MEMORY AND CPU RESOURCES

The tips and techniques that you work with in this chapter deal with minimizing both the memory and the CPU resources that your apps use. Unfortunately, these two objectives can be at odds with each other. As you'll see, sometimes when you take a step to decrease memory, you strain the CPU and vice versa.

One of the common questions that mobile AS3 developers ask is this: which should I be more concerned about — memory or CPU resources? For better or worse, this is not a simple yes or no question. It depends entirely on the nature of the app. However, truth be told, when the performance of your app is key, it's better to conserve CPU resources than to conserve memory.

ACTIONSCRIPT PRACTICES

When you code in AS3, you need to keep in mind several key principles.

Reuse Objects

Perhaps the single most important AS3 tip is to be sure to reuse objects rather than creating and removing them. Any time you instantiate an object, it is expensive, making object reuse far more efficient.

If your app requires you to constantly create objects and dispose of them, consider using an object pool. When you create an object pool, you create a batch of objects when your app launches. Rather than creating new instances, your app then requests objects from the pool and uses them. When the app is done with these instances, it deactivates and removes references to them, but it doesn't set them equal to null. This technique puts the object back into the pool, making it available for reuse later.

Listing 4-1 shows a sample pool that you could use to reuse Feed objects in an RSS app you are creating.

LISTING 4-1: FeedPool.as

```
{
   import com.richwagner.feeds.Feed;

   public final class FeedPool
   {
      private static var _pool:Vector.<Feed>;
      private static var _maxCount:int;
      private static var _counter:int;
      private static var _growthValue:int;

      public static function init(initialCount:int, growthValue:int):void
      {
         var i:int = initialCount;

         // Assign initial values to properties
         _maxCount = initialCount;
         _counter = initialCount;
         _growthValue = growthValue;

         // Create pool
         _pool = new Vector.<Feed>(initialCount);

         // Create Feed instances based on maxCount param
         while( --i >= 0 )
         {
```

```
      pool[i] = new Feed();
    }
  }


  public static function getFeed():Feed
  {
    var i:int = _growthValue;

    if ( _counter > 0 )
    {
      return = pool[--_counter];
    }

    while( --i >= 0 )
    {
      pool.unshift ( new Feed() );
    }

    _counter = _growthValue;

    return getFeed();
  }

  public static function disposeFeed(feed:Feed):void
  {
    pool[_counter++] = feed;
  }

  }
}
```

General Tips for Working with AS3

The following are general AS3 tips to consider:

➤   Always use the most efficient data type possible when working with variables. A Number is less efficient than uint or int, and a Vector is preferred over an Array.

➤   For string searching and management, use string methods (such as indexOf()) rather than working with less efficient regular expressions.

➤   When you do need to create objects, try to create them outside of loops.

➤   Referencing an object using square brackets slows performance. Therefore, notice the multiple references using square brackets in the for loop here:

```
public processFeeds(feeds:Vector.<Feed>):void
{

  var feed:Feed;
  var count:int = feeds.length;

  for (var i:int=0; i<count; i++)
  {
```

```
        feeds[i].name = "RSSFeed1";
        feeds[i].url = "www.myfeed.com/rss"
        feeds[i].fetch();
    }
}
```

A more efficient way to write would be as follows:

```
public processFeeds(feeds:Vector.<Feed>):void
{

  var feed:Feed;
  var count:int = feeds.length;

  for (var i:int=0; i<count; i++)
  {
    feed = feeds[i];
    feed.name = "RSSFeed1";
    feed.url = "www.myfeed.com/rss"
    feed.fetch();
  }
}
```

➤ When you are working with loops, avoid evaluations when possible. A common issue would be when you are iterating through an array and you use this:

```
for (var i:int=0; i<feeds.length; i++)
{
    // loop
}
```

Instead, a more efficient way would be to assign the value of the evaluation first to a local variable, and then use that variable in the loop:

```
var count:int = feeds.length;
for (var i:int=0; i<count; i++)
{
    // loop
}
```

➤ Function calls are more expensive than placing all or the majority of your code in one procedural unit. Minimizing functions improves speeds significantly in certain cases, but it comes at a significant cost from a code architecture and maintainability standpoint. But if you are struggling with performance and have tried everything else, function calls are your panic button.

➤ Be careful with any kind of timer activity you want to perform. Timers are acceptable for nonanimated apps in which the increment for the timer is fairly long. For animated apps, consider attaching a listener to the Event.ENTER_FRAME event, which is dispatched for every new frame.

However, timers do consume more CPU cycles than attaching a listener to an ENTER_FRAME event, so be prudent in their usage, especially if the timer increment is less than 100 ms. If you have to use a timer, use a centralized one for all your app's time-related tasks.

➤ Keep in mind that asynchronous operations (for example, for file or database access) are preferred over synchronous operations for performance, or at least perceived performance.

➤ Avoid using large AS3 code libraries that, despite adding functionality, add bloat to your code base.

Event Handling

Use these tips to handle events more efficiently:

➤ Use `removeEventListener()` to free event handlers that you no longer need.

➤ Consider using a callback rather than a normal event to bypass the event model and all its event bubbling. If you don't need events to propagate throughout the event model, call `Event.stopPropagation` in your listener.

UI PRACTICES

Consider each of the following tips related to the UI:

➤ In general, use the least expensive display object that you need for a job. For general purposes, developers often choose between a `MovieClip` and a `Sprite` object. `Sprite` takes less memory, so if you don't need to animate or work with the timeline, use it. Otherwise, use the `MovieClip` class.

➤ If you are drawing something that doesn't require interaction, use a `Shape` object, which is much less expensive than a `Sprite` or `MovieClip`.

➤ Each visible display object impacts performance. If you don't need an object, make it invisible or remove it.

➤ Avoid filters, blends, and other effects. As tempting as they may be to use, they double the size required to render a display object. Instead, put your creativity hat on and figure out how to achieve the same effect you want to achieve using something else more efficient.

➤ If you don't need touch interaction with a display object, consider disabling its mouse input to save on event bubbling. To do so, set its `mouseChildren` and `mouseEnabled` properties to `false`.

➤ Although motion tweens are perfectly acceptable for normal desktop-based Flash tasks, avoid them in your mobile apps. They consume a lot of CPU resources.

➤ When you need to add text, consider using the `TextLine` object, which is the best object Flash has for rendering read-only text. If you need to have user input, you can use `TextField`.

➤ When assigning text to a `TextField` object, using `appendText()` is actually more efficient than assigning a value to its `text` property.

➤ Avoid assigning a `TextField`'s `text` property inside a loop. Instead, assign the value to a string variable, and then assign it to the text property outside the loop.

➤ If you animate your text, boost performance by removing transparency settings and assigning an `opaqueBackground` property to a color value, which disables the alpha properties. What's more, set the `cacheAsBitmap` to `true` so you can cache the text content as bitmaps.

GRAPHICS PRACTICES

When it comes to rendering graphics, keep the following tips and techniques in mind.

Caching

The number-one rule when rendering graphics in your Android or iPhone app is to *cache whenever you can*. Redrawing is always costly, so render only when you have to.

You need to understand three key properties to properly cache your bitmaps. These are shown in Table 4-1. Use this table to determine when to set these properties to `true`.

TABLE 4-1: Properties for Caching Bitmaps

PROPERTY	WHAT IT DOES	WHEN TO USE (=TRUE)	WHEN TO AVOID (=FALSE)
cacheAsBitmap	Caches a bitmap off-screen so you can reuse it rather than re-creating the bitmap multiple times. Eliminates the need to rerender a display object.	Enable for display objects that won't have transformations applied to them.	Don't use if you are changing alpha, rotation, or colors. If you do, the transformation slows processing down because it needs to cache and draw rather than just draw. Don't use if the content of the display object changes frequently.
cacheAsSurface	Eliminates the need to rerender a display object. Matrix transformations, such as scaling and rotating, should be applied outside a cached object, rather than being done as children of a cached object. If so, GPU (Graphical Processing Unit) will handle it.	Enable for display objects that will have transformations applied to them. Enable for the container display object if you are animating display objects inside of it.	Don't use if the content of the display object changes frequently or if a display object descendent also changes frequently.

PROPERTY	WHAT IT DOES	WHEN TO USE (=TRUE)	WHEN TO AVOID (=FALSE)
`cacheAsBit-mapMatrix`	Caches the x, y, rotation, scale, and skew properties.	Use for display objects that aren't regularly updated.	Don't use if you modify alpha or color properties or the matrix of the children sprites. Doing so slows rendering down because it needs to cache and draw rather than just draw.

Miscellaneous Tips

The tips here don't fit neatly into a category, but they can help you write fast-running apps:

➤ Avoid using the `Graphics` class for drawing on the fly. Instead, use prerendered objects.

➤ When you are finished with a `BitmapData` instance, call its `dispose()` method. That method instantly clears memory and doesn't wait for garbage collection.

➤ Rendering vector graphics requires less memory than using bitmaps does, but vector graphics are more expensive in terms of CPU resources. Bitmaps take more memory but require less processing power to display.

➤ When sizing bitmaps for use in your app, set their size equal to a power of 2 or just under it. For example, 32×32 or 31×31 is recommended over 33×33.

➤ Set the background color of a display object container if you have animation going on inside of it.

GENERAL APPLICATION PRACTICES

The following are tips and techniques to keep in mind for general application development.

Frame Rate

The general rule of thumb is to use as low of a frame rate as possible to ensure better performance. If you have an app with no animation in it, aim to go between 4 and 12 fps (frames per second). If you do have animation, start out at 20 fps and increase it if needed. However, don't go more than 30 fps.

Keep in mind that you can adjust the `Stage.frameRate` property (or in Flex, `WindowsApplication.frameRate`) on the fly to optimize different parts of your application.

If your app runs video, you don't need to worry about adjusting the `Stage.frameRate` to account for it. Video takes over the frame rate settings and adjusts it as needed. In fact, your settings won't impact it.

GPU Rendering

Adobe Integrated Runtime (AIR) for Android and Packager for iPhone both support GPU hardware acceleration, which enables you to pass off some kinds of graphical rendering to the GPU for increased performance. To enable GPU rendering, set the `renderingMode` property in the application descriptor file to the following:

```
<renderMode>gpu</renderMode>
```

You can also do that selecting GPU from the Render Mode drop-down list box in the Android or iPhone Settings dialog boxes, as shown in Figure 4-1.

However, you need to know what you're doing if you're going to enable GPU rendering. It handles certain rendering tasks really well, but it won't handle certain others. And, if GPU rendering can't display the command, it won't. Your app won't degrade gracefully and use CPU processing for those tasks.

GPU rendering doesn't support the following:

➤ Filters.

➤ `PixelBender`.

➤ Blends (alpha, erase, overlay, hardlight, lighten, and darken modes).

➤ Texture sizes greater than 1024×1024.

➤ Video (not recommended).

➤ Adjusting the viewport to show text input fields when the software keyboard is displayed. As a result, you have to design your UI around that constraint or programmatically move the page up.

What's more, GPU rendering for iOS is limited to rendering bitmaps, solid shapes, and display objects with the `cacheAsBitmap` property set to `true`.

Garbage Collection

If you are an experienced Flash or Flex developer, chances are you've got at least a basic understanding of garbage collection. Garbage collection is an automatic memory cleanup process that involves clearing out objects that have been disposed from memory.

However, determining exactly when garbage collection will occur can be a guessing game. It occurs only when all references to the object are removed and the object is set to `null`. However,

FIGURE 4-1

even then, the collection may not be immediate, because if your app doesn't need memory, garbage collection won't run immediately. AIR allows you to force a garbage collection cleanup by calling the following:

```
System.gc();
```

However, the garbage collector is not a cure-all. If you call it constantly, you can actually slow down your app because of the CPU resources required to run it.

Kitchen Sink Tips

The following "kitchen sink" list contains some additional general purpose tips to keep in mind:

➤   Only embed objects (fonts, graphics, and so on) that you are actually using in your app. Don't leave orphaned content that you're not utilizing.

➤   Compress everything you can in your app. See if you can reduce the size of your JPGs, audio or video compression, and so on.

➤   Use device fonts whenever possible for Android or iOS apps so you don't have to embed font files.

➤   Create a single Sound instance in your app for each sound you want to play. Then reference that instance anytime you need it.

➤   Silently play any sounds you plan to use when the app is launched so that they are cached in memory. This preloading trick helps eliminate the chance of a lag when the sound is played the first time.

➤   For benchmarking your code in terms of the memory being used, use the getSize() function. For example:

```
var feed:Feed = new Feed();
// Return size of Feed instance
trace(getSize(feed));
// Return total memory available
trace(getSize(System.totalMemory/1024));
```

SUMMARY

In this chapter, I walked you through several important principles to keep in mind when developing mobile applications for Android and iOS devices. It's important to always keep in mind the sometimes conflicting goals of conserving memory and CPU resources. When performance is most critical, you'll often want to optimize CPU resources to provide the smoothest user experience.

5

Multitouch API

➤ Understanding the difference between touch and gesture events

➤ Enabling your app to respond to touches and gestures

➤ Adding a swipe to your app

➤ Zooming and rotating display objects

One of the core capabilities of any mobile app is effectively handling multitouch events: a finger press, a finger swipe, a multifinger gesture. With its multitouch interface, Android and iOS devices are designed for that intimate connection with the user. As you develop Flash apps, you'll want to pay close attention to this key method of user interaction.

This chapter walks you through touch events available to you and shows you how to listen and respond to them in your apps.

UNDERSTANDING THE MULTITOUCH JARGON

Before going into the actual touch API, the next sections highlight the three types of touch-related events.

Mouse Emulation Events

Mouse emulation events (`MouseEvent`) are the events that you are probably quite familiar with if you worked with ActionScript 3 (AS3) events in Flash. When a user touches a single finger to the device, a `MouseEvent` is dispatched, which in effect, simulates a mouse clicking a display object, such as a button. You can decide whether to listen for mouse events or respond only to touch events.

Touch Events

Touch events (TouchEvent) are dispatched when one or more fingers touch the screen. You can listen for a single finger press or multiple finger touches that occur at different points on the screen at the same time. (See Table 5-1.)

TABLE 5-1: Touch Events

EVENT	DESCRIPTION
TOUCH_BEGIN	Start of a single touch action
TOUCH_END	End of a single touch action
TOUCH_MOVE	Single touch movement
TOUCH_OUT	Touch outside a display object
TOUCH_OVER	Touch over a display object
TOUCH_ROLL_OUT	Rollout of display object
TOUCH_ROLL_OVER	Rollover display object
TOUCH_TAP	Tap

You can capture TouchEvent events for finger pressing instead of MouseEvent events. However, as a general rule, if you're just listening for basic button clicks and so on, use MouseEvent events when possible, because they are less expensive.

Gesture Events

Gesture events (GestureEvent), on the other hand, are combinations of touch events that also support such things as scaling and rotation. You can carry out some gestures with one finger, whereas others need multiple touch points. Table 5-2 displays the available types of gesture events.

TABLE 5-2: Gesture Events

EVENT	DESCRIPTION
TransformGestureEvent.GESTURE_PAN	Multi-finger press, hold, and move
TransformGestureEvent.GESTURE_ROTATE	Multi-finger rotation
TransformGestureEvent.GESTURE_SWIPE	Multi-finger swipe action (left to right, right to left, top to bottom, bottom to top)
TransformGestureEvent.GESTURE_ZOOM	

EVENT	DESCRIPTION
PressAndTapGestureEvent .GESTURE_PRESS_AND_TAP	Press a finger and then tap with another finger
GestureEvent.GESTURE_TWO_FINGER_TAP	Two finger tap

Listening for Touch Events

The `Multitouch.inputMode` property tells the app what type of touch-related events the app should be listening for. There are three possible values.

To listen for mouse events only and not listen for touches and gestures, use this:

```
Multitouch.inputMode=MultitouchInputMode.NONE
```

To listen for single touches, use this:

```
Multitouch.inputMode=MultitouchInputMode.TOUCH_POINT
```

To listen for gestures, use this:

```
Multitouch.inputMode=MultitouchInputMode.GESTURE
```

Event Bubbling

Beware of event bubbling when you are designing mobile apps. *Event bubbling* occurs when a child display object passes on an event to its parent to handle. If this display object has a parent, it continues to pass it up through the object hierarchy until the topmost parent handles the event. This chaining of events is costly for mobile apps.

You can minimize event bubbling by flattening the display object hierarchy as much as possible. What's more, it's a good practice to handle the event in the intended target display object and then stop the event bubbling by calling the event object's `stopPropagation()` method.

WORKING WITH TOUCH EVENTS

You'll learn how to work with the basic touch events with an app called `PhotoTouch`. This app displays two photos on the screen and enables you to move them around with your finger across the viewport. Before diving into the ActionScript code, set up the Flash app as follows:

1. Within the desired directory, create a new Flash document based on the Android or iPhone and name it **PhotoTouch.fla**.

2. In the Properties panel, enter **PhotoTouch** as the document class and click the pencil button to edit the class definition in your preferred editor.

Coding the Document Class

As you begin to code your document class, add the import statements that you'll need just inside the package:

```
import flash.display.Bitmap;
import flash.display.Sprite;
import flash.events.TouchEvent;
import flash.ui.Multitouch;
import flash.ui.MultitouchInputMode;
import flash.display.Loader;
import flash.events.Event;
```

Code snippet PhotoTouch.as

You then need to define the necessary properties for working with the two photo images used in the app. I reference two external JPG files named `WaterFrontImage.jpg` and `RoadImage.jpg`. (You can find these graphics on the book's website at `wrox.com`.) Here's the code:

```
Embed(source="waterfront.jpg")]
private var WaterFrontImage:Class;

Embed(source="fallroad.jpg")]
private var RoadImage:Class;

private var pic:Bitmap;
private var pic2:Bitmap;
```

Code snippet PhotoTouch.as

With the `Embed` metadata declarative, embed the external file into the app and associate it with the `Class` variable just beneath it. As discussed in Chapter 3, the `Embed` metadata tag requires the Flex Software Development Kit (SDK). As a result, when you first publish the app, Flash CS5 prompts you to add the Flex SDK path to the Library path of your project.

You now need to define your constructor. Begin by creating the bitmap instances for the two photos, and then add sprite containers for both:

```
// Create bitmap
pic= new WaterFrontImage();
pic.smoothing = true;

pic2= new RoadImage();
pic2.smoothing = true;

// Create sprite container for images
var picSprite:Sprite = new Sprite();
   picSprite.addChild(pic);
var picSprite2:Sprite = new Sprite();
   picSprite2.addChild(pic2);

// Add to stage
```

```
addChild(picSprite);
addChild(picSprite2)
```

Place both of these images at or near the center of the viewport. I add the first one to the middle:

```
// Center first picture
pic.x = stage.stageWidth/2 - pic.width/2;
pic.y = stage.stageHeight/2 - pic.height/2;
```

Then offset the second bitmap by 50 pixels:

```
// Offset second picture
pic2.x = pic.x + 50;
pic2.y = pic.y + 50;
```

Although your initial user interface (UI) is ready to go, you now need to add listeners for the TOUCH_
BEGIN, TOUCH_MOVE, and TOUCH_END events for both bitmaps. The code is shown here:

```
if (Multitouch.supportsTouchEvents)
{

// Enable Touch mode
Multitouch.inputMode = MultitouchInputMode.TOUCH_POINT;

// Assign touch event handlers
picSprite.addEventListener(TouchEvent.TOUCH_BEGIN, touchBeginHandler);
picSprite2.addEventListener(TouchEvent.TOUCH_BEGIN, touchBeginHandler);

addEventListener(TouchEvent.TOUCH_MOVE, touchMoveHandler);
addEventListener(TouchEvent.TOUCH_END, touchEndHandler);


}


}
```

First check to see that the device supports touch events. If it does, assign the touch input type by
assigning the Multitouch.inputMode property a value of MultitouchInputMode.TOUCH_POINT,
which tells the app to treat all touch-related events as touches, not gestures or mouse clicks.

The two Sprite instances are assigned listeners for TOUCH_BEGIN events. However, the stage actually is the better object to respond to TOUCH_MOVE and TOUCH_END events because a user's finger
could move outside the borders of the objects being dragged.

The next step is to define the three event handlers that respond to the touch events. The TOUCH_
BEGIN handler looks like this:

```
private function touchBeginHandler(event:TouchEvent)
{
    var sprite:Sprite = event.target as Sprite;
    // Init drag
    sprite.startTouchDrag(event.touchPointID);
```

```
                 // Bring to top
                 setChildIndex(sprite, numChildren-1);

       }
```

Code snippet PhotoTouch.as

The `Sprite startTouchDrag()` method initiates a touch event, much like `startDrag()` kicks off drag-and-drop mouse events. Its one required parameter is a unique `touchPointID` that the Flash run time assigns to identify the specific point that was touched. The `touchPointID` enables you to ensure that your events respond to the correct touch point, not another caused by another finger somewhere on the screen. So, an entire touch-and-drag sequence, such as the one being added to `PhotoTouch` app, will be characterized or identified with a single `touchPointID`.

Because a user can touch an object that is underneath another in the display order, the `setChildIndex()` method sets the sprite being touched to the top.

The `TOUCH_MOVE` handler comes next:

```
       private function touchMoveHandler(event:TouchEvent)
       {
            var sprite:Sprite = event.target as Sprite;
            // Set alpha
            sprite.alpha = 0.7;
       }
```

Code snippet PhotoTouch.as

When the user drags the sprite around on the stage, you'll want to set its `alpha` to `0.7` to show a difference for the object being dragged. You don't need to add additional code for this event handler, because Flash run time handles all the movement.

The `TOUCH_END` listener handles the end of a touch action:

```
       private function touchEndHandler(event:TouchEvent)
       {
               var sprite:Sprite = event.target as Sprite;
               sprite.stopTouchDrag(event.touchPointID);
               // Reset alpha
               sprite.alpha = 1;
       }
```

Code snippet PhotoTouch.as

The `stopTouchDrag()` method ends the drag action using the `touchPointID` of the event. The final action you need to take is resetting the `alpha` property to normal (1).

That's the end of document class.

Running the App

You can compile the Flash project and install the compiled app onto your device. After that, you are ready to launch it in Android or iOS. Figures 5-1 and 5-2 show the start and end of a touch-and-drag action.

FIGURE 5-1   FIGURE 5-2

Listing 5-1 shows the full source code listing for the PhotoTouch class.

LISTING 5-1: PhotoTouch.as

```
package {

    import flash.display.Bitmap;
    import flash.display.Sprite;
    import flash.events.TouchEvent;
    import flash.ui.Multitouch;
    import flash.ui.MultitouchInputMode;
     import flash.display.Loader;
    import flash.events.Event;


    /**
     * Document class for PhotoTouch application.
     * Sample application
     *
     * @author Rich Wagner
     *
     */
```

continues

LISTING 5-1 *(continued)*

```
public class PhotoTouch extends Sprite
{

    // External image
    [Embed(source="waterfront.jpg")]
    private var WaterFrontImage:Class;

    [Embed(source="fallroad.jpg")]
    private var RoadImage:Class;


    private var pic:Bitmap;
    private var pic2:Bitmap;


    /**
     * Constructor
     *
     */
    public function PhotoTouch()
    {

        // Create bitmap
        pic= new WaterFrontImage();
        pic.smoothing = true;

        pic2= new RoadImage();
        pic2.smoothing = true;

        // Create sprite container for images
        var picSprite:Sprite = new Sprite();
           picSprite.addChild(pic);
        var picSprite2:Sprite = new Sprite();
           picSprite2.addChild(pic2);

        // Add to stage
        addChild(picSprite);
        addChild(picSprite2)

        // Center first picture
        pic.x = stage.stageWidth/2 - pic.width/2;
        pic.y = stage.stageHeight/2 - pic.height/2;

        // Offset second picture
        pic2.x = pic.x + 50;
        pic2.y = pic.y + 50;


        if (Multitouch.supportsTouchEvents)
        {
            // Enable Touch mode
            Multitouch.inputMode = MultitouchInputMode.TOUCH_POINT;

            // Assign Touch Event handlers
```

```
                picSprite.addEventListener(TouchEvent.TOUCH_BEGIN,
touchBeginHandler);
                picSprite2.addEventListener(TouchEvent.TOUCH_BEGIN,
touchBeginHandler);
            addEventListener(TouchEvent.TOUCH_MOVE, touchMoveHandler);
            addEventListener(TouchEvent.TOUCH_END, touchEndHandler);


        }

    }

    /**
     * Handler for TouchBegin events
     *
     * @param event
     *
     */
    private function touchBeginHandler(event:TouchEvent)
    {
        var sprite:Sprite = event.target as Sprite;
        sprite.startTouchDrag(event.touchPointID);
        // Bring to top
        setChildIndex(sprite, numChildren-1);
    }

    /**
     * Handler for TouchMove events
     *
     * @param event
     *
     */
    private function touchMoveHandler(event:TouchEvent)
    {
        var sprite:Sprite = event.target as Sprite;
        // Set alpha
        sprite.alpha = 0.7;

    }

    /**
     * Handler for TouchEnd events
     *
     * @param event
     *
     */
    private function touchEndHandler(event:TouchEvent)
    {
        var sprite:Sprite = event.target as Sprite;
        sprite.stopTouchDrag(event.touchPointID);
        // Reset alpha
        sprite.alpha = 1;
    }

    }

}
```

WORKING WITH THE SWIPE GESTURE

Handling gestures is much like responding to touch events, as you'll see in a sample app called `PhotoPage`. This app demonstrates how you can use the swipe gesture to move to different frames inside your Flash timeline.

Begin by creating a new Flash document based on the Android or iPhone and naming it `PhotoPage` `.fla`. Before coding the document class, you need to add a set of frames to your timeline.

The image files for this sample app are sized for the default Adobe Integrated Runtime (AIR) for Android dimensions (480×800). If you're using these sample images for iOS, resize them accordingly in a graphics editor before continuing.

Setting Up the Timeline

For this sample app, you'll add four full-frame portrait-oriented photos to the Flash document, each displayed within separate frames of the timeline. After opening the Flash timeline (accessible from Window ⇨ Timeline), perform the following tasks:

1. With the first (and only) layer selected, click the first frame in the Timeline.

2. Choose Import ⇨ Import to Stage from the menu.

3. Select an image you want to display on the stage for this frame.

   If you're following along with my example, I chose `p1.jpg`.

4. Click the New Layer button in the Timeline, or choose Insert ⇨ Timeline ⇨ Layer from the menu.

5. Select the second frame in the Timeline for that layer.

6. Right-click and choose Insert Frame.

7. Select that frame with your mouse.

8. Select an image you want to display on the stage for this frame. In my case, I chose `p2.jpg`.

9. Repeat steps 4–8 for the next two frames, using `p3.jpg` and `p4.jpg` files (or your own).

   Figure 5-3 shows the Timeline with all images added. (Note that you optionally can name the layers accordingly.

Adding a Sound Asset

You also need to add an .mp3 sound file to the `.fla` that you'll use to play a swipe sound when a user performs that gesture. To do so, follow these steps:

1. Choose Import ⇨ Import to Library from the menu.

2. Select the sound file in the dialog box. I chose the file `Swipe.mp3`.

   The sound is added as an asset to your library (Window ⇨ Library). However, before you can use it inside your AS3 code, you need to export it for use in ActionScript.

FIGURE 5-3

3. Right-click the sound asset in the Library and choose Properties.

4. In the Sound Properties dialog box (see Figure 5-4), name the sound asset swipesound.

5. Check the Export for ActionScript check box.

6. Enter **SwipeSound** in the Class text box.

7. Click OK.

Coding the Document Class

With the Timeline set up and the sound asset added to your Flash document, you are ready to create and code the AS3 document class. In the Properties panel, enter **PhotoPage** as the document class, and click the pencil button to edit the class definition in your preferred editor.

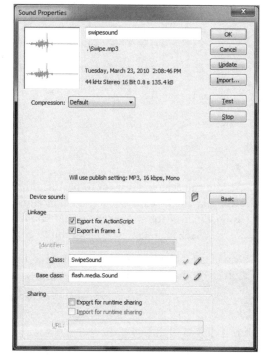

FIGURE 5-4

Inside the package, begin by adding the import statements that you'll need:

```
import flash.display.MovieClip;
import flash.events.TransformGestureEvent;
import flash.events.Event;
import flash.ui.Multitouch;
import flash.ui.MultitouchInputMode;
import flash.media.Sound;
```

Code snippet PhotoPage.as

Next, add one private property inside the PhotoPage class for the sound asset:

```
private var swipe:SwipeSound;
```

Code snippet PhotoPage.as

The SwipeSound class is the class that Flash generated when you exported the asset to ActionScript.

Continuing on, you are ready to create the class constructor:

```
public function PhotoPage()
{
    // Need to stop playing of movie since
    // we have multiple frames for this app
    stop();

    // Create sound instance
    swipe = new SwipeSound();

    // If support multitouch
    if (Multitouch.supportsTouchEvents)
    {
        Multitouch.inputMode = MultitouchInputMode.GESTURE;
        stage.addEventListener(TransformGestureEvent.GESTURE_SWIPE,
swipeHandler);
    }

}
```

Code snippet PhotoPage.as

As you can see, you'll want to perform three actions in the constructor. First, stop the Flash movie from playing by calling stop(). This causes the movie to stop playing at Frame 1. Second, create an instance of the SwipeSound that you'll use later. Third, if touch events are supported, assign the Multitouch.inputMode to respond to gestures. Then add a listener for the GESTURE_SWIPE event.

My idea for the app is to move between frames each time the user performs a swipe action on the screen. To handle that, the GESTURE_SWIPE event handler is shown here:

```
private function swipeHandler(event:TransformGestureEvent):void
{
    // Swipe Left
    if (event.offsetX == 1 )
    {
        if (currentFrame > 1)
```

```
        {
            gotoAndStop(currentFrame-1);
        }
        else
        {
            gotoAndStop(totalFrames);
        }

    }
    //Swipe Right
    else if (event.offsetX == -1)
    {
        if (currentFrame < totalFrames)
        {
            gotoAndStop(currentFrame+1);
        }
        else
        {
            gotoAndStop(1);
        }
    }

    swipe.play();

}
```

Code snippet PhotoPage.as

Use the `offsetX` property of the `TransformGestureEvent` object to determine the direction of the swipe. A value of 1 indicates that the swipe is leftward, whereas a value of –1 indicates a swipe to the right.

Therefore, if the user performs a right swipe, the intended action is to move to the next frame in the Timeline using `gotoAndStop(currentFrame+1)`. However, once the user gets to the last frame, the app should take the user to the first frame.

When the user swipes left, the app should take the user to the previous frame. If the user performs a leftward swipe on the first frame, it wraps around and takes the user to the final frame of the Timeline.

Once that action is performed, the swipe sound is played.

After you finish entering the code, it should look like what is shown in Listing 5-2. Save the results, and you'll be ready to run the app.

LISTING 5-2: PhotoPage.as

```
package   {

    import flash.display.MovieClip;
    import flash.events.TransformGestureEvent;
    import flash.events.Event;
    import flash.ui.Multitouch;
    import flash.ui.MultitouchInputMode;
```

continues

LISTING 5-2 *(continued)*

```actionscript
import flash.media.Sound;


/**
 * Document class for PhotoPage application.
 * Sample application
 *
 * @author Rich Wagner
 *
 */
public class PhotoPage extends MovieClip {

    // SwipeSound is a Flash asset
    private var swipe:SwipeSound;

    /**
     * Constructor
     *
     */
    public function PhotoPage()
    {
        // Need to stop playing of movie since
        // we have multiple frames for this app
        stop();

        // Create sound instance
        swipe = new SwipeSound();

        // If support multitouch
        if (Multitouch.supportsTouchEvents)
        {
            Multitouch.inputMode = MultitouchInputMode.GESTURE;
            stage.addEventListener(TransformGestureEvent.GESTURE_SWIPE,
swipeHandler);
        }

    }


    /**
     * Handler for Swipe event
     *
     * @param event
     *
     */
    private function swipeHandler(event:TransformGestureEvent):void
    {

        // Swipe Left
        if (event.offsetX == 1 )
        {
            if (currentFrame > 1)
```

```
        {
              gotoAndStop(currentFrame-1);
        }
        else
        {
              gotoAndStop(totalFrames);
        }

    }
    //Swipe Right
    else if (event.offsetX == -1)
    {
        if (currentFrame < totalFrames)
        {
              gotoAndStop(currentFrame+1);
        }
        else
        {
              gotoAndStop(1);
        }
    }

    swipe.play();

  }

 }

}
```

Running the App

You have everything ready to publish and install the app. Choose File ⇨ Publish to compile the Flash project and install the compiled app onto your Android or iOS device.

WORKING WITH ROTATE AND ZOOM GESTURES

Another set of gestures that you can perform is rotating and zooming display objects on your stage. To demonstrate, I'll create a sample app called GestureMania. Its narrow purpose is to display a photo on the stage and allow the user to perform rotation and zoom actions on using multifinger gestures.

This is an AS3-based app for Android or iOS. But before diving into the ActionScript code, set up the Flash app as follows:

1. Within the desired directory, create a new Flash document based on the Android or iPhone and name it **GestureMania.fla**.

2. In the Properties panel, enter **GestureMania** as the document class, and click the pencil button to edit the class definition in your preferred editor.

CODING THE DOCUMENT CLASS

As is usual, start by adding `import` statements of the packages that you'll be referencing inside the package:

```
import flash.display.Bitmap;
import flash.display.Sprite;
import flash.display.MovieClip;
import flash.events.TouchEvent;
import flash.ui.Multitouch;
import flash.ui.MultitouchInputMode;
import flash.display.Loader;
import flash.events.Event;
```

Code snippet GestureMania.as

Inside the class, add three private properties:

```
// External image
[Embed(source="waterfront.jpg")]
private var WaterFrontImage:Class;

private var pic:Bitmap;
private var picSprite:Sprite;
```

Code snippet GestureMania.as

The constructor for the `GestureMania` class needs to create an instance of the `Bitmap`, add it to a `Sprite` instance, add the `Sprite` to the stage, and then center the `Bitmap` instance onto the stage. Here's the code:

```
public function GestureMania()
{

        // Create bitmap
        pic= new WaterFrontImage();
        pic.smoothing = true;
        pic.scaleX = 1.3;
        pic.scaleY = 1.3;

        // Create sprite container for image
        picSprite = new Sprite();
        picSprite.addChild(pic);

        // Add to stage
        addChild(picSprite);

        // Center picture
        pic.x = stage.stageWidth/2 - pic.width/2;
        pic.y = stage.stageHeight/2 - pic.height/2;

        // If support multitouch
        if (Multitouch.supportsTouchEvents)
        {
                Multitouch.inputMode = MultitouchInputMode.GESTURE;
```

```
                picSprite.addEventListener(TransformGestureEvent.GESTURE_ZOOM,
    GestureZoomandler);
                picSprite.addEventListener(TransformGestureEvent.GESTURE_ROTATE,
    GestureRotateHandler);
        }
    }
```

As you can see, the gesture support is added by checking for touch event support. If the support exists, the gestures are enabled for `Multitouch.inputMode` and `GESTURE_ZOOM`, and `GESTURE_ROTATE` event listeners are added.

The following function responds to all `GESTURE_ZOOM` events for the `Sprite`:

Available for download on Wrox.com

```
private function GestureZoomHandler(event:TransformGestureEvent):void
{
    // Zoom in proportion to gesture
    pic.scaleX *= event.scaleX;
    pic.scaleY *= event.scaleY;

    // Always reset picture to center
    pic.x = stage.stageWidth/2 - pic.width/2;
    pic.y = stage.stageHeight/2 - pic.height/2;
}
```

Code snippet GestureMania.as

The `Bitmap` instance is scaled in proportion to the `scaleX` and `scaleY` properties of the `TransformGestureEvent` instance. It is then recentered in the stage.

The handler for the `GESTURE_ROTATE` is slightly trickier:

Available for download on Wrox.com

```
private function GestureRotateHandler(event:TransformGestureEvent):void
{
    var matrix:Matrix = picSprite.transform.matrix;
    var rotatePoint:Point =
        matrix.transformPoint(new Point((picSprite.width/2),
(picSprite.height/2)));
    matrix.translate(-rotatePoint.x, -rotatePoint.y);
    matrix.rotate(event.rotation*(Math.PI/180));
    matrix.translate(rotatePoint.x, rotatePoint.y);
    picSprite.transform.matrix = matrix;
}
```

Code snippet GestureMania.as

This handler uses a `Matrix` object to help in the rotation transformation:

```
    var matrix:Matrix = picSprite.transform.matrix;
```

The `Matrix` object serves as a "transformation matrix" that helps map points between different coordinate spaces:

```
    var rotatePoint:Point =
      matrix.transformPoint(new Point((picSprite.width/2),
(picSprite.height/2)));
```

You can then work with a `Matrix` instance, attach it to a `Transform` instance, and then apply that transformation to the `Sprite` instance. You'll need to perform some math to change the radians in the *event.rotation* to degrees:

```
matrix.translate(-rotatePoint.x, -rotatePoint.y);
matrix.rotate(event.rotation*(Math.PI/180));
matrix.translate(rotatePoint.x, rotatePoint.y);
picSprite.transform.matrix = matrix;
```

Listing 5-3 shows the full source code for `GestureMania.as`.

LISTING 5-3: GestureMania.as

```actionscript
package {

    import flash.display.Bitmap;
    import flash.display.Sprite;
    import flash.display.MovieClip;
    import flash.events.TransformGestureEvent;
    import flash.geom.Matrix;
    import flash.ui.Multitouch;
    import flash.ui.MultitouchInputMode;
    import flash.events.Event;
    import flash.geom.Point;

    /**
     * Document class for GestureMania application.
     * Sample application
     *
     * @author Rich Wagner
     *
     */
    public class GestureMania extends MovieClip
    {

        // External image
        [Embed(source="waterfront.jpg")]
        private var WaterFrontImage:Class;

        private var pic:Bitmap;
        private var picSprite:Sprite;

        /**
         * Constructor
         *
         */
        public function GestureMania()
        {

            // Create bitmap
            pic= new WaterFrontImage();
            pic.smoothing = true;
```

```
            pic.scaleX = 1.3;
            pic.scaleY = 1.3;

            // Create sprite container for image
            picSprite = new Sprite();
            picSprite.addChild(pic);

            // Add to stage
            addChild(picSprite);

            // Center picture
            pic.x = stage.stageWidth/2 - pic.width/2;
            pic.y = stage.stageHeight/2 - pic.height/2;

            // If support multitouch
            if (Multitouch.supportsTouchEvents)
            {
                Multitouch.inputMode = MultitouchInputMode.GESTURE;
                picSprite.addEventListener(TransformGestureEvent.GESTURE_ZOOM,
GestureZoomandler);
                picSprite.addEventListener(TransformGestureEvent.GESTURE_ROTATE,
  GestureRotateHandler);
            }
        }


        /**
         * Handler for Zoom event
         *
         * @param event
         *
         */
        private function GestureZoomHandler(event:TransformGestureEvent):void
        {
            // Zoom in proportion to gesture
            pic.scaleX *= event.scaleX;
            pic.scaleY *= event.scaleY;

            // Always reset picture to center
            pic.x = stage.stageWidth/2 - pic.width/2;
            pic.y = stage.stageHeight/2 - pic.height/2;
        }


        /**
         * Handler for Rotate event
         *
         * @param event
         *
         */
        private function
GestureRotateHandler(event:TransformGestureEvent):void
        {
            var matrix:Matrix = picSprite.transform.matrix;
```

continues

LISTING 5-3 *(continued)*

```
            var rotatePoint:Point = matrix.transformPoint(new
   Point((picSprite.width/2), (picSprite.height/2)));
            matrix.translate(-rotatePoint.x, -rotatePoint.y);
            matrix.rotate(event.rotation*(Math.PI/180));
            matrix.translate(rotatePoint.x, rotatePoint.y);
            picSprite.transform.matrix = matrix;
        }



    }
}
```

Running the App

With the document class completed, you are ready to publish your Flash project and install the compiled app onto your Android or iOS device. Figure 5-5 shows the app in its default state, whereas Figure 5-6 shows the photo after it has been zoomed in. Figures 5-7 and 5-8 show two stages of a rotation.

FIGURE 5-5

FIGURE 5-6

FIGURE 5-7

FIGURE 5-8

SUMMARY

In this chapter, you discovered how to work with touch and gesture events in your Android and iOS apps. You began by exploring the differences between the various multitouch events and how to trap them within your apps. You then walked through three sample applications that focused on different multitouch events. PhotoTouch illustrates how to use TOUCH_START, TOUCH_MOVE, and TOUCH_END events to touch and drag objects around a screen. PhotoPage explores how to use the swipe gesture as an intuitive way to switch frames inside a Flash document. Finally, GestureMania illustrates how to work with rotation and zoom gestures to manipulate a display object on-screen.

Detecting Motion with Accelerometer

➤ Detecting motions in your app

➤ Working with Accelerometer and AccelerometerEvent classes

➤ Detecting when the user shakes the device

Android and iOS devices have built-in motion detectors that enable programmers to capture the motion that occurs on a three-dimensional axis. This capability enables you to detect all sorts of user motions — tilting the phone, shaking back and forth, and rotating it in a circular fashion.

This chapter introduces you to the `Accelerometer` and `AccelerometerEvent` classes and shows you how to detect motion in your apps. It walks you through the creation of three apps that demonstrate different aspects of motion detection:

➤ `AccelerateInfo`, which lists raw data from the motion sensor

➤ `SphereAcceleration`, which uses the Accelerometer to guide a sphere around the viewport

➤ `Shakey`, which captures a `shake` event

However, before beginning, it's important to introduce you to the two classes you'll work with to detect motion.

INTRODUCING ACCELEROMETER AND ACCELEROMETEREVENT

There are two main classes that you work with to use a mobile device's motion sensor: Accelerometer and AccelerometerEvent. Android and iOS enable you to return movement data of the device along the x, y, and z axes to your app. The data you receive is in Gs. One G is the gravitational constant equal to 9.8m/sec^2.

The Accelerometer class is used for basic setup purposes: checking for motion sensor support on the device, assigning a listener for motion sensor updates, and setting the requested interval time between updates. Its primary method is setRequestedUpdateInterval(), which sets up time intervals (in milliseconds) for updates from the motion sensor. The time you specify is only a request and can vary based on the OS and motion sensor. If not specified, the default update time is 100 ms.

The AccelerometerEvent class provides the update event that is fired each time the motion sensor updates based on the requested or OS-determined time interval or whenever the motion sensor updates when the Android wakes from sleep.

The AccelerometerEvent contains the following properties:

➤ accelerationX — Acceleration along the x axis (in Gs)

➤ acceleration — Acceleration along the y axis (in Gs)

➤ accelerationZ — Acceleration along the z axis (in Gs)

➤ timestamp — Time since motion detection began (in milliseconds)

The skeleton code for checking for motion detection support and setting up a listener is shown here:

```
private function initAccelerator():void
{
    if (Accelerometer.isSupported)
    {
        accelerometer = new Accelerometer();
        accelerometer.addEventListener(AccelerometerEvent.UPDATE,
            accelerometerUpdateHandler);
    }
    else
    {
        trace("Motion sensor detection is not supported on this device.");
    }
}


private function accelerometerUpdateHandler(event:AccelerometerEvent):void
{
    // event.accelerationX available
    // event.accelerationY available
    // event.accelerationZ available
}
```

LISTENING FOR ACCELEROMETER EVENTS

To demonstrate basic functionality, this section shows you how to create an app called
`AccelerateInfo`, which simply displays real-time accelerator data on the screen.

Before diving into the ActionScript code, set up the Flash app as follows:

1. Within the desired directory, create a new Flash document based on the Android or iPhone
    and name it **AccelerateInfo.fla**.

2. In the Properties panel, enter **AccelerateInfo** as the document class and click the pencil
    button to edit the class definition in your preferred editor.

Coding the Document Class

As you code your `AccelerateInfo` class, begin by setting up class properties. You only need two: a
`TextField` and an `Accelerometer` instance:

**Available for
download on
Wrox.com**

```
private var tfInfo:TextField;
private var accelerometer:Accelerometer;
```

Code snippet AccelerateInfo.as

In the constructor, set up and configure the stage and TextField. I set up the Accelerometer and
assigned a handler for the `AccelerometerEvent.UPDATE` event. Here it is:

**Available for
download on
Wrox.com**

```
public function AccelerateInfo()
{
    stage.align = StageAlign.TOP_LEFT;
    stage.scaleMode = StageScaleMode.NO_SCALE;

    // Create Text Field
    tfInfo = new TextField();
    var format:TextFormat = new TextFormat("Helvetica", 26);
    format.color = 0xffffffff;
    tfInfo.defaultTextFormat = format;
    tfInfo.border = true;
    tfInfo.wordWrap = true;
    tfInfo.multiline = true;
    tfInfo.background = true;
    tfInfo.backgroundColor = 0xFF5500;
    tfInfo.x = 0;
    tfInfo.y = 0;
    tfInfo.height = stage.stageHeight;
    tfInfo.width = stage.stageWidth;
    addChild(tfInfo);

    // Determine Accelerator support
    if (Accelerometer.isSupported)
    {
        accelerometer = new Accelerometer();
        accelerometer.setRequestedUpdateInterval(500);
        accelerometer.addEventListener(AccelerometerEvent.UPDATE,
```

```
                accelerometerUpdateHandler);
        }
        else
        {
            tfInfo.text = "Motion sensor detection is not support on " +
                    this device. No Accelerator for you!";
        }


    }
```

The event handler gets the values of the `accelerationX`, `accelerationY`, and `accelerationZ` properties, converts them to string values, and outputs them in the `TextField`. It is shown here:

```
    private function accelerometerUpdateHandler(event:AccelerometerEvent):void
    {

        var s:String = "X:" + event.accelerationX.toString() + "\n" +
                    "Y:" + event.accelerationY.toString() + "\n" +
                    "Z:" + event.accelerationZ.toString() + "\n" +
                    "Duration:" + event.timestamp.toString() + "\n";

        tfInfo.text = s;


    }
```

This simple app gives you a feel for a range of values that you can expect working with acceleration.

Listing 6-1 lists the full source code for `AccelerateInfo.as`.

LISTING 6-1: AccelerateInfo.as

```
package
{
    import flash.display.MovieClip;
    import flash.events.AccelerometerEvent;
    import flash.sensors.Accelerometer;
    import flash.text.*;
    import flash.display.*;

    /**
     * Document class for AccelerateInfo application.
     * Sample code for Professional Flash Mobile Development     *
     *
     * @author Rich Wagner
     *
     */
    public class AccelerateInfo extends MovieClip
    {

        private var tfInfo:TextField;
```

```
private var accelerometer:Accelerometer;

/**
 *  Constructor
 *
 */
public function AccelerateInfo()
{
    stage.align = StageAlign.TOP_LEFT;
    stage.scaleMode = StageScaleMode.NO_SCALE;

    // Create Text Field
    tfInfo = new TextField();
    var format:TextFormat = new TextFormat("Helvetica", 26);
    format.color = 0xffffffff;
    tfInfo.defaultTextFormat = format;
    tfInfo.border = true;
    tfInfo.wordWrap = true;
    tfInfo.multiline = true;
    tfInfo.background = true;
    tfInfo.backgroundColor = 0xFF5500;
    tfInfo.x = 0;
    tfInfo.y = 0;
    tfInfo.height = stage.stageHeight;
    tfInfo.width = stage.stageWidth;
    addChild(tfInfo);

    // Determine Accelerator support
    if (Accelerometer.isSupported)
    {
        accelerometer = new Accelerometer();
        accelerometer.setRequestedUpdateInterval(500);
        accelerometer.addEventListener(AccelerometerEvent.UPDATE,
          accelerometerUpdateHandler);
    }
    else
    {
        tfInfo.text = "Motion sensor detection is not support on this" +
          "device. No Accelerator for you!";
    }

}


/**
 * Handler for Accelerometer updates
 */
private function accelerometerUpdateHandler(event:AccelerometerEvent):void
{

    var s:String = "X:" + event.accelerationX.toString() + "\n" +
                   "Y:" + event.accelerationY.toString() + "\n" +
                   "Z:" + event.accelerationZ.toString() + "\n" +
```

continues

LISTING 6-1 *(continued)*

```
                                "Duration:" + event.timestamp.toString() + "\n";

                tfInfo.text = s;

            }


        }
    }
```

Running the App

You can compile the Flash project and install the compiled app onto the device. After that, you are ready to try it out on Android (see Figure 6-1) or iPhone (see Figure 6-2).

FIGURE 6-1   **FIGURE 6-2**

RESPONDING TO ACCELEROMETER EVENTS

Now that you've seen the basic display of acceleration info, it's time to start responding to that data. You'll learn how to create an app that displays a sphere in motion. The sphere responds to the acceleration data, going in the direction of the tilt of the Android.

Set up the Flash file by performing the following steps:

1. Within the desired directory, create a new Flash document based on the Android/iPhone template, and name it SphereAcceleration.fla.

2. In the Properties panel, enter **SphereAcceleration** as the document class, and click the pencil button to edit the class definition in your preferred editor.

Before you actually code the document class, create a support class called Sphere.

Creating the Sphere Class

In your preferred code editor (Flash IDE or Flash Builder), create a new ActionScript class called Sphere. Choose the appropriate package in which to locate it; I placed mine in com .richwagner.Spheres.

Listing 6-2 shows the class code. Notice that Sphere is a child of Sprite and contains two physical properties and two properties related to the acceleration of the object. The constructor creates a circle based on its size and color parameters.

LISTING 6-2: Sphere.as

```
package com.richwagner.Spheres
{
    import flash.display.Sprite;

    /**
     * Sphere class for SphereAcceleration application.
     * Sample code for Professional Flash Mobile Development
     *
     * @author Rich Wagner
     *
     */
    public class Sphere extends Sprite
    {

        public var size:Number = 25;
        public var color:Number = 0x000000;
        public var xSpeed:Number = 0;
        public var ySpeed:Number = 0;

        /**
         * Constructor
         *
         * @param size - diameter of sphere
         * @param color - color of sphere
         *
         */
        public function Sphere(size:Number, color:Number)
        {
            size = size;
            color = color;

            graphics.beginFill(color);
            graphics.drawCircle(0, 0, size/2);
            graphics.endFill();

        }

    }
}
```

With the Sphere class created, you are ready to return to the document class.

Coding the Document Class

You are ready to fill the `SphereAcceleration` class shell structure that was created earlier. Begin by defining two properties:

```
private var accelerometer:Accelerometer;
private var sphere:Sphere;
```

Code snippet SphereAcceleration.as

Before creating the constructor, you want to create a helper function called `createSphere()`. This method creates the `Sphere` instance using the `size` and `color` parameters and adds it to the stage in the center. You are creating only one instance in this example, so you could add it inside the constructor. However, if you expand the app to include multiple `Sphere` objects, this helper comes in handy. Here's the code:

```
private function createSphere(size:Number, color:Number):void
{
    sphere = new Sphere(size, color);
    sphere.x = (stage.stageWidth / 2);
    sphere.y = (stage.stageHeight / 2);
    sphere.cacheAsBitmap = true;
    addChild(sphere);
}
```

Code snippet SphereAcceleration.as

You use the constructor to set up the stage, create a sphere, and set up a listener for motion sensor updates:

```
public function SphereAcceleration()
{

    stage.align = StageAlign.TOP_LEFT;
    stage.scaleMode = StageScaleMode.NO_SCALE;

    createSphere(50, 0x65c8c6);

    // Determine Accelerator support
    if (Accelerometer.isSupported)
    {
        accelerometer = new Accelerometer();
        accelerometer.addEventListener(AccelerometerEvent.UPDATE,
            accelerometerUpdateHandler);

        addEventListener(Event.ENTER_FRAME, onEnterFrame);

    }
    else
    {
        trace("Motion sensor detection is not support on this " +
            "device. No Accelerator for you!");
    }

}
```

Code snippet SphereAcceleration.as

Notice that you also set up a handler for the ENTER_FRAME event. You get to that later, but first you need to set up the accelerometerUpdateHandler(). Inside this function, you update the xSpeed and ySpeed properties of the Sphere object based on the accelerationX and accelerationY properties from the AccelerometerEvent. Multiplying both of those values by 2 gives a good result to simulate a speeding sphere on-screen. Here's the code:

```
private function accelerometerUpdateHandler(event:AccelerometerEvent):void
{
    sphere.xSpeed += event.accelerationX * 2;
    sphere.ySpeed -= event.accelerationY * 2;
}
```

Code snippet SphereAcceleration.as

You can use the real-time acceleration data provided by the Accelerometer to animate the ball in response. To perform the animation, you need to update the sphere position. You do that by triggering the animation from the ENTER_FRAME event. The handler that you assigned in the constructor simply references a private method you will define called roll():

```
private function onEnterFrame(event:Event):void
{
    roll();
}
```

Code snippet SphereAcceleration.as

You could have also used a timer instead of ENTER_FRAME, but ENTER_FRAME provides smoother animation of the sphere.

The heart of the SphereAcceleration app is in the roll() method, which animates the sphere based on the data received from the Accelerometer. The code is shown here:

```
private function roll():void
{
    var sphereRadius:Number = 25;

    var newX:Number = sphere.x + sphere.xSpeed;
    var newY:Number = sphere.y + sphere.ySpeed;

    // Left side boundary
    if (newX < sphereRadius)
    {
        sphere.x = sphereRadius;
        sphere.xSpeed *= -0.5;
    }
    // Right side boundary
    else if (newX > stage.stageWidth - sphereRadius)
    {
        sphere.x = stage.stageWidth - sphereRadius;
        sphere.xSpeed *= -0.5;
    }
    // Otherwise, go at normal speed
    else
    {
        sphere.x += sphere.xSpeed;
```

```
    }

    // Top boundary
    if (newY < sphereRadius)
    {
        sphere.y = sphereRadius;
        sphere.ySpeed *= -0.5;
    }
    // Bottom boundary
    else if (newY > stage.stageHeight - sphereRadius)
    {
        sphere.y = stage.stageHeight - sphereRadius;
        sphere.ySpeed *= -0.5;
    }
    // Otherwise, go at normal speed
    else
    {
        sphere.y += sphere.ySpeed;
    }

}
```

Code snippet SphereAcceleration.as

The `newX` and `newY` variables determine the new x, y position of the `Sphere` object based on the existing coordinates plus the acceleration values provided by the `accelerometerUpdateHandler()`. The method then examines the current position of the sphere and determines whether it is in a left, right, top, or bottom boundary area or whether it is somewhere in the middle of the viewport.

If the sphere is not in a boundary area, the new x, y positions are simply based on the acceleration data and continue in the sphere's current direction. But if a boundary area is detected, the `xSpeed` or `ySpeed` property is multiplied by a negative value to send it in the reverse direction, giving the effect of bouncing off the walls. I used a −0.5 value, which seemed to provide the most natural reverse speed, although you can alter it if you want to speed up the bouncing effect.

The full source code for the `SphereAnimation` document class is shown in Listing 6-3.

Available for download on Wrox.com

LISTING 6-3: SphereAnimation.as

```
package
{
    import com.richwagner.Spheres.Sphere;

    import flash.display.MovieClip;
    import flash.display.StageAlign;
    import flash.display.StageScaleMode;
    import flash.events.AccelerometerEvent;
    import flash.events.Event;
    import flash.events.TimerEvent;
    import flash.media.Sound;
    import flash.media.SoundChannel;
    import flash.net.URLRequest;
```

```
import flash.sensors.Accelerometer;
import flash.utils.Timer;


/**
 * Document class for SphereAcceleration application.
 * Sample code for Professional Flash Mobile Development
 *
 * @author Rich Wagner
 *
 */
public class SphereAcceleration extends MovieClip
{

    private var accelerometer:Accelerometer;
    private var sphere:Sphere;

    /**
     * Constructor
     *
     */
    public function SphereAcceleration()
    {

        stage.align = StageAlign.TOP_LEFT;
        stage.scaleMode = StageScaleMode.NO_SCALE;

        createSphere(50, 0x65c8c6);


        // Determine Accelerator support
        if (Accelerometer.isSupported)
        {
            accelerometer = new Accelerometer();
            accelerometer.addEventListener(AccelerometerEvent.UPDATE,
                accelerometerUpdateHandler);

            addEventListener(Event.ENTER_FRAME, onEnterFrame);

        }
        else
        {
            trace("Motion sensor detection is not support on this " +
                    "device. No Accelerator for you!");
        }

    }


    /**
     * Creates a Sphere instance and adds to the stage center.
     */
    private function createSphere(size:Number, color:Number):void
    {
        sphere = new Sphere(size, color);
```

continues

LISTING 6-3 *(continued)*

```
        sphere.x = (stage.stageWidth / 2);
        sphere.y = (stage.stageHeight / 2);
        sphere.cacheAsBitmap = true;
        addChild(sphere);
    }


    /**
     * Handler for Accelerometer updates
     */
    private function accelerometerUpdateHandler(event:AccelerometerEvent):void
    {
        sphere.xSpeed += event.accelerationX * 2;
        sphere.ySpeed -= event.accelerationY * 2;
    }

    /**
     * Handler for ENTER_FRAME updates
     */
    private function onEnterFrame(event:Event):void
    {
        roll();
    }


    /**
     * Animates the sphere based on accelerometer data
     */
    private function roll():void
    {
        var sphereRadius:Number = 25;

        var newX:Number = sphere.x + sphere.xSpeed;
        var newY:Number = sphere.y + sphere.ySpeed;

        // Left side boundary
        if (newX < sphereRadius)
        {
            sphere.x = sphereRadius;
            sphere.xSpeed *= -0.5;
        }
        // Right side boundary
        else if (newX > stage.stageWidth - sphereRadius)
        {
            sphere.x = stage.stageWidth - sphereRadius;
            sphere.xSpeed *= -0.5;
        }
        // Otherwise, go at normal speed
        else
        {
            sphere.x += sphere.xSpeed;
        }

        // Top boundary
```

```
            if (newY < sphereRadius)
            {
                sphere.y = sphereRadius;
                sphere.ySpeed *= -0.5;
            }
            // Bottom boundary
            else if (newY > stage.stageHeight - sphereRadius)
            {
                sphere.y = stage.stageHeight - sphereRadius;
                sphere.ySpeed *= -0.5;
            }
            // Otherwise, go at normal speed
            else
            {
                sphere.y += sphere.ySpeed;
            }

        }


    }
}
```

Running the App

After you publish the Flash .fla and install the app onto your mobile device, you can run it. Figures 6-3 and 6-4 show the sphere as it moves around the screen under Android, while Figures 6-5 and 6-6 show it under iPhone.

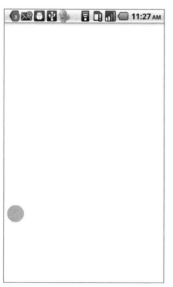

FIGURE 6-3   **FIGURE 6-4**   **FIGURE 6-5**

DETECTING SHAKING

One of the real-world motions that application developers frequently want to capture and utilize in their apps is the shake. Although the `Accelerometer` class doesn't explicitly provide a shake event, you can analyze the data received from the motion sensor and identify when a shake action occurs.

I'll show you how I did it in an app I call `Shakey`, which simply displays the number of shakes that the app detected since the app began. To create this project, begin by setting up the Flash project in a typical fashion:

1. Within the desired directory, create a new Flash document using the AIR for Android template and name it **Shakey.fla**.

2. In the Properties panel, enter **Shakey** as the document class and click the pencil button to edit the class definition in your preferred editor.

FIGURE 6-6

Coding the Document Class

As you begin to fill out the `Shakey` class definition, you will have several properties to define. Start with the standard objects that you'll need: an `Accelerometer` instance and a `TextField` component that will be the sole UI for the app.

```
private var accelerometer:Accelerometer;
private var tfInfo:TextField;
```

Code snippet Shakey.as

Then you define several variables that will be used to analyze the motion of the device:

```
private var deltaX:Number;
private var deltaY:Number;
private var deltaZ:Number;
private var accX:Number;
private var accY:Number;
private var accZ:Number;
```

Code snippet Shakey.as

I'll discuss how those are used later in the example.

Next, define one more variable, which is simply a counter to the number of shakes detected:

```
private var shakes:int = 0;
```

Code snippet Shakey.as

The constructor begins with straightforward code to set up the stage and `TextField` and then attach a handler for the `Accelerometer` update event:

```
public function Shakey()
{
    stage.scaleMode = StageScaleMode.NO_SCALE;
    stage.align = StageAlign.TOP_LEFT;

    // Create text field
    tfInfo = new TextField();
    var format:TextFormat = new TextFormat("Helvetica", 26);
    format.color = 0x000000;
    tfInfo.defaultTextFormat = format;
    tfInfo.border = false;
    tfInfo.wordWrap = true;
    tfInfo.multiline = true;
    tfInfo.x = 10;
    tfInfo.y = 10;
    tfInfo.height = stage.stageHeight - 80;
    tfInfo.width = stage.stageWidth - 20;
    addChild(tfInfo);

    // Determine accelerator support
    if (Accelerometer.isSupported)
    {
        accelerometer = new Accelerometer();
        accelerometer.addEventListener(AccelerometerEvent.UPDATE,
          accelerometerUpdateHandler);
    }
    else
    {
        tfInfo.text = "Motion sensor detection is not support on this " +
            "device. No shaking for you!";
    }

}
```

Code snippet Shakey.as

One of the key purposes of this app is to detect when a shake occurs. To that end, you want to define a custom `shake` event that you will write your application to dispatch when your app experiences a shake. To define the custom event, add the `[Event]` metatag above the `Shakey` class definition:

```
[Event("shake", "flash.events.Event")]
public class Shakey extends Sprite
{
    ...
}
```

Code snippet Shakey.as

Before you leave the constructor code you started earlier, add the following line:

```
addEventListener("shake", shakeHandler);
```

Therefore, when a shake event occurs, the shakeHandler() function is called.

The accelerometerUpdateHandler() contains the key logic that the app uses to determine whether a shake occurs. Here's the code:

```
private function accelerometerUpdateHandler(event:AccelerometerEvent):void
{
    // Constant used to determine whether a movement is strong enough
    // to constitute a "shake"
    var threshold:Number   = 0.7;

    // Determine delta for each dimension
    deltaX = Math.abs(accX - event.accelerationX);
    deltaY = Math.abs(accY - event.accelerationY);
    deltaZ = Math.abs(accZ - event.accelerationZ);

    // Algorithm to determine whether a shake occurred.
    if ((deltaX > threshold && deltaY > threshold) ||
        (deltaX > threshold && deltaZ > threshold) ||
        (deltaY > threshold && deltaZ > threshold))
    {
        dispatchEvent(new Event("shake"));
    }

    // Save acceleration data from this read
    accX = event.accelerationX;
    accY = event.accelerationY;
    accZ = event.accelerationZ;

}
```

Code snippet Shakey.as

The threshold is a number that determines whether a movement is strong enough to be called a shake. You may want to experiment with this number slightly. I settled at 0.7. Next, delta values are obtained for the x, y, and z axes based on the difference between the previous Accelerometer data and the current data set. These delta values are then compared to the threshold variable. If two of the three axes register values greater than 0.7, a shake event is dispatched.

The Accelerometer values are then saved with the accX, accY, and accZ variables for the next pass through.

The shakeHandler() method simply needs to increment the counter variable and display the information on-screen:

```
private function shakeHandler(event:Event):void
{
    shakes++;
    tfInfo.text = "Shakes detected: " + shakes.toString();
}
```

Code snippet Shakey.as

Listing 6-4 shows the full source code for the document class.

LISTING 6-4: Shakey.as

```
package
{
    import flash.display.Sprite;
    import flash.display.StageAlign;
    import flash.display.StageScaleMode;
    import flash.events.AccelerometerEvent;
    import flash.events.Event;
    import flash.events.EventDispatcher;
    import flash.sensors.Accelerometer;
    import flash.text.TextField;
    import flash.text.TextFormat;

    /**
     * Document class for Shakey application.
     * Sample code for Professional Flash Mobile Development
     *
     * @author Rich Wagner
     *
     */
    [Event("shake", "flash.events.Event")]
    public class Shakey extends Sprite
    {
        // Class properties
        private var accelerometer:Accelerometer;
        private var tfInfo:TextField;

        // Data used to determine a shake
        private var deltaX:Number;
        private var deltaY:Number;
        private var deltaZ:Number;
        private var accX:Number;
        private var accY:Number;
        private var accZ:Number;

        // Number of shakes captured
        private var shakes:int = 0;

        /**
         * Constructor
         *
         */
        public function Shakey()
        {
            stage.scaleMode = StageScaleMode.NO_SCALE;
            stage.align = StageAlign.TOP_LEFT;

            // Create text field
            tfInfo = new TextField();
            var format:TextFormat = new TextFormat("Helvetica", 26);
            format.color = 0x000000;
            tfInfo.defaultTextFormat = format;
```

continues

LISTING 6-4 *(continued)*

```
            tfInfo.border = false;
            tfInfo.wordWrap = true;
            tfInfo.multiline = true;
            tfInfo.x = 10;
            tfInfo.y = 10;
            tfInfo.height = stage.stageHeight - 80;
            tfInfo.width = stage.stageWidth - 20;
            addChild(tfInfo);

            // Determine accelerator support
            if (Accelerometer.isSupported)
            {
                accelerometer = new Accelerometer();
                accelerometer.addEventListener(AccelerometerEvent.UPDATE,
                  accelerometerUpdateHandler);
            }
            else
            {
                tfInfo.text = "Motion sensor detection is not supported on
this " + "device. No shaking for you!";
            }

            // Add custom shake event
            addEventListener("shake", shakeHandler);

        }


        /**
         * Handler for Accelerator updates
         *
         * @param event
         *
         */
        private function accelerometerUpdateHandler(event:AccelerometerEvent):void
        {
            // Constant used to determine whether a movement is strong enough
            // to constitute a "shake"
            var threshold:Number  = 0.72;

            // Determine delta for each dimension
            deltaX = Math.abs(accX - event.accelerationX);
            deltaY = Math.abs(accY - event.accelerationY);
            deltaZ = Math.abs(accZ - event.accelerationZ);

            // Algorithm to determine whether a shake occurred.
            if ((deltaX > threshold && deltaY > threshold) ||
                (deltaX > threshold && deltaZ > threshold) ||
                (deltaY > threshold && deltaZ > threshold))
            {
                dispatchEvent(new Event("shake"));
```

```
        }

        // Save acceleration data from this read
        accX = event.accelerationX;
        accY = event.accelerationY;
        accZ = event.accelerationZ;

    }

    /**
     * Handler for shake event
     *
     * @param event
     *
     */
    private function shakeHandler(event:Event):void
    {
        shakes++;
        tfInfo.text = "Shakes detected: " + shakes.toString();
    }


    }
}
```

Running the App

Figure 6-7 shows the on-screen results of running the app and shaking it vigorously. If too many shakes are being dispatched, you can adjust the time in which the Accelerometer updates with `setRequestedIntervalTime()` of the `Accelerometer` class, or you can try adjusting the threshold value.

SUMMARY

In this chapter, you discovered how to use the accelerometer, one of the core hardware components of any mobile device. I began by showing you how to listen for accelerometer events and then walked you through how to respond to these events in the user interface. Finally, while AS3 doesn't currently provide a shake event, I showed how you can combine your own logic with existing accelerometer events to detect shaking.

Shakes detected: 2

FIGURE 6-7

7

Implementing Auto Orientation

WHAT'S IN THIS CHAPTER?

➤ Rotating your app automatically

➤ Working with StageOrientationEvent

➤ Detecting an orientation change

If you are experienced in creating Flash or Flex applications for the Web or for Adobe Integrated Runtime (AIR) for Desktop, you are probably used to dealing with issues surrounding stretched versus fixed widths to account for different browser sizes or monitor resolutions. When you're developing for Android and iOS, it's a different world, because there is a new issue to contend with — screen orientation (or rotation).

Android and iOS users can change the orientation of their screens by physically turning the device with their hands. If an application changes its UI based on this change, it supports *auto orientation*. Therefore, application developers must face two key design questions:

➤ Will my app support auto orientation? Or will it stay fixed at portrait or landscape?

➤ If my app supports auto orientation, how should the UI change?

This chapter walks you through how to implement auto orientation into your Flash apps by focusing on how to respond to `StageOrientationEvent` events.

ENABLING YOUR APP TO ROTATE

Before you can implement auto orientation, you need to enable this feature in your Flash project. You can do this through the AIR Android Settings dialog box or by modifying the application descriptor XML file.

For Android apps, access the Android Settings dialog box (see Figure 7-1) by clicking the Android OS Settings Edit button in the Properties panel of your `.fla` document. Check the Auto Orientation check box and click OK.

For iPhone apps, access the iPhone Settings dialog box (see Figure 7-2) by clicking the iPhone OS Settings Edit button in the Properties panel. Check the Auto Orientation check box and click OK.

Or, if you prefer to work with the application descriptor XML file, set the `<autoOrients>` tag to `true`:

```
<initialWindow>
  <autoOrients>true</autoOrients>
</initialWindow>
```

Don't be misled by the "auto" in auto orientation. That setting doesn't mean that Flash will automatically reorient your app for you. Instead, it simply flips on the switch and allows your app to listen for `StageOrientationEvent` events.

FIGURE 7-1

FIGURE 7-2

STAGEORIENTATIONEVENT

When the user rotates the mobile device by hand, the stage dispatches a `StageOrientationEvent` event. You can listen for events at two stages of the orientation process:

➤ `StageOrientationEvent.ORIENTATION_CHANGE` is dispatched as the screen changes into a new orientation. When you're working with auto orientation, `orientationChange` is the primary event you'll work with.

➤ `StageOrientationEvent.ORIENTATION_CHANGING` is triggered before the bounds have changed. You'll usually want to trap for this event to perform a task (such as saving the current state) prior to the new orientation. The `StageOrientationEvent` has two key properties:

➤ `afterOrientation` provides a string value of the orientation after the change from a fixed set of options (the current orientation for an `orientationChange` event).

➤ `beforeOrientation` provides a string value of the orientation before the change from the same fixed set of options.

Here's the basic setup:

```
stage.addEventListener(StageOrientationEvent.ORIENTATION_CHANGE,
 myOrientationChangeHandler);

stage.addEventListener(StageOrientationEvent.ORIENTATION_CHANGING,
 myOrientationChangingHandler);

public function myOrientationChangeHandler(event:StageOrientationEvent):void
{
    // event.beforeOrientation - indicates previous orientation
    // event.afterOrientaion - indicates current orientation


}

public function myOrientationChangingHandler(event:StageOrientationEvent):void
{
    // event.beforeOrientation - indicates current orientation
    // event.afterOrientation - indicates new orientation
(unless the event is cancelled)
}
```

The `StageOrientationEvent` event is not triggered when the app loads. Therefore, to evaluate the orientation at this start-up, you need to explicitly call the handler function on your own.

TWO ESSENTIALS FOR UI REORIENTATION

Before any `StageOrientationEvent` events occur, you need to set two critical `stage` properties for auto orientation to work as intended: `align` and `scaleMode`. Specifically, be sure to set these properties as follows:

```
stage.align = StageAlign.TOP_LEFT;
stage.scaleMode = StageScaleMode.NO_SCALE;
```

Both of these ensure that when the screen rotation occurs, the stage is reset to align to the top left and doesn't scale to the original setting. Without these two property settings, any reorientation code you add fails to adjust to your new viewport dimensions.

DETECTING AN ORIENTATION CHANGE

You can detect an orientation change with the viewport and then perform an action based on the new orientation. You'll see a simple example of creating an app that contains a single TextField sized to the boundaries of the stage. When an orientation occurs, you can adjust the size as needed to match the new dimensions. What's more, you put information about the new orientation into the TextField.

Before diving into the AS3 code, perform the following steps to create the project:

1. Within the target directory, create a new Flash document based on the desired template and name it OrientationSimple.fla.

2. In the Properties panel, enter **OrientationSimple** as the document class, and click the pencil button to edit the class definition in your preferred editor.

Inside your editor, the OrientationSimple class is created as a child of Sprite. You begin by adding a single class property, which is a reference to the TextField:

```
public var tfInfo:TextField;
```

Then you set up the stage properties, TextField settings, and event handlers in the constructor:

```
public function OrientationSimple():void
{
    // Required property assignments if you want to
    // manually orient your app
    stage.align = StageAlign.TOP_LEFT;
    stage.scaleMode = StageScaleMode.NO_SCALE;

    // Create TextField
    tfInfo = new TextField();
    var format:TextFormat = new TextFormat("Helvetica", 26);
    format.color = 0xffffffff;
    tfInfo.defaultTextFormat = format;
    tfInfo.border = true;
    tfInfo.wordWrap = true;
    tfInfo.multiline = true;
    tfInfo.background = true;
    tfInfo.backgroundColor = 0xFF5500;
    tfInfo.x = 0;
    tfInfo.y = 0;
    tfInfo.height = stage.stageHeight;
    tfInfo.width = stage.stageWidth;
    addChild(tfInfo);

    // Set up stage orientation
    try
    {
        stage.addEventListener(StageOrientationEvent.ORIENTATION_CHANGE,
            orientationChangeListener);
        print("Rotate me");

    }
```

```
        catch(e:Error)
        {
            print("Stage orientation not supported.");
        }

    }
```

You begin by setting the key `align` and `scaleMode` properties for the stage to ensure that auto orientation works as expected. You then instantiate the `TextField`, format it, set its x, y coordinates to the top-left of the stage, and size it the same dimensions as the stage.

Inside the `try/catch` block, you attempt to add an event listener for the `StageOrientationEvent` `.ORIENTATION_CHANGE` event. If this attempt fails, the user is notified with a call to a custom `print()` method:

```
        public function print(obj:Object):void
        {
            tfInfo.text = obj as String;
        }
```

If you're creating an Android app, the event handler is defined as follows:

```
        public function orientationChangeListener(event:StageOrientationEvent):void
        {

            // Reassign dimensions
            tfInfo.width = stage.stageWidth;
            tfInfo.height = stage.stageHeight

            if (event.afterOrientation)
            {
                if (stage.orientation == StageOrientation.DEFAULT )
                    print("Portrait");
                else if (stage.orientation == StageOrientation.ROTATED_RIGHT)
                    print("Landscape");
            }
        }
```

In this function, the dimensions of the `TextField` are reassigned to be the same as the new stage width and height. The `event.afterOrientation` is checked, so the code block inside it is executed only after the orientation has changed, not before.

The conditional block inside evaluates the `screen.orientation` property with the `ScreenOrientation` object, which provides the possible orientation values:

➤   `ScreenOrientation.DEFAULT`

➤   `ScreenOrientation.ROTATED_RIGHT`

If you're developing for iOS, you can take advantage of some additional orientation return values. See the expanded handler code:

```
public function orientationChangeListener(event:StageOrientationEvent):void
{

    // Reassign dimensions
    tfInfo.width = stage.stageWidth;
    tfInfo.height = stage.stageHeight;

    if(event.afterOrientation)
    {
        if (stage.orientation == StageOrientation.DEFAULT )
            print("Portrait");
        else if (stage.orientation == StageOrientation.UPSIDE_DOWN)
            print("Portrait (upside down)")
        else if (stage.orientation == StageOrientation.ROTATED_LEFT )
            print("Landscape (left, screen turned counterclockwise")
        else if (stage.orientation == StageOrientation.ROTATED_RIGHT)
            print("Landscape (right, screen turned clockwise)");
        else
            print("Where am I? I am totally disoriented");
    }


     if (event.afterOrientation)
     {
         if (stage.orientation == StageOrientation.DEFAULT )
            print("Portrait");
         else if (stage.orientation == StageOrientation.ROTATED_RIGHT)
            print("Landscape");
     }
 }
}
```

Code snippet OrientationSimple.as

Android does not currently support the following ScreenOrientation *constants:*

➤ ScreenOrientation.ROTATED_LEFT

➤ ScreenOrientation.UPSIDE_DOWN

➤ ScreenOrientation.UNKNOWN

Listing 7-1 provides the full source code for a version of OrientationSimple.as that would work under both Android and iOS.

LISTING 7-1: OrientationSimple.as

```
package
{
    import flash.display.MovieClip;
    import flash.display.*;
```

```
import flash.display.Sprite;
import flash.events.*;
import flash.text.*;

/**
 * Document class for OrientationSimple application.
 * Sample code for Professional Flash Mobile Development app
 *
 * @author Rich Wagner
 *
 */
public class OrientationSimple extends Sprite
{
    public var tfInfo:TextField;

    /**
     * Constructor
     *
     */
    public function OrientationSimple():void
    {
        // Required property assignments if you want to
        // manually orient your app
        stage.align = StageAlign.TOP_LEFT;
        stage.scaleMode = StageScaleMode.NO_SCALE;

        tfInfo = new TextField();
        var format:TextFormat = new TextFormat("Helvetica", 26);
        format.color = 0xffffffff;
        tfInfo.defaultTextFormat = format;
        tfInfo.border = true;
        tfInfo.wordWrap = true;
        tfInfo.multiline = true;
        tfInfo.background = true;
        tfInfo.backgroundColor = 0xFF5500;
        tfInfo.x = 0;
        tfInfo.y = 0;
        tfInfo.height = stage.stageHeight;
        tfInfo.width = stage.stageWidth;
        addChild(tfInfo);

        try
        {
            print("Rotate me");
            stage.addEventListener(StageOrientationEvent.ORIENTATION_CHANGE,
             orientationChangeListener);
        }
        catch(e:Error)
        {
            print("Stage orientation not supported.");
        }

    }

    /**
```

continues

LISTING 7-1 *(continued)*

```
           * Listener for orientation changes
           *
           * @param event
           *
           */
          public function orientationChangeListener(event:StageOrientationEvent):void
          {
              tfInfo.width = stage.stageWidth;
              tfInfo.height = stage.stageHeight;

              if(event.afterOrientation)
              {
                  if (stage.orientation == StageOrientation.DEFAULT ||
        stage.orientation == StageOrientation.UPSIDE_DOWN )
                          print("Portrait");
                  else if (stage.orientation == StageOrientation.ROTATED_RIGHT
        || stage.orientation == StageOrientation.ROTATED_LEFT)
                          print("Landscape");
              }
          }


          /**
           * Prints specified param to UI
           *
           * @param obj
           *
           */
          public function print(obj:Object):void
          {
              tfInfo.text = obj as String;
          }

      }
  }
```

Listing 7-2 provides an alternative version that provides additional iOS-specific feedback.

LISTING 7-2: OrientationSimple.as (alternative version)

```
package
{
    import flash.display.MovieClip;
    import flash.display.*;
    import flash.display.Sprite;
```

```
import flash.events.*;
import flash.text.*;

/**
 * Document class for OrientationSimple application.
 * Sample code for Professional Flash Mobile Development app
 *
 * @author Rich Wagner
 *
 */
public class OrientationSimple extends Sprite
{
    public var tfInfo:TextField;

    /**
     * Constructor
     *
     */
    public function OrientationSimple():void
    {
        // Required property assignments if you want to
        // manually orient your app
        stage.align = StageAlign.TOP_LEFT;
        stage.scaleMode = StageScaleMode.NO_SCALE;

        tfInfo = new TextField();
        var format:TextFormat = new TextFormat("Helvetica", 26);
        format.color = 0xffffffff;
        tfInfo.defaultTextFormat = format;
        tfInfo.border = true;
        tfInfo.wordWrap = true;
        tfInfo.multiline = true;
        tfInfo.background = true;
        tfInfo.backgroundColor = 0xFF5500;
        tfInfo.x = 0;
        tfInfo.y = 0;
        tfInfo.height = stage.stageHeight;
        tfInfo.width = stage.stageWidth;
        addChild(tfInfo);

        try
        {
            print("Rotate me");

stage.addEventListener(StageOrientationEvent.ORIENTATION_CHANGE,
                    orientationChangeListener);
        }
        catch(e:Error)
        {
            print("Stage orientation not supported.");
```

continues

LISTING 7-2 *(continued)*

```
            }

    }

    /**
     * Listener for orientation changes
     *
     * @param event
     *
     */
    public function orientationChangeListener(event:StageOrientationEvent):void
    {

        tfInfo.width = stage.stageWidth;
        tfInfo.height = stage.stageHeight;

        if(event.afterOrientation)
        {
            if (stage.orientation == StageOrientation.DEFAULT )
                print("Portrait");
            else if (stage.orientation == StageOrientation.UPSIDE_DOWN)
                print("Portrait (upside down)")
            else if (stage.orientation == StageOrientation.ROTATED_LEFT )
                print("Landscape (left, screen turned counterclockwise")
            else if (stage.orientation == StageOrientation.ROTATED_RIGHT)
                print("Landscape (right, screen turned clockwise)");
            else
                print("Where am I? I am totally disoriented");
        }
    }


    /**
     * Prints specified param to UI
     *
     * @param obj
     *
     */
    public function print(obj:Object):void
    {
        tfInfo.text = obj as String;
    }

    }
}
```

Figures 7-3 through 7-6 show the iOS-specific app running in all different orientations.

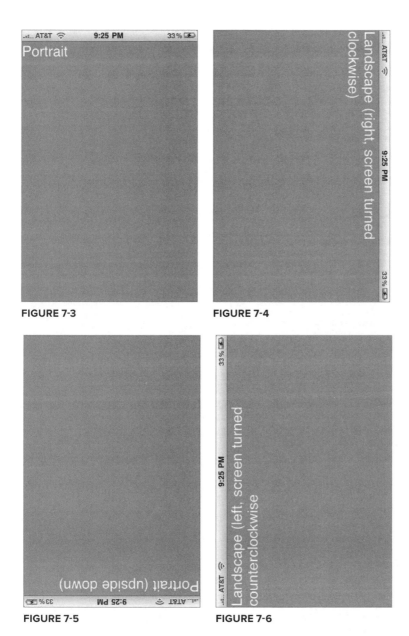

FIGURE 7-3 **FIGURE 7-4**

FIGURE 7-5 **FIGURE 7-6**

CHANGING POSITIONING BASED ON ORIENTATION CHANGES

Using the StageOrientationEvent event, you can begin to position components of the UI dynamically based on whether the viewport is in portrait or landscape mode.

To illustrate how this is done, this section shows you how to create an app with two objects on the stage that are repositioned when the screen rotates.

You begin by setting up the project and calling it `OrientExpress`, creating a new `OrientExpress.fla` based on the AIR for Android template, and then creating the document class of the same name that extends the `Sprite` class. You edit the `OrientExpress` class in your editor.

You define the two UI components to be used in the app:

➤   `public var tfInfo:TextField;`

➤   `public var btnDefault:Button;`

The constructor looks similar to the `OrientationSimple` example, except that a `Button` object is added to the stage:

```
// Manually orient your app
stage.align = StageAlign.TOP_LEFT;
stage.scaleMode = StageScaleMode.NO_SCALE;

// Set up TextField
tfInfo = new TextField();
var format:TextFormat = new TextFormat("Helvetica", 26);
format.color = 0xffffffff;
tfInfo.defaultTextFormat = format;
tfInfo.border = true;
tfInfo.wordWrap = true;
tfInfo.multiline = true;
tfInfo.background = true;
tfInfo.backgroundColor = 0x7AB900;
tfInfo.x = 10;
tfInfo.y = 10;
tfInfo.height = stage.stageHeight - 80;
tfInfo.width = stage.stageWidth - 20;
addChild(tfInfo);

// Set up Button
btnDefault = new Button();
btnDefault.width = stage.stageWidth-20;
btnDefault.height = 44;
btnDefault.x = 10;
btnDefault.y = stage.stageHeight - 54;
addChild(btnDefault);

try
{
    tfInfo.text = stage.orientation;
    stage.addEventListener(StageOrientationEvent.ORIENTATION_CHANGE,
      orientationChangeHandler);
}
catch(e:Error)
{
    print("Stage orientation not supported.");
}
```

Code snippet OrientExpress.as

Note that the TextField is sized to be 80 pixels smaller than the stage height and 20 pixels smaller than the stage width. The Button y positioning is then set to be 54 pixels smaller than the stage height.

In the orientationChange handler, the width and height properties of tfInfo are set to new sizes based on the new sizes of the stage. The btnDefault button is then repositioned based on the stage's new height, and its width is adjusted relative to the stage.StageWidth value:

```
public function orientationChangeHandler(event:StageOrientationEvent):void
{

    if(event.afterOrientation)
    {
        if (stage.orientation == StageOrientation.DEFAULT || stage.orientation
== StageOrientation.UPSIDE_DOWN)
        {
            tfInfo.width = stage.stageWidth - 20;
            tfInfo.height = stage.stageHeight - 80;

            btnDefault.x = 10;
            btnDefault.y = stage.stageHeight - 54;
            btnDefault.width = stage.stageWidth - 20;

        }
        else if (stage.orientation == StageOrientation.ROTATED_RIGHT ||
stage.orientation == StageOrientation.ROTATED_LEFT)
        {
            tfInfo.width = stage.stageWidth - 20;
            tfInfo.height = stage.stageHeight - 80;

            btnDefault.width = stage.stageWidth - 20;
            btnDefault.x = 10;
            btnDefault.y = stage.stageHeight - 54;
        }
        else
        {
            // Do something
        }

        print("orientation:" + stage.orientation);
    }
}
```

Code snippet OrientExpress.as

Listing 7-3 shows the full source code for OrientExpress.as.

LISTING 7-3: OrientExpress.as

```
package
{
    import flash.display.*;
    import flash.display.Sprite;
    import flash.events.*;
```

continues

LISTING 7-3 *(continued)*

```
import flash.text.*;
import fl.controls.Button;
import fl.controls.Label;
import fl.controls.LabelButton;

/**
 * Document class for OrientExpress application
 * Sample code for Professional Flash Mobile Developmentapp
 *
 * @author Rich Wagner
 *
 */
public class OrientExpress extends Sprite
{
    public var tfInfo:TextField;
    public var btnDefault:Button;

    /**
     * Constructor
     *
     */
    public function OrientExpress():void
    {
        // Required property assignments if you want to
        // manually orient your app
        stage.align = StageAlign.TOP_LEFT;
        stage.scaleMode = StageScaleMode.NO_SCALE;

        // Set up TextField
        tfInfo = new TextField();
        var format:TextFormat = new TextFormat("Helvetica", 26);
        format.color = 0xffffffff;
        tfInfo.defaultTextFormat = format;
        tfInfo.border = true;
        tfInfo.wordWrap = true;
        tfInfo.multiline = true;
        tfInfo.background = true;
        tfInfo.backgroundColor = 0x7AB900;
        tfInfo.x = 10;
        tfInfo.y = 10;
        tfInfo.height = stage.stageHeight - 80;
        tfInfo.width = stage.stageWidth - 20;
        addChild(tfInfo);

        // Set up Button
        btnDefault = new Button();
        btnDefault.width = stage.stageWidth-20;
        btnDefault.height = 44;
        btnDefault.x = 10;
        btnDefault.y = stage.stageHeight - 54;
```

```actionscript
        addChild(btnDefault);

        try
        {
            tfInfo.text = stage.orientation;
            stage.addEventListener(StageOrientationEvent.ORIENTATION_CHANGE,
              orientationChangeHandler);
        }
        catch(e:Error)
        {
            print("Stage orientation not supported.");
        }
    }


    /**
     * Listener for orientation changes
     *
     * @param event
     *
     */
    public function orientationChangeHandler(event:StageOrientationEvent):void
    {

        if(event.afterOrientation)
        {
            if (stage.orientation == StageOrientation.DEFAULT ||
                stage.orientation == StageOrientation.UPSIDE_DOWN)
            {
                tfInfo.width = stage.stageWidth - 20;
                tfInfo.height = stage.stageHeight - 80;

                btnDefault.x = 10;
                btnDefault.y = stage.stageHeight - 54;
                btnDefault.width = stage.stageWidth - 20;

            }
            else if (stage.orientation == StageOrientation.ROTATED_LEFT ||
                    stage.orientation == StageOrientation.ROTATED_RIGHT)
            {
                tfInfo.width = stage.stageWidth - 20;
                tfInfo.height = stage.stageHeight - 80;

                btnDefault.width = stage.stageWidth - 20;
                btnDefault.x = 10;
                btnDefault.y = stage.stageHeight - 54;
            }
            else
            {
        // Do something
            }

            print("orientation:" + stage.orientation);
```

continues

LISTING 7-3 *(continued)*

```
            }
        }

        /**
         * Prints specified param to UI
         *
         * @param obj
         *
         */
        public function print(obj:Object):void
        {
            tfInfo.text = obj as String;
        }


    }
}
```

Figures 7-7 and 7-8 show the app running first in default portrait mode and then shifted left. The components are resized and positioned when they are in landscape mode.

FIGURE 7-7

FIGURE 7-8

SUMMARY

In this chapter, you discovered how to configure your Flash-based Android or iOS application to support auto orientation. You learned how to listen to and create a handler for the `StageOrientationEvent`. You then walked through an example that showed how to detect an orientation change. Finally, you discovered how to reposition the UI based on the current orientation.

8

Geolocation API

WHAT'S IN THIS CHAPTER?

➤ Working with the Geolocation class

➤ Enabling GPS support on Android devices

➤ Getting speed and altitude info from the Geolocation class

Where do you want to go today? may have been an old Microsoft advertising campaign, but with access to the GPS location services of Android and iPhone, you can build apps with a slightly different slogan: *Go where you want, but we can guide you every step of the way.*

AIR for Android and Packager for iPhone provide access to mobile location services through two classes: `Geolocation` and `GeolocationEvent`. This chapter shows you how to work with these two classes to make your apps location aware. It highlights four sample apps that utilize geolocation:

➤ `Geolocate` — A simple raw display of location data

➤ `Poorman Compass` — A simple compass app

➤ `Speedometer` — A simple speedometer app

➤ `FindMeAPizza` — An app that finds the nearest pizza shop

GETTING GEOLOCATION DATA

You can use a combination of the `Geolocation` and `GeolocationEvent` classes to retrieve geolocation data into your app. The `Geolocation` class is the controller that dispatches events triggered by the Android location sensor. Table 8-1 displays the properties, methods, and events of `Geolocation`.

TABLE 8-1: Geolocation Members

TYPE	NAME	DESCRIPTION
Property	`isSupported:Boolean (static)`	Indicates whether the device supports geolocation services
Property	`muted:Boolean`	Specifies whether the user has given permission to access geolocation information in the app
Methods	`setRequestedUpdateInterval(interval)`	Sets the time interval for updates (milliseconds)
Event	`StatusEvent.Status`	Dispatched when the user changes the access permission to geolocation
Event	`GeolocationEvent.Update`	Dispatched when the location sensor updates the app

However, because your app may or may not be running on a mobile device that doesn't have built-in GPS, you first need to check to see whether a geolocation sensor is available using the static `Geolocation` method `isSupported()`, which returns a Boolean value indicating support.

After you establish the fact that geolocation services are available, you can instantiate a `Geolocation` object and configure it for use. A typical scenario looks something like this:

```
if (Geolocation.isSupported)
{
    var geo:Geolocation = new Geolocation();
    geo.setRequestedUpdateInterval(200);
    geo.addEventListener(GeolocationEvent.UPDATE, geolocationUpdateHandler);
    geo.addEventListener(StatusEvent.STATUS, geolocationStatusHandler);
}
else
{
    Trace("Geolocation not available.);
}
```

The `setRequestedUpdateInterval()` method sets up a requested time interval (in milliseconds) in which to receive location updates. However, note the usage of the word `requested`. The actual time may vary, because the OS and location sensor ultimately are responsible for determining the interval.

Depending on the OS, the default interval will be around 100 ms when working with geolocation services. Therefore, you don't have to specifically call the `setRequestedUpdateInterval()` method to get `Geolocation` to provide updates.

The `setRequestedUpdateInterval()` method can be helpful for conserving battery power, particularly if your app doesn't need constant real-time updates. So, if you would like to request an update only every one second instead of every tenth of a second, you'd be making 90 percent fewer calls.

Next, a handler for the `GeolocationEvent.UPDATE` event is assigned with `addEventListener()`. The `update` event is dispatched each time the location sensor provides an update based on the requested or OS-determined time interval or whenever the location sensor updates following a device coming back from sleep or from being out of GPS range.

When the `update` event is dispatched, the `GeolocationEvent` object returns the geolocation information shown in Table 8-2. (Support for `GeolocationEvent` depends on the device.)

TABLE 8-2: GeolocationEvent Properties

NAME	DESCRIPTION
altitude	Altitude (meters).
heading	Direction of movement in degrees (0–359) from north pole (north = 0).
horizontalAccuracy	Horizontal accuracy (meters).
latitude	Latitude in degrees between 90 and –90. Positive latitude is north, whereas negative latitude is south.
longitude	Longitude in degrees between 180 and –180. Positive longitude is east, whereas negative longitude is west.
speed	Current speed (meters per second).
timestamp	Amount of time (milliseconds) between the current event and the initialization of the `Geolocation` instance.
verticalAccuracy	Vertical accuracy (meters).

A final event that you need to listen for is a change in the geolocation's status. The `status` event is dispatched whenever the user changes access permissions to the geolocation sensor. You can use this event in combination with the `muted` property to determine whether you have access to the geolocation sensor.

ENABLING GPS SUPPORT FOR ANDROID

To enable `Geolocation` services in your Android app, the application descriptor file of your app needs to specify permission to use GPS services. You give permission with the `android.permission` `.ACCESS_FINE_LOCATION` parameter inside of the Android manifest section:

```
<android>
    <manifestAdditions>
      <manifest>
        <data>
          <![CDATA[
          <uses-permission android:name="android.permission.ACCESS_FINE_LOCATION" />
          ]]>
        </data>
```

```
      </manifest>
    </manifestAdditions>
  </android>
```

Without this explicit permission, your app will not have access to geolocation data.

CREATING A BASIC GEOLOCATION APPLICATION

To demonstrate how this all works, I lead you through the process of building an app called `Geolocate` that simply accesses geolocation services on the Android and iPhone and periodically returns current data to the app. The app then logs the incoming data to the UI.

Before diving into the code, here's how to set up the project:

1.   Within the target directory, create a new Flash document using the desired template and name it `Geolocate.fla`.

2.   Set the background color of the stage to black (#000000). (I use white text on a black background.)

3.   In the Properties panel, enter **Geolocate** as the document class, and click the pencil button to edit the class definition in your preferred editor.

Coding the Document Class

In defining the `Geolocate` class, you begin by setting up class properties. In this case, you need to define `Geolocation` and `TextField` variables. The app uses the `TextField` variables to display the geolocation information it receives from the `update` event:

```
private var geo:Geolocation;

private var tfInfo:TextField;
```

Code snippet Geolocate.as

`Geolocate`'s constructor instantiates the `tfInfo` `TextField`, adds it to the display list, and sets up the UI. It then tests `Geolocation.isSupported` to see whether location services are available. If they are available, the `Geolocation` object is created and assigned an `update` event handler. Here's the code:

```
public function Geolocate()
{
    // Set up the stage.
    stage.scaleMode = StageScaleMode.NO_SCALE;
    stage.align = StageAlign.TOP_LEFT;

    // Create TextField.
    tfInfo = new TextField();
    var format:TextFormat = new TextFormat("Helvetica", 18);
    format.color = 0xffffff;
    tfInfo.defaultTextFormat = format;
```

```
        tfInfo.border = true;
        tfInfo.wordWrap = true;
        tfInfo.multiline = true;
        tfInfo.x = 10;
        tfInfo.y = 10;
        tfInfo.height = stage.stageHeight - 20;
        tfInfo.width = stage.stageWidth - 20;
        addChild(tfInfo);

        // Is geolocation supported?
        if (Geolocation.isSupported)
        {
            // If so, set it up.
            geo = new Geolocation();
            geo.setRequestedUpdateInterval(500);
            geo.addEventListener(GeolocationEvent.UPDATE, geolocationUpdateHandler);
            geo.addEventListener(StatusEvent.STATUS, geolocationStatusHandler);

        }
        // If not, let the user know.
        else
        {
            tfInfo.text =  "No geolocation services available.";
        }
    }
```

Code snippet Geolocate.as

You are now ready to set up the listener method for the update event. This Geolocate app provides only a raw data feed of the information received from the location sensor; just turn it around and display it on the screen using tfInfo:

Available for download on Wrox.com

```
private function geolocationUpdateHandler(event:GeolocationEvent):void
{
    tfInfo.text = "Raw Geolocation Data:\n";
    tfInfo.appendText("Latitude:" +  Math.round(event.latitude).toString() +
        "°\n");
    tfInfo.appendText("Longitude:" + Math.round(event.longitude).toString() +
        "°\n");
    tfInfo.appendText("Altitude:" + Math.round(event.altitude).toString() +
        " m\n");
    tfInfo.appendText("Speed:" + Math.round(event.speed).toString() + "
        m/s\n");
    tfInfo.appendText("Horizontal Accuracy:" +
        Math.round(event.horizontalAccuracy).toString() + " m\n");
    tfInfo.appendText("Vertical Accuracy:" +
        Math.round(event.verticalAccuracy).toString() + " m\n");
    tfInfo.appendText("Heading:" + Math.round(event.heading).toString() +
        "°");
}
```

Code snippet Geolocate.as]

For this demo, you round the numbers received to make them easier to read.

Also watch for status changes, and display appropriate user feedback if access is denied:

```
private function geolocationStatusHandler(event:StatusEvent):void
{
    // If the user is not allowing updates, then display
    if (geo.muted)
    tfInfo.text =  "No geolocation services available.";
}
```

Listing 8-1 shows the complete source code for the `Geolocate.as` document class.

LISTING 8-1: Geolocate.as

```
package
{

    import flash.display.Sprite;
    import flash.display.StageAlign;
    import flash.display.StageScaleMode;
    import flash.events.GeolocationEvent;
    import flash.events.StatusEvent;
    import flash.sensors.Geolocation;
    import flash.text.TextField;
    import flash.text.TextFormat;

    /**
     * Document class for Geolocate application.
     * Sample code for Professional Flash Mobile Development
     *
     * @author Rich Wagner
     *
     */
    public class Geolocate extends Sprite
    {

        // Geolocation
        private var geo:Geolocation;

        // TextField
        private var tfInfo:TextField;

        /**
         * Constructor
         *
         */
        public function Geolocate()
        {

            // Set up the stage.
            stage.scaleMode = StageScaleMode.NO_SCALE;
            stage.align = StageAlign.TOP_LEFT;

            // Create TextField.
            tfInfo = new TextField();
            var format:TextFormat = new TextFormat("Helvetica", 18);
```

```
            format.color = 0xffffff;
            tfInfo.defaultTextFormat = format;
            tfInfo.border = true;
            tfInfo.wordWrap = true;
            tfInfo.multiline = true;
            tfInfo.x = 10;
            tfInfo.y = 10;
            tfInfo.height = stage.stageHeight - 20;
            tfInfo.width = stage.stageWidth - 20;
            addChild(tfInfo);

            // Is geolocation supported?
            if (Geolocation.isSupported)
            {
                // If so, set it up.
                geo = new Geolocation();
                geo.setRequestedUpdateInterval(500);
                geo.addEventListener(GeolocationEvent.UPDATE,
geolocationUpdateHandler);
                geo.addEventListener(StatusEvent.STATUS,
geolocationStatusHandler);
            }
            // If not, let the user know.
            else
            {
                tfInfo.text =  "No geolocation services available.";
            }
        }


        /**
         * Called each time the geolocation services update app
         *
         * @param event
         *
         */
        private function geolocationUpdateHandler(event:GeolocationEvent):void
        {
            tfInfo.text = "Raw Geolocation Data:\n";
            tfInfo.appendText("Latitude:" +
Math.round(event.latitude).toString() +
                "°\n");
            tfInfo.appendText("Longitude:" +
Math.round(event.longitude).toString() +
                "°\n");
            tfInfo.appendText("Altitude:" +
Math.round(event.altitude).toString() +
                " m\n");
            tfInfo.appendText("Speed:" + Math.round(event.speed).toString() +
                " m/s\n");
            tfInfo.appendText("Horizontal Accuracy:" +
                Math.round(event.horizontalAccuracy).toString() + " m\n");
            tfInfo.appendText("Vertical Accuracy:" +
                Math.round(event.verticalAccuracy).toString() + " m\n");
            tfInfo.appendText("Heading:" +
```

continues

LISTING 8-1 *(continued)*

```
Math.round(event.heading).toString() + "°");
        }

        /**
         * Called each time the status changes
         *
         * @param event
         *
         */
        private function geolocationStatusHandler(event:StatusEvent):void
        {
            // If the user is not allowing updates, then display
            if (geo.muted)
                tfInfo.text =  "No geolocation services available.";
        }


    }


}
```

Testing and Running the App

Going back to the `.fla` document, you can test this app on your computer before installing it on your Android device by using the Debug feature in Flash CS5. As you would expect, however, AIR's debugger tool fails the `Geolocation.isSupported` test, as shown in Figure 8-1.

After publishing the Flash project and installing the app onto your device, you are ready to try it. Figure 8-2 shows the app running on iPhone.

FIGURE 8-1

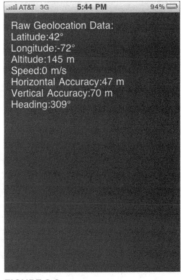

FIGURE 8-2

If you're testing your Android app using the SDK's Android emulator, you can simulate geographical location. For details, go to `http://developer.android.com/guide/developing/tools/emulator.html#geo`.

CREATING A COMPASS APP

Although `Geolocate` displays raw geolocation data on the screen, you can use the heading data from the location sensor to build a compass. The Android Market has plenty of compass apps already and iPhone comes with one included with the OS, but here you learn how to build a "poor man's compass," telling the user the general direction in which he is pointed: north, south, east, or west. This app displays one of four bitmap images that offer directional information to the user.

To begin, you set up the project by doing the following:

1. Within the target directory, create a new Flash document using the desired template and name it **PoorManCompass.fla**.

2. In the Properties panel, enter **Compass** as the document class, and click the pencil button to edit the class definition in your preferred editor.

Coding the Document Class

Inside the `Compass` class, begin by defining several class properties. In addition to a `Geolocation` variable, you need to define four image classes and bitmap variables:

Available for download on Wrox.com

```
// Geolocation
private var geo:Geolocation;

// External images
[Embed(source="north.jpg")]
private var NorthImage:Class;

[Embed(source="south.jpg")]
private var SouthImage:Class;

[Embed(source="east.jpg")]
private var EastImage:Class;

[Embed(source="west.jpg")]
private var WestImage:Class;

// Bitmaps for each direction
private var north:Bitmap;
private var south:Bitmap;
private var east:Bitmap;
private var west:Bitmap;
```

Code snippet Compass.as

You use the `[Embed]` tag to embed the four `.jpg` images into the app and associate it with a variable. As discussed in Chapter 3, the `[Embed]` metadata tag requires the Flex SDK. As a result, when you first publish the app, Flash CS5 prompts you for the Flex SDK path to the Library path of your project. (If you have Flex installed on your computer, simply provide your existing Flex SDK directory. Or, if you don't have the Flex SDK, it's a free download at www.adobe.com/cfusion/ entitlement/index.cfm?e=flex4sdk

You then associate these image files with the Bitmap variables in the constructor.

You use the constructor to set up the stage and geolocation services as well as create the bitmaps that the app will use. Here's the code:

```
public function Compass()
{

    stage.scaleMode = StageScaleMode.NO_SCALE;
    stage.align = StageAlign.TOP_LEFT;

    if (Geolocation.isSupported)
    {
        geo = new Geolocation();
        geo.setRequestedUpdateInterval(200);
        geo.addEventListener(GeolocationEvent.UPDATE, geolocationUpdateHandler);
        geo.addEventListener(StatusEvent.STATUS, geolocationStatusHandler);

        // Create bitmaps.
        north = new NorthImage();
        north.smoothing = true;
        north.visible = false;
        addChild(north);

        south = new SouthImage();
        south.smoothing = true;
        south.visible = false;
        addChild(south);

        east = new EastImage();
        east.smoothing = true;
        east.visible = false;
        addChild(east);

        west = new WestImage();
        west.smoothing = true;
        west.visible = false;
        addChild(west);

    }
    else
    {
        noSupportNotify();
    }


}
```

Code snippet Compass.as

If geolocation services are supported, the `geolocation` instance is instantiated and set up. The four bitmapped images are created and added to the stage. But the `visible` property of each is set to `false` initially. If geolocation services are not available, the `noSupportNotify()` method is called, which informs the user that the location sensor is not available. This private method is defined as follows:

```
private function noSupportNotify():void
{
    var tfInfo:TextField = new TextField();
    var format:TextFormat = new TextFormat("Helvetica", 22);
    format.color = 0x000000;
    tfInfo.defaultTextFormat = format;
    tfInfo.border = false;
    tfInfo.wordWrap = true;
    tfInfo.multiline = true;
    tfInfo.x = 10;
    tfInfo.y = 10;
    tfInfo.height = stage.stageHeight - 20;
    tfInfo.width = stage.stageWidth - 20;
    tfInfo.text =  "No geolocation services available.";
    addChild(tfInfo);
}
```

Code snippet Compass.as

The heart of the app is `geolocationUpdateHandler()`. The heading `property` will be evaluated to determine which bitmap to display. Here's the logic for the simplified compass. If the heading is:

➤ Above 316 degrees or less than 45, display the north image

➤ Between 46 and 135, display the east image

➤ Between 136 and 225, display the south image

➤ Between 226 and 315, display the west image

Here's the code:

```
private function geolocationUpdateHandler(event:GeolocationEvent):void
{
    var h:Number = event.heading;

    if ( (h > 316) || (h < 45))
        updateUI(north)
    else if ( (h > 46) && (h < 135))
        updateUI(east)
    else if ( (h > 136) && (h < 225))
        updateUI(south)
    else if ( (h > 226) && (h < 315))
        updateUI(west)

}
```

Code snippet Compass.as

The `updateUI()` utility function toggles the visibility of the images based on the incoming parameter:

```
private function updateUI(bitmap:Bitmap):void
{
    north.visible = (north == bitmap);
    south.visible = (south == bitmap);
    east.visible = (east == bitmap);
    west.visible = (west == bitmap);
}
```

Code snippet Compass.as

Listing 8-2 shows the complete source code for the `Compass.as` document class.

LISTING 8-2: Compass.as

```
package
{
    import flash.display.Bitmap;
    import flash.display.Sprite;
    import flash.text.TextField;
    import flash.text.TextFormat;
    import flash.display.MovieClip;
    import flash.events.StatusEvent;
    import flash.events.GeolocationEvent;
    import flash.sensors.Geolocation;
    import flash.display.StageAlign;
    import flash.display.StageScaleMode;

    /**
     * Document class for PoorManCompass application
     * Sample code for Professional Flash Mobile Development      *
     * @author Rich Wagner
     *
     */
    public class Compass extends MovieClip
    {
        // Geolocation
        private var geo:Geolocation;

        // External images
        [Embed(source="north.jpg")]
        private var NorthImage:Class;

        [Embed(source="south.jpg")]
        private var SouthImage:Class;

        [Embed(source="east.jpg")]
        private var EastImage:Class;

        [Embed(source="west.jpg")]
        private var WestImage:Class;

        // Bitmaps for each direction
```

```
private var north:Bitmap;
private var south:Bitmap;
private var east:Bitmap;
private var west:Bitmap;

/**
 * Constructor
 *
 */
public function Compass()
{

    stage.scaleMode = StageScaleMode.NO_SCALE;
    stage.align = StageAlign.TOP_LEFT;

    if (Geolocation.isSupported)
    {
        geo = new Geolocation();
        geo.setRequestedUpdateInterval(200);
        geo.addEventListener(GeolocationEvent.UPDATE,
geolocationUpdateHandler);
        geo.addEventListener(StatusEvent.STATUS,
geolocationStatusHandler);

        // Create bitmaps.
        north = new NorthImage();
        north.smoothing = true;
        north.visible = false;
        addChild(north);

        south = new SouthImage();
        south.smoothing = true;
        south.visible = false;
        addChild(south);

        east = new EastImage();
        east.smoothing = true;
        east.visible = false;
        addChild(east);

        west = new WestImage();
        west.smoothing = true;
        west.visible = false;
        addChild(west);

    }
    else
    {
        noSupportNotify();
    }


}

/**
```

continues

LISTING 8-2 *(continued)*

```
 * Toggles visibility of bitmaps to display current direction
 *
 * @param bitmap
 *
 */
private function updateUI(bitmap:Bitmap):void
{
    north.visible = (north == bitmap);
    south.visible = (south == bitmap);
    east.visible = (east == bitmap);
    west.visible = (west == bitmap);
}


/**
 * Called each time the geolocation service updates app
 *
 * @param event
 *
 */
private function geolocationUpdateHandler(event:GeolocationEvent):void
{
    var h:Number = event.heading;

    if ( (h > 316) || (h < 45))
        updateUI(north)
    else if ( (h > 46) && (h < 135))
        updateUI(east)
    else if ( (h > 136) && (h < 225))
        updateUI(south)
    else if ( (h > 226) && (h < 315))
        updateUI(west)

}


/**
 * Notifies the user that no service is available due to lack
 * of geo-awareness of device
 *
 */
private function noSupportNotify():void
{
    var tfInfo:TextField = new TextField();
    var format:TextFormat = new TextFormat("Helvetica", 22);
    format.color = 0x000000;
    tfInfo.defaultTextFormat = format;
    tfInfo.border = false;
    tfInfo.wordWrap = true;
    tfInfo.multiline = true;
    tfInfo.x = 10;
    tfInfo.y = 10;
    tfInfo.height = stage.stageHeight - 20;
```

```
                tfInfo.width = stage.stageWidth - 20;
                tfInfo.text =  "No geolocation services available.";
                addChild(tfInfo);
        }


        /**
         * Called each time the status changes
         *
         * @param event
         *
         */
        private function geolocationStatusHandler(event:StatusEvent):void
        {
            // If the user is not allowing updates, then display
            if (geo.muted)
                noSupportNoify();
        }


    }
}
```

Running the App

After you publish the project and install the app onto the device, you can begin to use it (see Figure 8-3).

Figure 8-4 shows the iPhone pointing north.

Figure 8-5 shows the iPhone pointing east.

FIGURE 8-3   **FIGURE 8-4**   **FIGURE 8-5**

CREATING A SPEEDOMETER AND ALTIMETER

Another popular use case for geolocation services is tracking real-time speed or altitude. This section covers how to create a simple speedometer and altimeter app that displays the current speed and altitude. However, to give the app a little more pizzazz, you put an automobile dash background image behind the text and use a special digital-looking font that resembles an LCD readout. Finally, you set this app only in Landscape mode, so you need to adjust the graphics and app orientation accordingly.

 *I am using a background image I downloaded from stock.xchng (*www.sxc .hu*) and modified in Photoshop to be sized 320×480. I also downloaded the Digital-7 font from* www.dafont.com/. *Figure 8-6 shows the landscape-oriented background to be used in the app.*

You begin by creating a new Flash document using the AIR for Android or iPhone template and naming it **Speedometer.fla**.

Embedding a Font in Your App

Before continuing with coding the document class, you need to embed the special font to use for displaying the speed and altitude. You can do that inside the Speedometer.fla by performing the following steps:

FIGURE 8-6

1. In the Library panel, click the top-right menu and choose the New Font item.

    The Font Embedding dialog box is displayed, as shown in Figure 8-7.

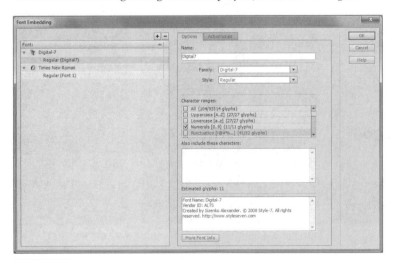

FIGURE 8-7

2. Click the + button to add a new font.

   A new font is added to the font list.

3. Enter a name for the font.

   I named mine Digital7.

4. Select the desired font from the Family combo box.

   I am using Digital 7 font, which is available at www.dafont.com/digital-7.font.

5. Select the font style from the Style combo box.

6. Select the range of characters you'll need for use in your app by checking the appropriate check box(s) in the Character Ranges list box.

   Select only the range of characters you'll need to minimize the size that the embedded font will take. I will be displaying only numbers, so I check only the Numerals check box.

7. Click the ActionScript tab.

8. Check the Export for ActionScript check box.

   The Export in Frame 1 check box will automatically be checked, and the Class and Base class will be populated.

9. Click OK.

   The font is embedded into the .fla and can be utilized in ActionScript code.

Coding the Document Class

With the embedded font ready for use, you can continue by creating the document class. To do so, you enter **Speedometer** as the document class in the Properties panel and click the pencil button to edit the class definition in your preferred editor.

You need to define a few variables at the class level: Geolocation, two TextField instances, and a reference to the background image you are using:

Available for download on Wrox.com

```
// Geolocation
private var geo:Geolocation;

// Speed text
private var tfSpeed:TextField;
private var tfAlt:TextField;

// Background image
[Embed(source="bg.jpg")]
private var BgImage:Class;
```

Code snippet Speedometer.as

The constructor allows you to perform a variety of tasks to set up the app UI and geolocation services. First, you prepare the stage and bitmap background:

```
stage.scaleMode = StageScaleMode.NO_SCALE;
stage.align = StageAlign.TOP_LEFT;

// Add a background.
var bg:Bitmap = new BgImage();
bg.smoothing = true;
addChild(bg);
```

Code snippet Speedometer.as

Four `TextField` objects are created and configured — `tfSpeed` and `tfAlt` are updated to show the current data, whereas `tfSpeedLabel` and `tfAltLabel` display unit measurements for these other fields. All four are assigned the Digital7 font. The x and y coordinates of the four objects are designed to fit exactly into the white boxes of the background image. Here's the code:

```
// Digital7 font
var digital7Font:Font = new Digital7();

var format:TextFormat = new TextFormat();
format.color = 0x000000;
format.align = "right";
format.font =  digital7Font.fontName;
format.size = 35;

// Create TextFields
tfSpeed = new TextField();
tfSpeed.defaultTextFormat = format;
tfSpeed.selectable = false;
tfSpeed.antiAliasType = AntiAliasType.ADVANCED;
tfSpeed.x = 309;
tfSpeed.y = 182;
tfSpeed.height = 42;
tfSpeed.width = 60;
tfSpeed.text =  "25";
tfSpeed.embedFonts = true;
addChild(tfSpeed);

tfAlt = new TextField();
tfAlt.defaultTextFormat = format;
tfAlt.selectable = false;
tfAlt.antiAliasType = AntiAliasType.ADVANCED;
tfAlt.x = 89;
tfAlt.y = 179;
tfAlt.height = 42;
tfAlt.width = 66;
tfAlt.text =  "3419";
tfAlt.embedFonts = true;
addChild(tfAlt);

var format2:TextFormat = new TextFormat();
format2.color = 0x000000;
format2.align = "left";
```

```
    format2.font =  digital7Font.fontName;
    format2.size = 12;

    var tfAltLabel:TextField = new TextField();
    tfAltLabel.defaultTextFormat = format2;
    tfAltLabel.selectable = false;
    tfAltLabel.antiAliasType = AntiAliasType.ADVANCED;
    tfAltLabel.x = 156;
    tfAltLabel.y = 185;
    tfAltLabel.height = 42;
    tfAltLabel.width = 67;
    tfAltLabel.text =  "m.";
    tfAltLabel.embedFonts = true;
    addChild(tfAltLabel);

    var tfSpeedLabel:TextField = new TextField();
    tfSpeedLabel.defaultTextFormat = format2;
    tfSpeedLabel.selectable = false;
    tfSpeedLabel.antiAliasType = AntiAliasType.ADVANCED;
    tfSpeedLabel.x = 369;
    tfSpeedLabel.y = 187;
    tfSpeedLabel.height = 42;
    tfSpeedLabel.width = 63;
    tfSpeedLabel.text =  "mph";
    tfSpeedLabel.embedFonts = true;
    addChild(tfSpeedLabel);
```

Code snippet Speedometer.as

As should be familiar by now, you configure the geolocation services in the constructor after checking to ensure that the location sensor is available:

Available for download on Wrox.com

```
    if (Geolocation.isSupported)
    {
        geo = new Geolocation();
        geo.setRequestedUpdateInterval(300);
        geo.addEventListener(GeolocationEvent.UPDATE, geolocationUpdateHandler);
        geo.addEventListener(StatusEvent.STATUS, geolocationStatusHandler);
    }
    else
    {
        tfSpeed.text = "N/A";
        tfAlt.text = "N/A";
    }

}
```

Code snippet Speedometer.as

The geolocationUpdateHandler() method is the listener for update events. When triggered, it assigns the current speed and altitude to the tfSpeed and tfAlt text fields, respectively. However, before displaying the speed, you need to convert the speed from meters per second to miles per hour.

You do that by taking the `event.speed` property value and multiplying by the constant value of 2.23693629. Here's the code:

```
private function geolocationUpdateHandler(event:GeolocationEvent):void
{

    // The speed is returned at meters per second multiplied by
    // a constant to give miles per hour.
    var speed:Number = event.speed * 2.23693629;
    // Altitude
    var alt:Number = event.altitude;

    tfSpeed.text = Math.round(speed).toString();
    tfAlt.text = Math.round(alt).toString();

}
```

Code snippet Speedometer.as

Listing 8-3 shows the complete source code for the `Speedometer` document class.

LISTING 8-3: Speedometer.as

```
package
{
    import flash.display.Bitmap;
    import flash.display.MovieClip;
    import flash.display.Sprite;
    import flash.display.StageAlign;
    import flash.display.StageScaleMode;
    import flash.events.GeolocationEvent;
    import flash.sensors.Geolocation;
    import flash.text.AntiAliasType;
    import flash.text.Font;
    import flash.text.TextField;
    import flash.text.TextFormat;
    import flash.text.engine.FontWeight;
    import flash.events.StatusEvent;

    /**
     * Document class for Speedometer application.
     * Sample code for Professional Flash Mobile Development
     *
     * @author Rich Wagner
     *
     */
    public class Speedometer extends flash.display.MovieClip    {
        // Geolocation
        private var geo:Geolocation;

        // Speed text
        private var tfSpeed:TextField;
```

```
        private var tfAlt:TextField;


        // Background image
        [Embed(source="bg.jpg")]
        private var BgImage:Class;

        [Embed(source='digital-7.ttf', fontName='DigitalSeven',
fontWeight="normal", advancedAntiAliasing="true", mimeType="application/x-
font")]
        private var digital7:Class;

        /**
         * Constructor
         *
         */
        public function Speedometer()
        {
            Font.registerFont(digital7);

            stage.scaleMode = StageScaleMode.NO_SCALE;
            stage.align = StageAlign.TOP_LEFT;

            // Digital7 font
            var digital7Font:Font = new Digital7();

            // Add background
            var bg:Bitmap = new BgImage();
            bg.smoothing = true;
            addChild(bg);

            var format:TextFormat = new TextFormat();
            format.color = 0x000000;
            format.align = "right";
            format.font =  digital7Font.fontName;
            format.size = 35;

            // Create TextFields
            tfSpeed = new TextField();
            tfSpeed.defaultTextFormat = format;
            tfSpeed.selectable = false;
            tfSpeed.antiAliasType = AntiAliasType.ADVANCED;
            tfSpeed.x = 520;
            tfSpeed.y = 290;
            tfSpeed.height = 42;
            tfSpeed.width = 60;
            tfSpeed.text =  "25";
                tfSpeed.embedFonts = true;
            addChild(tfSpeed);

            tfAlt = new TextField();
            tfAlt.defaultTextFormat = format;
            tfAlt.selectable = false;
            tfAlt.antiAliasType = AntiAliasType.ADVANCED;
```

continues

LISTING 8-3 *(continued)*

```
                tfAlt.x = 185;
                tfAlt.y = 290;
                tfAlt.height = 42;
                tfAlt.width = 66;
                tfAlt.text =  "3419";
                tfAlt.embedFonts = true;
                addChild(tfAlt);

                var format2:TextFormat = new TextFormat();
                format2.color = 0x000000;
                format2.align = "left";
                format2.font =  digital7Font.fontName;
                format2.size = 12;

                var tfAltLabel:TextField = new TextField();
                tfAltLabel.defaultTextFormat = format2;
                tfAltLabel.selectable = false;
                tfAltLabel.antiAliasType = AntiAliasType.ADVANCED;
                tfAltLabel.x = 262;
                tfAltLabel.y = 287;
                tfAltLabel.height = 42;
                tfAltLabel.width = 67;
                tfAltLabel.text =  "m.";
                tfAltLabel.embedFonts = true;
                addChild(tfAltLabel);


                var tfSpeedLabel:TextField = new TextField();
                tfSpeedLabel.defaultTextFormat = format2;
                tfSpeedLabel.selectable = false;
                tfSpeedLabel.antiAliasType = AntiAliasType.ADVANCED;
                tfSpeedLabel.x = 595;
                tfSpeedLabel.y = 287;
                tfSpeedLabel.height = 42;
                tfSpeedLabel.width = 63;
                tfSpeedLabel.text =  "mph";
                tfSpeedLabel.embedFonts = true;
                addChild(tfSpeedLabel);


                if (Geolocation.isSupported)
                {
                    geo = new Geolocation();
                    geo.setRequestedUpdateInterval(300);
                    geo.addEventListener(GeolocationEvent.UPDATE,
        geolocationUpdateHandler);
                    geo.addEventListener(StatusEvent.STATUS,
        geolocationStatusHandler);
                }
                else
                {
                    tfSpeed.text = "N/A";
```

```
                    tfAlt.text = "N/A";
                }

            }


            /**
             * Called each time the geolocation services update app
             *
             * @param event
             *
             */
            private function geolocationUpdateHandler(event:GeolocationEvent):void
            {

                    // Speed is returned at meters/second multiplied by
                    // constant to give miles per hour
                    var speed:Number = event.speed * 2.23693629;
                    // Altitude
                    var alt:Number = event.altitude;

                    tfSpeed.text = Math.round(speed).toString();
                    tfAlt.text = Math.round(alt).toString();

            }


            /**
             * Called each time the status changes
             *
             * @param event
             *
             */
            private function geolocationStatusHandler(event:StatusEvent):void
            {
                // If user is not allowing updates, then display
                if (geo.muted)
                {
                    tfSpeed.text = "N/A";
                    tfAlt.text = "N/A";
                }

            }

        }
    }
```

Configuring Landscape Orientation

As mentioned at the start of the chapter, Speedometer is designed to be a landscape-only app. Therefore, you need to perform a few tasks to configure the app for this orientation depending on whether you are developing for Android or iPhone.

Landscape Orientation with Android

1.   **Change dimensions of** `Speedometer.fla` — With the `.fla` document active, select the Properties panel and then click the Edit button next to the Size property. In the Document Settings dialog box, change the size to 800 px (width) and 480 px (height).

2.   **Change AIR Android settings** — In the Properties panel of the `.fla`, click the AIR Android Settings Edit button. Select `Landscape` from the Aspect Ratio combo box. Also, click the Full screen check box, because the background image extends to the complete dimensions of the viewport. (See Figure 8-8.)

FIGURE 8-8

Landscape Orientation with iPhone

1.   **Change dimensions of** `Speedometer.fla` — With the `.fla` document active, select the Properties panel and then click the Edit button next to the Size property. In the Document Settings dialog box, change the size to 480px (width) and 320px (height).

2.   **Adjust** `Default.png` **orientation** — Make sure the `Default.png` splash screen is land-scape oriented as well to provide a consistent orientation for the user. Figure 8-9 shows the Speedometer splash screen.

3. **Change iPhone Settings** — In the Properties panel of the `.fla`, click the iPhone Settings Edit button. Select `Landscape` from the Aspect ratio combo box. What's more, be sure to click the Full screen check box, because the background image extends to the complete dimensions of the viewport.

Running the App

When the `Speedometer` app is installed onto your Android or iPhone device, you can run it to display your current speed and altitude. Figure 8-10 displays the app when I ran it on an iPhone while driving my car.

FIGURE 8-9

FIGURE 8-10

SENDING GEOLOCATION TO A WEB SERVICE

A final geolocation use case covers how you can fetch geolocation data from the location sensor and, rather than displaying any of it, pass that information on to a web service and retrieve location-specific data from it.

To demonstrate, I'll walk you through an app called `FindMeAPizza`. When the user clicks a button on-screen, the app retrieves the current longitude and latitude readings from the location sensor. This information is then passed to Yahoo Local web services to retrieve the closest pizza shop. The user is also passed this information.

Set up the project by performing the following tasks:

1. Within the target directory, create a new Flash document using the desired template and name it **FindMeAPizza.fla**.

2. Set the background color of the stage to black (#000000). (I'll use white text on a black background.)

3 From the Components panel, add a Button component to the stage. Set its size to be 230 px (width) by 44 px (height), and position it at the bottom of the stage (see Figure 8-11). Name it **btnFind** in the top Name box.

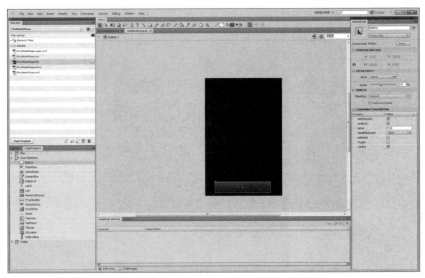

FIGURE 8-11

4. In the Properties panel, enter **FindMeAPizza** as the document class and click the pencil button to edit the class definition in your preferred editor.

Coding the Document Class

Once you're inside the editor, you are ready to begin coding the document class. Before filling out the constructor, add the following class properties:

```
// Geolocation
private var geo:Geolocation;

// TextField
private var tfInfo:TextField;

// Coordinates
private var longitude:Number;
private var latitude:Number;
```

Code snippet FindMeAPizza.as

The constructor creates a `TextField` instance and adds it to the stage. The `Geolocation` instance is created and configured:

```
public function FindMeAPizza()
{

    stage.scaleMode = StageScaleMode.NO_SCALE;
    stage.align = StageAlign.TOP_LEFT;

    tfInfo = new TextField();
    var format:TextFormat = new TextFormat("Helvetica", 20);
    format.color = 0xffffff;
    tfInfo.defaultTextFormat = format;
    tfInfo.border = true;
    tfInfo.wordWrap = true;
    tfInfo.multiline = true;
    tfInfo.x = 10;
    tfInfo.y = 10;
    tfInfo.height = stage.stageHeight - 80;
    tfInfo.width = stage.stageWidth - 20;
    addChild(tfInfo);

    // Geolocation setup
    if (Geolocation.isSupported)
    {
        geo = new Geolocation();
        geo.setRequestedUpdateInterval(5000);
        geo.addEventListener(GeolocationEvent.UPDATE,
geolocationUpdateHandler);
        geo.addEventListener(StatusEvent.STATUS, geolocationStatusHandler);

        // Enable the button if a location is provided.
        btnFind.addEventListener(MouseEvent.CLICK,
buttonClickHandler);
        tfInfo.text =  "Click the Find button to find your nearest
pizza shop.";
    }
    else
    {
        tfInfo.text =  "Can't find where you are. No pizza for you.";
    }
}
```

Code snippet FindMeAPizza.as

As you can see, an event handler is added to `btnFind` if geolocation services are available.

Inside the `update` handler for the Geolocation instance, you simply assign the current longitude and latitude readings to the class properties:

```
private function geolocationUpdateHandler(event:GeolocationEvent):void
{
    latitude = event.latitude;
    longitude = event.longitude;
}
```

Code snippet FindMeAPizza.as

The heart of this app, however, is the `click` handler for `btnFind`, which only calls the `fetch()` command to begin the fetching process from Yahoo local services:

```
private function buttonClickHandler(event:MouseEvent):void
{
    fetch();
}
```

Code snippet FindMeAPizza.as

The `fetch()` method prepares the URL and variables to send to Yahoo local services as a REST request:

```
public function fetch():void
{

    var url:String "http://local.yahooapis.com/LocalSearchService/V3/
localSearch";
    var variables:URLVariables = new URLVariables();
    variables.appid=

"x77v8JvV34GL7auv9T_1FPBhWqJIEwk..3DpsJ3Ds0LODlQA1qdshBHMreEbYEI3y_iGUuMGBvVJr
Q";
    variables.query="pizza";
    variables.latitude = latitude;
    variables.longitude = longitude;
    variables.radius = "300";
    variables.results = "1";
    sendData(url, variables);
}
```

Code snippet FindMeAPizza.as

The following variables are passed to the Yahoo web service:

➤ The `appid` is an ID that you receive from Yahoo upon registration. (Note that the `appid` provided previously is not usable; you need to register on your own.)

➤ The `query` variable provides a search term for the locale-specific search, which in this case is simply `pizza`.

➤ The `latitude` and `longitude` variables provide the location-specific information for this query.

➤ The `radius` tells Yahoo to search within a 300-mile radius.

➤ The `results` variable indicates how many results you want to receive from the server. In most cases, you want to display multiple results. But for this simple case, I am limiting the result set to 1.

This information is passed to a `sendData()` method, which makes the server request:

```
public function sendData(url:String, vars:URLVariables):void
{
    var request:URLRequest = new URLRequest(url);
    var loader:URLLoader = new URLLoader();
    request.data = vars;
    request.method = URLRequestMethod.POST;
    loader.addEventListener(Event.COMPLETE, loaderCompleteHandler);
```

```
        loader.addEventListener(IOErrorEvent.IO_ERROR, iOErrorHandler);
        loader.load(request);
    }
```

Code snippet FindMeAPizza.as

The `loaderCompleteHandler()` method is called when a response is received from the server. It is responsible for processing the XML data received from the server and displaying key pizza shop information in the `tfInfo` `TextField`. The code for the handler is provided here:

```
private function loaderCompleteHandler(event:Event):void
{
    // Get the response and convert it to XML.
    var response:String = event.target.data as String;
    try
    {
        var xml:XML = cleanResponse(response);
    }
    catch(error:TypeError)
    {
        writeLn("The response data was not in valid XML format");
    }

    // Get all <Result> children. There's only one in this case, but
    // you could expand to handle multiple results.
    var item:XML;
    var results:XMLList = xml.descendants("Result");

    // If no matches, let the user know the bad news.
    if (results.length() == 0)
    {
        writeLn("You are at least 300 miles from the nearest pizza shop.
No pizza for you. ");
    }
    // Otherwise, write out the closest match.
    else
    {
        for each(item in results)
        {
            var s:String = "Your closest pizza shop is: \n" +
                            item.Title + "\n" +
                            item.Address + "\n" +
                            item.City + ", " +
                            item.State + "\n" +
                            item.Phone;
            writeLn(s);
        }
    }

}
```

Code snippet FindMeAPizza.as

As you can see, the response variable receives the raw XML data, which is then cleaned up and converted to an XML variable by `cleanResponse()`. The XML fragment is processed and displayed on-screen.

The complete source code is provided in Listing 8-4.

LISTING 8-4: FindMeAPizza.as

```
package
{
    import flash.display.SimpleButton;
    import flash.display.Sprite;
    import flash.display.StageAlign;
    import flash.display.StageScaleMode;
    import flash.events.*;
    import flash.events.GeolocationEvent;
    import flash.net.*;
    import flash.net.URLVariables;
    import flash.sensors.Geolocation;
    import flash.text.TextField;
    import flash.text.TextFormat;

    /**
     * Document class for FindMeAPizza application.
     * Sample code for Professional Flash Mobile Development
     *
     * @author Rich Wagner
     *
     */
    public class FindMeAPizza extends Sprite
    {

        // Geolocation
        private var geo:Geolocation;

        // TextField
        private var tfInfo:TextField;

        // Coordinates
        private var longitude:Number;
        private var latitude:Number;

        /**
         * Constructor
         *
         */
        public function FindMeAPizza()
        {

            stage.scaleMode = StageScaleMode.NO_SCALE;
            stage.align = StageAlign.TOP_LEFT;

            tfInfo = new TextField();
            var format:TextFormat = new TextFormat("Helvetica", 20);
            format.color = 0xffffff;
            tfInfo.defaultTextFormat = format;
            tfInfo.border = true;
```

```
            tfInfo.wordWrap = true;
            tfInfo.multiline = true;
            tfInfo.x = 10;
            tfInfo.y = 10;
            tfInfo.height = stage.stageHeight - 80;
            tfInfo.width = stage.stageWidth - 20;
            addChild(tfInfo);

            // Geolocation setup
            if (Geolocation.isSupported)
            {
                geo = new Geolocation();
                geo.setRequestedUpdateInterval(5000);
                geo.addEventListener(GeolocationEvent.UPDATE,
geolocationUpdateHandler);
    geo.addEventListener(StatusEvent.STATUS, geolocationStatusHandler);

                // Enable the button if the location is provided.
                btnFind.addEventListener(MouseEvent.CLICK,
buttonClickHandler);
                tfInfo.text =  "Click the Find button to find your nearest
pizza shop.";
            }
            else
            {
                tfInfo.text =  "Can't find where you are. No pizza for you.";
            }
        }

        /**
         * Triggers a pizza lookup
         *
         * @param event
         *
         */
        private function buttonClickHandler(event:MouseEvent):void
        {
            fetch();
        }


        /**
         * Main routine for fetching pizza data. Sets up URL params.
         *
         */
        public function fetch():void
        {

            var url:String =
"http://local.yahooapis.com/LocalSearchService/V3/localSearch";
            var variables:URLVariables = new URLVariables();
            variables.appid=
"x77v8JvV34GL7auv9T_lFPBhWqJIEwk..3DpsJ3Ds0LODlQA1qdshBHMreEbYEI3y_iGUuMGBvVJr
Q";
```

continues

LISTING 8-4 *(continued)*

```
        variables.query="pizza";
        variables.latitude = latitude;
        variables.longitude = longitude;
        variables.radius = "300";
        variables.results = "1";
        sendData(url, variables);
    }

    /**
     * Helper function that makes the URL request to Yahoo
     *
     * @param url
     * @param vars
     *
     */
    public function sendData(url:String, vars:URLVariables):void
    {
        var request:URLRequest = new URLRequest(url);
        var loader:URLLoader = new URLLoader();
        request.data = vars;
        request.method = URLRequestMethod.POST;
        loader.addEventListener(Event.COMPLETE, loaderCompleteHandler);
        loader.addEventListener(IOErrorEvent.IO_ERROR, iOErrorHandler);
        loader.load(request);
    }

    /**
     * Handler for server response
     *
     * @param event
     *
     */
    private function loaderCompleteHandler(event:Event):void
    {
        // Get the response and convert it to XML.
        var response:String = event.target.data as String;
        try
        {
            var xml:XML = cleanResponse(response);
        }
        catch(error:TypeError)
        {
            writeLn("The response data was not in valid XML format");
        }

        // Get all <Result> children. There's only one in this
        // case, but you could expand to handle multiple results.
        var item:XML;
        var results:XMLList = xml.descendants("Result");

        // If no matches, let the user know the bad news.
        if (results.length() == 0)
        {
```

```
                writeLn("You are at least 300 miles from the nearest pizza
shop. No pizza
for you. ");
            }
            // Otherwise, write out the closest match.
            else
            {
                for each(item in results)
                {
                    var s:String = "Your closest pizza shop is: \n" +
                                   item.Title + "\n" +
                                   item.Address + "\n" +
                                   item.City + ", " +
                                   item.State + "\n" +
                                   item.Phone;
                    writeLn(s);
                }
            }

        }

        /**
         * Handler for IO errors with server
         *
         * @param event
         *
         */
        private function iOErrorHandler(event:IOErrorEvent):void
        {
            writeLn("Error loading URL.");
        }


        /**
         * Called each time the geolocation service updates app
         *
         * @param event
         *
         */
        private function geolocationUpdateHandler(event:GeolocationEvent):void
        {
            latitude = event.latitude;
            longitude = event.longitude;
        }

        /**
         * Helper utility method for writing text to the UI.
         *
         * @param s - text to write
         *
         */
        private function writeLn(s:String):void
        {
            tfInfo.text = s;
```

continues

LISTING 8-4 *(continued)*

```
        }


    /**
     * Strips out unneeded namespace and schema definitions
     *
     * @param response - raw XML feed
     *
     * @returns XML instance
     *
     */
    private function cleanResponse(response:String):XML
    {
        const NP1:String =  'xmlns="urn:yahoo:lcl"';
        const NP2:String =  'xmlns:xsi="http://www.w3.org/2001/XMLSchema-
instance"';
        const NP3:String =  'xsi:schemaLocation="urn:yahoo:lcl
http://local.yahooapis.com/LocalSearchService/V3/LocalSearchResponse.xsd"';

        response = response.replace(NP1, "");
        response = response.replace(NP2, "");
        response = response.replace(NP3, "");

        return new XML(response);

    }


    }
}
```

Running the App

After installing the `FindMeAPizza` app onto your Android or iPhone device, you can run it to display your local pizza shop (see Figure 8-12).

SUMMARY

In this chapter, you discovered how to work with the geographical sensor of Android and iPhone and the geolocation API. You looked at four sample apps, each of which uses various aspects of geolocation services. In one of the examples, you learned how to work with directional data to create a compass app. Then you read about measuring speed and altitude. Finally, you learned how to send the geolocation data to a web service to create real-time geographical-based apps.

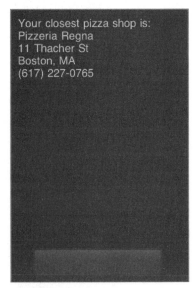

Your closest pizza shop is:
Pizzeria Regna
11 Thacher St
Boston, MA
(617) 227-0765

FIGURE 8-12

Service Integration Using URL Protocols

WHAT'S IN THIS CHAPTER?

➤ Make phone calls and send SMS messages

➤ Send e-mails

➤ Use GoogleMaps in your apps

Certainly, one of the most potentially exciting aspects of an application that is written specifically for Android or iPhone is the ability to integrate your app with mobile services, such as phone, e-mail, and Google Maps. After all, if you can do so, you break out of the solo application silo and extend its reach across mobile devices.

There's two types of integration that's possible: through AIR API and through URL protocols. Using the AIR API, you can directly access Camera, Camera Roll, and Microphone for Android devices. I'll cover that in Chapter 10. (As of the time of writing, iOS devices do not provide support for Camera, CameraRoll, and Microphone.)

Other Android and iOS services don't have direct API access through AS3. As a result, you need to use a special set of URLs to integrate with these services. I'll cover how to do this in this chapter.

This chapter shows you how to integrate your app with Android and iOS services using URL protocols for the following services:

➤ Phone

➤ SMS

➤ Mail

➤ Google Maps

At the same time, it demonstrates how to add an ActionScript wrapper around these protocols to provide your own custom-made AS3 API for Android and iPhone Services.

ABSTRACTING URL PROTOCOLS

Rather than work directly with URL protocols in my application code, I decided that I'd rather create a set of classes that can be called. What's more, should the access method of calling these Android services ever change, I'd have the option to alter the underlying implementation of these classes rather than modify my application source code.

To follow along with this example, you develop the specific classes for each of the services that you will integrate with throughout the chapter. But you begin by creating an abstract class called MobileService that implements one static method, executeCommand(). As you can see by the code shown in Listing 9-1, this method takes the string parameter and sends it as a URL request using navigateToUrl(). Subclasses of MobileService can then call this method internally.

LISTING 9-1: MobileService.as

```
package com.richwagner.mobileservices
{

    import flash.net.URLRequest;
    import flash.net.navigateToURL;

    /**
     * Abstract class for mobile service access
     * Sample code for Professional Flash Mobile Development
     *
     * @author Rich Wagner
     *
     */
    public class MobileService
    {
        /**
         * Performs the specified URL-based command.
         *
         * @param command - URL with special protocol
         *
         */
        protected static function executeCommand(command:String):void
        {
            var request:URLRequest = new URLRequest(command);
            try
            {
                navigateToURL(request);
            }
            catch (e:Error)
            {
                trace("Error occurred!");
            }
```

```
            }
        }
    }
```

With that groundwork out of the way, you begin with the phone dialer.

MAKING PHONE CALLS FROM YOUR APPLICATION

You can initiate a phone call from your app by using the `tel:` protocol. The basic URL syntax is:

```
tel:978-555-1212
```

Here's how you'd call it ActionScript:

```
var request:URLRequest = new URLRequest("tel:812-555-1212");
navigateToURL(request);
```

When that code is executed in your app, the mobile OS exits your app and starts the call using the device phone.

In addition to basic phone number support, Android and iOS provide partial support for the RFC 2086 protocol (`www.ietf.org/rfc/rfc2806.txt`), which allows you to use some advanced telephone-based URLs. The following call, for example, dials the U.S. Postal Service, pauses for 3 seconds, and then presses 2 to get a Spanish version:

```
tel:1-800-ASK-USPS;ppp2
```

The p keyword creates a one-second pause. You can stack those as needed to form multisecond delays.

Creating PhoneDialer.as

Next, you create a subclass of `MobileService` that adds support for phone dialing. The class, which I am calling `PhoneDialer`, has a single static method called `dial()`. The `dial()` method takes a phone number as a parameter, adds the `tel:` protocol to it, and then passes that onto `executeCommand()`. The class code is shown in Listing 9-2.

Available for download on Wrox.com

LISTING 9-2: PhoneDialer.as

```
package com.richwagner.mobileservices
{
    /**
     * PhoneDialer
     * Sample code for Professional Flash Mobile Development
     *
     * @author Rich Wagner
     *
     */
```

continues

LISTING 9-2 *(continued)*

```
public class PhoneDialer extends MobileService
{
    /**
     * Calls the specified phone number via the phone
     *
     * @param phoneNumber - number to call
     *
     */
    public static function dial(phoneNumber:String):void
    {
        // In a real-world situation, you'd want to add
        // validation to the phone number
        var cmd:String = "tel:" + phoneNumber;
        executeCommand(cmd);
    }
}
}
```

Using PhoneDialer in an App

To demonstrate how you can add PhoneDialer in an app, I am going to create a simple app that contains two UI components:

➤ `TextInput` for user entry of the phone number to call

➤ `Button` to trigger the call

Setting Up Your Project

To set up your project, perform the following steps:

1. Within the root project directory, create a new document using the desired template, and name it `PhoneServices.fla`.

2. Add a `com.richwagner.mobileservices` package to the project (or you can reference a common library) that contains `MobileService.as` and `PhoneDialer.as`.

3. In the Properties panel for the `.fla`, enter **PhoneServices** as the document class, and click the pencil button to edit the class definition in your preferred editor.

Coding the PhoneServices Class

Inside the `PhoneServices` document class, begin by adding two properties:

Available for download on Wrox.com

```
public var tiNumber:TextInput;
public var btnPhone:Button;
```

Code snippet PhoneServices.as

These will serve as the basic UI for my app.

Inside the constructor, instantiate the two UI components, two text formatters, and assign the text formatters to the components using `setStyle()`:

```
// Formatters
var format:TextFormat = new TextFormat("Helvetica", 44);
format.color = 0xffffffff;

var btnFormat:TextFormat = new TextFormat("Helvetica", 32);
btnFormat.color = 0x000000;
btnFormat.bold = true;


// Create TextInput
tiNumber = new TextInput();
tiNumber.textField.background = true;
tiNumber.textField.backgroundColor = 0x7AB900;
tiNumber.x = 10;
tiNumber.y = 10;
tiNumber.height = 60;
tiNumber.textField.multiline = true;
tiNumber.textField.wordWrap = true;
tiNumber.width = stage.stageWidth - 20;
tiNumber.text = "978-555-1212
tiNumber.setStyle("textFormat", format);
addChild(tiNumber);

// Create Call button
btnPhone = new Button();
btnPhone.width = stage.stageWidth-20;
btnPhone.height = 44;
btnPhone.x = 10;
btnPhone.alpha = 0.9;
btnPhone.label = "Call";
btnPhone.setStyle("textFormat", btnFormat);
btnPhone.y = stage.stageHeight - 54;
btnPhone.addEventListener(MouseEvent.CLICK, btnPhoneMouseClickHandler);
addChild(btnPhone);
```

Code snippet PhoneServices.as

Although the focus of this app is on phone dialing, I want to make sure the app is easy to use. Specifically, I want to make it easy for a user to close out the keyboard when he is finished entering the phone number. To that end, you add a `click` listener for the stage, prompting a change in focus from the `TextInput` to the button, thus hiding the on-screen keyboard:

```
stage.addEventListener(MouseEvent.CLICK, stageClickHandler);
```

code snippet PhoneServices.as

You also need to add a handler for the `TextInput`:

```
tiNumber.addEventListener(MouseEvent.CLICK, tiNumberClickHandler);
```

code snippet PhoneServices.as

There are three event handlers to create. Begin with the `stageClickHandler()`, which simply sets the focus to `btnPhone`:

```
private function stageClickHandler(event:Event):void
{
    btnPhone.setFocus();
}
```

Code snippet PhoneServices.as

The `click` handler for the `TextInput` stops the `click` event from rippling down to the stage:

```
private function tiNumberClickHandler(event:Event):void
{
    event.stopPropagation();
}
```

code snippet PhoneServices.as

Add the code that you and I are most concerned with here: the handler for the Dial button. When clicked, it calls the `PhoneDialer.dial()` command using the text of the `TextInput`:

```
private function btnPhoneMouseClickHandler(event:Event):void
{
    event.stopPropagation();
    PhoneDialer.dial(tiNumber.text);
}
```

code snippet PhoneServices.as

The full source code for `PhoneServices.as` is shown in Listing 9-3.

LISTING 9-3: PhoneServices.as

```
package
{
    import com.richwagner.mobileservices.PhoneDialer;

    import fl.controls.Button;
    import fl.controls.Label;
    import fl.controls.LabelButton;
    import fl.controls.TextInput;

    import flash.display.Sprite;
    import flash.events.Event;
    import flash.events.MouseEvent;
    import flash.net.URLRequest;
    import flash.net.navigateToURL;
    import flash.text.*;

    /**
     * Document class for PhoneServices application.
     * Sample code for Professional Flash Mobile Development
     *
```

```
 * @author Rich Wagner
 *
 */
public class PhoneServices extends Sprite
{

    public var tiNumber:TextInput;
    public var btnPhone:Button;
    public var btnSMS:Button;

    /**
     * Constructor
     *
     */
    public function PhoneServices()
    {

        // Formatters
        var format:TextFormat = new TextFormat("Helvetica", 44);
        format.color = 0xffffffff;

        var btnFormat:TextFormat = new TextFormat("Helvetica", 32);
        btnFormat.color = 0x000000;
        btnFormat.bold = true;


        // Create TextInput
        tiNumber = new TextInput();
        tiNumber.textField.background = true;
        tiNumber.textField.backgroundColor = 0x7AB900;
        tiNumber.x = 10;
        tiNumber.y = 10;
        tiNumber.height = 60;
        tiNumber.textField.multiline = true;
        tiNumber.textField.wordWrap = true;
        tiNumber.width = stage.stageWidth - 20;
        tiNumber.text = "978-270-1889";
        tiNumber.setStyle("textFormat", format);
        tiNumber.addEventListener(MouseEvent.CLICK, tiNumberClickHandler);
        addChild(tiNumber);

        // Create Service buttons
        btnPhone = new Button();
        btnPhone.width = stage.stageWidth-20;
        btnPhone.height = 44;
        btnPhone.x = 10;
        btnPhone.alpha = 0.9;
        btnPhone.label = "Call";
        btnPhone.setStyle("textFormat", btnFormat);
        btnPhone.y = stage.stageHeight - 54;
        btnPhone.addEventListener(MouseEvent.CLICK, btnPhoneMouseClickHandler);
        addChild(btnPhone);

        // Stage event handler
```

continues

LISTING 9-3 *(continued)*

```
        stage.addEventListener(MouseEvent.CLICK, stageClickHandler);

    }


    /**
     * Dials phone
     *
     * @param event
     *
     */
    private function btnPhoneMouseClickHandler(event:Event):void
    {
        event.stopPropagation();
        PhoneDialer.dial(tiNumber.text);
    }


    /**
     * Click handler for Text Input
     *
     * @param event
     *
     */
    private function tiNumberClickHandler(event:Event):void
    {
        event.stopPropagation();
    }


    /**
     * Click handler for stage
     *
     * @param event
     *
     */
    private function stageClickHandler(event:Event):void
    {
        btnPhone.setFocus();
    }

    }
}
```

 If you get compiler errors saying that the TextInput *or* Button *classes cannot be found, go back to the Flash document and drop a* TextInput *or* Button *instance from the Components panel into your library. (Or you can drop them both onto your document and then delete them — they'll stay added to your library.)*

Android: Adding Permissions

You're done with the AS3 source code, but before you publish for Android, you need to enable your app for accessing the Internet and using the `tel:` protocol. To do so, add the `android.permission.INTERNET` parameter to your application descriptor file (`PhoneServices-app.xml`):

Available for download on Wrox.com

```
<android>
  <manifestAdditions>
    <manifest>
      <data>
      <![CDATA[
        <uses-permission android:name="android.permission.INTERNET"/>
      ]]>
      </data>
    </manifest>
  </manifestAdditions>
</android>
```

Code snippet PhoneServices-app.xml

Figure 9-1 shows the app being run on my Nexus One. When the Call button is clicked, the Phone app is activated, as shown in Figure 9-2.

FIGURE 9-1

FIGURE 9-2

Figure 9-3 shows the app being run on my iPhone. When the Call button is clicked, the iPhone phone is activated, as shown in Figure 9-4.

SENDING SMS MESSAGES

Similar to phone calls, you can send SMS messages using the `sms:` protocol. The following code launches your mobile phone's SMS app, addressing the text to 978-555-1211:

```
sms:978-545-1211
```

FIGURE 9-3

FIGURE 9-4

Inside the SMS app, the user is prompted to enter the actual message using the keyboard and send it when finished.

You can also launch the SMS app without needing a specific number to text by using a blank `sms:` call:

```
sms:
```

There are a couple of limitations to SMS support. First, you cannot send an SMS directly from within your app. You can only initiate the process in your app, which you then hand off to an SMS app. Second, you can't supply the message, only the number the user wants to text.

Creating SMS.as

This example creates a `MobileService` subclass that supports SMS, which essentially emulates the same structure as the `PhoneDialer` but uses the `sms:` protocol:

LISTING 9-4: SMS.as

```
package com.richwagner.mobileservices
{
    /**
     * SMS
     * Sample code for Professional Flash Mobile Development
     *
     * @author Rich Wagner
     *
     */
    public class SMS extends MobileService
    {
        /**
         * Opens the SMS app to a message window to the specified
```

```
      * number.
      *
      * @param phoneNumber - number to text
      *
      */
     public static function send(phoneNumber:String):void
     {
         // In a real-world situation, you'd want to add
         // validation to the phone number
         var cmd:String = "sms:" + phoneNumber;
         executeCommand(cmd);
     }
   }
}
```

Adding SMS Support to the PhoneServices App

To demonstrate SMS texts from a mobile app, you simply add SMS capabilities to the PhoneServices app created earlier in the chapter. About the only thing you need to add to the document class is a new button called btnSMS and have its click handler call the SMS.send() method.

The following code is added to the constructor:

```
btnSMS = new Button();
btnSMS.width = stage.stageWidth-20;
btnSMS.height = 44;
btnSMS.x = 10;
btnSMS.alpha = 0.9;
btnSMS.label = "Send SMS";
btnSMS.setStyle("textFormat", btnFormat);
btnSMS.y = stage.stageHeight - 104;
btnSMS.addEventListener(MouseEvent.CLICK, btnSMSMouseClickHandler);
addChild(btnSMS);
```

code snippet PhoneServies.as

Next, the following event handler is added:

```
private function btnSMSMouseClickHandler(event:Event):void
{
    event.stopPropagation();
    SMS.send(tiNumber.text);
}
```

code snippet PhoneServies.as

Therefore, when the SMS button is clicked, the number the user enters in the TextField is passed to the SMS.send() method.

Running the App

When you publish the app and run it on an Android device, a new button appears, as shown in Figure 9-5.

When you type in a number to text and click the SMS button, a prompt asks you whether to complete the action using the Google Voice or Messaging app, as shown in Figure 9-6.

FIGURE 9-5   **FIGURE 9-6**

If you press Messaging, the number is added to the prompt of the Messaging app and sets the prompt for the user to type a message (see Figure 9-7).

Or, when you recompile the app and reinstall onto your iPhone via iTunes, a new button appears, as shown in Figure 9-8. When you type in a number to text and click the SMS button, the app exits and the SMS app displays an open conversion window (Figure 9-9).

FIGURE 9-7   **FIGURE 9-8**   **FIGURE 9-9**

SENDING E-MAILS

Your application can also initiate e-mails using the `mailto:` protocol. Here's the most basic syntax:

```
mailto:rich@mycompany.com
```

When you execute this code, the Android or iPhone Mail app launches, and a new message window is displayed. If you supplied just the recipient e-mail address, the user could then fill out the subject and body of the message and send from that window.

As with SMS, you cannot automatically send an e-mail message directly from within your app. Instead, the `mailto:` protocol always closes your app and takes the user to a new message window in Mail.

You can provide additional parameters to Mail, however. In this way, you can specify the Subject, Cc addresses, Bcc addresses, and body of the message. In fact, you can even embed basic HTML tags inside the body text.

Table 9-1 details the `mailto:` parameters available to you.

TABLE 9-1: mailto: Protocol Parameters

PARAMETER	SYNTAX
Message recipient(s)	Add a comma to separate multiple e-mail addresses
Message subject	`subject=Subject%20Text`
Cc recipients	`cc=myname@mycompany.com`
Bcc recipients	`bcc=myname@mycompany.com`
Message text	`body=Message%20text`

Creating Mail.as

Before creating a sample app demonstrating the use of the `mailto:` protocol, I will create a `MobileService` subclass called `Mail` that wraps the mailing functionality into an easy-to-call abstract method. Unlike the `PhoneDialer` or `SMS` classes, the `mailto:` call is slightly more involved, as shown by the `Mail.as` code in Listing 9-5.

Available for download on Wrox.com

LISTING 9-5: Mail.as

```
package com.richwagner.mobileservices
{
    /**
     * Mail
     * Sample code for Professional Flash Mobile Development
     *
     * @author Rich Wagner
     *
     */
```

continues

LISTING 9-5 *(continued)*

```
public class Mail extends MobileService
{
    public static var recipient:String = null;
    public static var ccList:String = null;
    public static var bccList:String = null;
    public static var subject:String = null;
    public static var body:String = null;

    /**
     * Opens the Mail app and provides message details based on
     * the class static properties.
     *
     */
    public static function sendMail():void
    {
        var cmd:String = "mailto:";

        var firstParam:Boolean = false;


        if (!recipient)
        {
            trace("Error: You need to specify one or more recipients.");
            return;
        }

        // Add recipient list
        cmd += recipient;

        // Add subject
        if (subject)
        {
            var subjectArr:Array=subject.split(' ');
            subject = subjectArr.join('%20');

            cmd+= "?subject=" + subject;
            firstParam = true;
        }

        if (ccList)
        {
            var ccListArr:Array=ccList.split(' ');
            ccList = ccListArr.join('%20');

            if (!firstParam)
                cmd += "?cc=" + ccList
            else
                cmd += "&cc=" + ccList;

            firstParam = true;
        }

        if (bccList)
```

```
            {
                var bccListArr:Array=bccList.split(' ');
                bccList = bccListArr.join('%20');

                if (!firstParam)
                    cmd += "?bcc=" + bccList
                else
                    cmd += "&bcc=" + bccList;

                firstParam = true;
            }


            // Add message text
            if (body)
            {

                var bodyArr:Array= body.split(' ');
                body = bodyArr.join('%20');

                if (!firstParam)
                    cmd += "?body=" + body
                else
                    cmd += "&body=" + body;

            }

            executeCommand(cmd);



        }
    }
```

You begin this class by defining static properties for each of the `mailto:` parameters. The only required parameter is the `recipient` property. If that property is not present, `sendMail()` does not continue. But for each of the other parameters, the method checks for them and adds them to the command string that will be passed to the `executeCommand()` method.

Per HTTP conventions (you are building a URL after all), you must precede the initial parameter after the recipient list with a ? (such as `?subject=`) and precede any additional parameters with an &.

Notice, however, that preprocessing is being performed with the string values before they are added to the command string. Before passing the string via `mailto:`, you need to escape encode it to get rid of any spaces. I do the search and replace using a combo of `split()` and `join()`:

```
var subjectArr:Array=subject.split(' ');
subject = subjectArr.join('%20');
```

code snippet Mail.as

The `mailto:` protocol calls for line breaks to be supported in the body parameter by using %0A for a line break and %0A%0A for a line break followed by a new line. Unfortunately, Android ignores the %0A codes and puts the full string on a single line. There is a workaround for line breaks, however. Because you can embed HTML inside the message body, you could use a `<br/>` tag for a line break.

Sending Mail from an App

With the `Mail` class created, you can now use it to send mail from within an app. To demonstrate, this example creates a simple mail app called `KindaSortMail`, which will contain fields for inputting `mailto:` parameters and a button that calls `Mail.sendMail()`.

For this app, you create the UI components in Flash and then code the app in the document class.

1. Create a new Flash document using the desired template and name it **KindaSortaMail.fla**.

2. Lay out the UI in Flash, adding `Label` and `TextInput` components for To, Cc, Bcc, and Subject parameters. For the Message parameter, use a `TextArea`. For each of these text entry components, name them `tiRecipient`, `tiCcAddress`, `tiBccAddress`, `tiSubject`, and `taMessage` respectively. Next, you add a `Button` component and label it `Send`.

Figure 9-10 shows the UI in the Flash designer for my Android app, while Figure 9-11 shows the layout for my iPhone app.

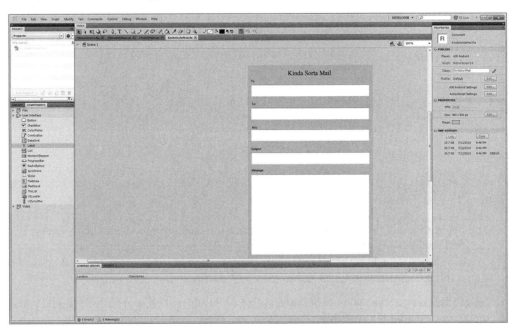

FIGURE 9-10

3. You are now ready to write the accompanying ActionScript code that powers the app. First, you want to link to the `com.richwagner.mobileservices` package or copy it into my project so that you can access the `Mail` class.

4. In the Properties panel, enter **KindaSortaMail** as the document class, and click the pencil button to edit the class definition in your preferred editor.

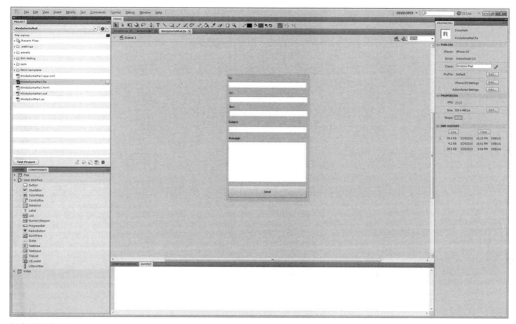

FIGURE 9-11

Because the UI is already created, the code needed is minimal. In fact, the only thing you need to add is a handler for the Send button's `click` event. In the constructor, place the following:

```
btnSend.addEventListener(MouseEvent.CLICK, sendClickHandler);
```

code snippet KindaSortaMail.as

The `sendClickHandler()` simply captures the input text from the app and passes it to the `Mail` object:

```
Mail.recipient = tiRecipient.text;
Mail.subject = tiSubject.text;
Mail.ccList = tiCcAddress.text;
Mail.bccList = tiBccAddress.text;
Mail.body = taMessage.text;
```

code snippet KindaSortaMail.as

Listing 9-6 provides the full source code.

LISTING 9-6: KindaSortMail.as

```
package
{
    import flash.display.Sprite;
    import flash.events.MouseEvent;
```

continues

LISTING 9-6 *(continued)*

```
import flash.events.Event;

import com.richwagner.mobileservices.Mail;

/**
 * Document class for KindaSortMail application.
 * Sample code for Professional Flash Mobile Development
 *
 * @author Rich Wagner
 *
 */
public class KindaSortMail extends Sprite
{
    /**
     * Constructor
     *
     */
    public function KindaSortMail()
    {
        btnSend.addEventListener(MouseEvent.CLICK, sendClickHandler);
    }

    /**
     * Handler for Send button click
     *
     * @param event
     *
     */
    private function sendClickHandler(event:Event):void
    {
        Mail.recipient = tiRecipient.text;
        Mail.subject = tiSubject.text;
        Mail.ccList = tiCcAddress.text;
        Mail.bccList = tiBccAddress.text;
        Mail.body = taMessage.text;
        Mail.sendMail();

    }


    }
}
```

Android: Adding Permissions

As with `PhoneServices`, you first need to enable an Android app for accessing the Internet and using the `mailto:` protocol. To do so, add the `android.permission.INTERNET` parameter to your application descriptor file (`KindaSortaMail-app.xml`):

```
<android>
  <manifestAdditions>
    <manifest>
```

```
            <data>
            <![CDATA[
              <uses-permission android:name="android.permission.INTERNET"/>
            ]]>
            </data>
          </manifest>
        </manifestAdditions>
      </android>
```

code snippet KindaSortaMail-app.xml

Running the App

When you install and run the app on your Android device, you can enter the message information in the text inputs (see Figure 9-12).

When you click Send, a pop-up window appears asking you whether to complete the action using Compose or Email (see Figure 9-13).

If you choose Email, a message window is pre-populated with the parameters specified in the KindaSortaMail app (see Figure 9-14).

FIGURE 9-12

FIGURE 9-13

FIGURE 9-14

Alternatively, when you install and run the app on my iPhone, you can enter the message information in the text inputs (see Figure 9-15). When you click Send, the app closes and iPhone's Mail app is launched. A new message is pre-populated with the parameters specified in the KindaSortaMail app (see Figure 9-16).

FIGURE 9-15   **FIGURE 9-16**

POINTING ON GOOGLE MAPS

Although the Maps app doesn't have a special URL protocol, Android does optionally route any URL requests pointing to maps.google.com to the Maps application. Therefore, by composing a URL string, you can point to a specific place on a map or display driving directions between two places.

The map displayed may be shown in Map or Satellite view, depending on the last view the user selected.

For example, the following are typical URLs that would be used to display a map, one by address and one by geographical coordinates:

```
http://maps.google.com/maps?q=Boston,+MA
http://maps.google.com/maps?q=52.123N,2.456W
```

For addresses, start with the q= parameter, and then type the address as normal, substituting + (plus signs) for blank spaces. For example:

```
http://maps.google.com/maps?q=108+State+Street,Boston,+MA
```

The label shown in the Maps app defaults to the location info provided in the URL. However, if you'd like to supply a more descriptive label, you can add one by tagging on a label in parentheses after the location details. For example:

```
http://maps.google.com/maps?q=Lapel,+IN+(My+Old+Stomping+Grounds)
```

To show driving directions, use the saddr= parameter to indicate the starting address and the daddr= parameter to specify the destination address, as shown in the following example:

```
http://maps.google.com/maps?saddr=Princeton+MA&daddr=108+State+Street,+Boston,+MA
```

Table 9-2 shows the Google Maps parameters that are supported.

TABLE 9-2: Google Maps Parameters

PARAMETER	DESCRIPTION
q=	Basic query parameter used for normal addresses, geographical coordinates, and so on
saddr=	Source address for driving directions
daddr=	Destination address for driving directions
ll=	Latitude and longitude points for the center point of the map
sll=	Latitude and longitude points to perform a business search
spn=	Approximate latitude and longitude span of the map
t=	Type of map to display
z=	Zoom level of the map

Creating GoogleMaps.as

This section demonstrates how you can create a subclass of MobileService that provides basic mapping support for addresses and latitude and longitude points. However, it would not take much to enhance it to provide full support for all the Google Maps parameters.

Listing 9-7 shows the source code for the GoogleMaps class.

LISTING 9-7: GoogleMaps.as

```
package com.richwagner.mobileservices
{

    /**
     * GoogleMaps
     * Sample code for Professional Flash Mobile Development
     *
     * @author Rich Wagner
     *
     */
    public class GoogleMaps extends MobileService
    {

        /**
         * Shows a map in Maps app based on the coordinates.
         *
         * @param longitude to display
         * @param latitude to display
         *
         */
```

continues

LISTING 9-7 *(continued)*

```
public static function pointToCoordinates(latitude:Number,
    longitude:Number):void
{
    var cmd:String = "http://maps.google.com/maps?q=" +
        latitude.toString() + "," + longitude.toString();
    executeCommand(cmd);
}

/**
 * Shows a map in Maps app based on address supplied.
 *
 * @param address - address to display
 *
 */
public static function pointToAddress(address:String):void
{
    var addressArr:Array=address.split(' ');
    address = addressArr.join('+');
    var cmd:String = "http://maps.google.com/maps?q=" + address;
    executeCommand(cmd);
}


    }
}
```

The `GoogleMaps` class provides two static methods. The `pointToCoordinates()` method takes the latitude and longitude values and displays the map. The `pointToAddress()` method takes a basic address query string and passes it to the `Maps` app for display.

Notice that the `pointToAddress()` method converts any spaces in the address to + characters.

Using GoogleMaps in an App

With the `GoogleMaps` wrapper class now completed, you are ready to create an app that utilizes this to display maps. For this sample, you want the app to do two things:

➤ Display a map by address

➤ Display a map based on geolocation data obtained from the phone's GPS

To set up your project, perform these steps:

1. Create a new Flash document using the desired template, and name it **MapServices.fla**.

2. Add the `com.richwagner.mobileservices` package to the project (or reference a common library) that contains `MobileService.as` and `GoogleMaps.as`.

3. In the Properties panel for the `.fla`, enter **MapServices** as the document class, and click the pencil button to edit the class definition in your preferred editor.

In writing the `MapServices` document class, there are several properties to declare:

```
public var btnAddress:Button;
public var btnGPS:Button;
public var tiAddress:TextInput;

public var latitude:Number;
public var longitude:Number;
private var geo:Geolocation;
```

code snippet MapServices.as

The first three properties are UI components that you'll be creating via ActionScript. The final three properties are used in gathering GPS information.

In the constructor, create the UI components and their text formatters. You also set up event handlers for the two buttons as a `Geolocation` event handler (which is described in full detail in Chapter 8).

```
public function MapServices()
{

    // Formatters
    var format:TextFormat = new TextFormat("Helvetica", 44);
    format.color = 0xffffffff;

    var btnFormat:TextFormat = new TextFormat("Helvetica", 26);
    btnFormat.color = 0x000000;
    btnFormat.bold = true;


    // Create TextInput
    tiAddress = new TextInput();
    tiAddress.textField.background = true;
    tiAddress.textField.backgroundColor = 0x7AB900;
    tiAddress.x = 10;
    tiAddress.y = 10;
    tiAddress.height = 300;
    tiAddress.textField.multiline = true;
    tiAddress.textField.wordWrap = true;
     tiAddress.width = stage.stageWidth - 20;
     tiAddress.text = "Address, City, State, Zip";
     tiAddress.setStyle("textFormat", format);
     tiAddress.addEventListener(MouseEvent.CLICK, tiAddressClickHandler);
    addChild(tiAddress);

    // Create Service buttons
    btnAddress = new Button();
    btnAddress.width = stage.stageWidth-20;
    btnAddress.height = 44;
    btnAddress.x = 10;
    btnAddress.alpha = 0.9;
    btnAddress.label = "Map Address";
    btnAddress.setStyle("textFormat", btnFormat);
```

```
        btnAddress.y = tiAddress.y + tiAddress.height + 5;
        btnAddress.addEventListener(MouseEvent.CLICK, btnAddressMouseClickHandler);
        addChild(btnAddress);


        btnGPS = new Button();
        btnGPS.width = stage.stageWidth-20;
        btnGPS.height = 44;
        btnGPS.x = 10;
        btnGPS.alpha = 0.9;
        btnGPS.label = "Map by GPS";
        btnGPS.setStyle("textFormat", btnFormat);
        btnGPS.y = stage.stageHeight - 54;
        btnGPS.addEventListener(MouseEvent.CLICK, btnGPSMouseClickHandler);
        addChild(btnGPS);

        // Stage event handler
        stage.addEventListener(MouseEvent.CLICK, stageClickHandler);


        // Is geolocation supported?
        if (Geolocation.isSupported)
        {
            // If so, set it up
            geo = new Geolocation();
            geo.setRequestedUpdateInterval(500);
            geo.addEventListener(GeolocationEvent.UPDATE,
                geolocationUpdateHandler);
        }

    }
```

code snippet MapServices.as

For the `geolocationUpdateHandler()`, you want to update the `latitude` and `longitude` proper-ties each time you update the `Geolocation` object:

```
    private function geolocationUpdateHandler(event:GeolocationEvent):void
    {
        latitude = event.latitude;
        longitude = event.longitude;
    }
```

code snippet MapServices.as

For the Map Address button, call `GoogleMaps.pointToAddress()` using the text that the user supplies:

```
    private function btnAddressMouseClickHandler(event:Event):void
    {
        event.stopPropagation();
        GoogleMaps.pointToAddress(tiAddress.text);
    }
```

code snippet MapServices.as

For the Map GPS button, pass the latitude and longitude data obtained from the `Geolocation` object onto `GoogleMaps.pointToCoordinates()`:

```
private function btnGPSMouseClickHandler(event:Event):void
{
    event.stopPropagation();
    GoogleMaps.pointToCoordinates(latitude, longitude);
}
```

code snippet MapServices.as

Listing 9-8 provides the source code for the `MapServices.as` document class.

LISTING 9-8: MapServices.as

```
package
{

    import com.richwagner.mobileservices.GoogleMaps;

    import fl.controls.Button;
    import fl.controls.Label;
    import fl.controls.LabelButton;
    import fl.controls.TextInput;
    import flash.events.GeolocationEvent;
    import flash.sensors.Geolocation;
    import flash.display.Sprite;
    import flash.events.Event;
    import flash.events.MouseEvent;
    import flash.net.URLRequest;
    import flash.net.navigateToURL;
    import flash.text.*;

    /**
     * Document class for Services application.
     * Sample code for Professional Flash Mobile Development
     *
     * @author Rich Wagner
     *
     */
    public class MapServices extends Sprite
    {

        public var btnAddress:Button;
        public var btnGPS:Button;
        public var tiAddress:TextInput;

        public var latitude:Number;
        public var longitude:Number;

        // Geolocation
        private var geo:Geolocation;

        /**
```

continues

LISTING 9-8 *(continued)*

```
 * Constructor
 *
 */
public function MapServices()
{

    // Formatters
    var format:TextFormat = new TextFormat("Helvetica", 44);
    format.color = 0xffffffff;

    var btnFormat:TextFormat = new TextFormat("Helvetica", 26);
    btnFormat.color = 0x000000;
    btnFormat.bold = true;


    // Create TextInput
    tiAddress = new TextInput();
    tiAddress.textField.background = true;
    tiAddress.textField.backgroundColor = 0x7AB900;
    tiAddress.x = 10;
    tiAddress.y = 10;
    tiAddress.height = 300;
    tiAddress.textField.multiline = true;
    tiAddress.textField.wordWrap = true;
    tiAddress.width = stage.stageWidth - 20;
    tiAddress.text = "Address, City, State, Zip";
    tiAddress.setStyle("textFormat", format);
    tiAddress.addEventListener(MouseEvent.CLICK, tiAddressClickHandler);
    addChild(tiAddress);

    // Create Service buttons
    btnAddress = new Button();
    btnAddress.width = stage.stageWidth-20;
    btnAddress.height = 44;
    btnAddress.x = 10;
    btnAddress.alpha = 0.9;
    btnAddress.label = "Map Address";
    btnAddress.setStyle("textFormat", btnFormat);
    btnAddress.y = tiAddress.y + tiAddress.height + 5;
    btnAddress.addEventListener
        (MouseEvent.CLICK, btnAddressMouseClickHandler);
    addChild(btnAddress);


    btnGPS = new Button();
    btnGPS.width = stage.stageWidth-20;
    btnGPS.height = 44;
    btnGPS.x = 10;
    btnGPS.alpha = 0.9;
    btnGPS.label = "Map by GPS";
```

```
        btnGPS.setStyle("textFormat", btnFormat);
        btnGPS.y = stage.stageHeight - 54;
        btnGPS.addEventListener(MouseEvent.CLICK, btnGPSMouseClickHandler);
        addChild(btnGPS);

        // Stage event handler
        stage.addEventListener(MouseEvent.CLICK, stageClickHandler);


        // Is geolocation supported?
        if (Geolocation.isSupported)
        {
            // If so, set it up
            geo = new Geolocation();
            geo.setRequestedUpdateInterval(500);
            geo.addEventListener(GeolocationEvent.UPDATE,
                geolocationUpdateHandler);
        }

}

/**
 * Called each time the geolocation service updates app
 *
 * @param event
 *
 */
private function geolocationUpdateHandler(event:GeolocationEvent):void
{
    latitude = event.latitude;
    longitude = event.longitude;
}

/**
 * Shows Google map of specified address
 *
 * @param event
 *
 */
private function btnAddressMouseClickHandler(event:Event):void
{
    event.stopPropagation();
    GoogleMaps.pointToAddress(tiAddress.text);
}

/**
 * Shows Google map based on current latitude, longitude coordinates
 *
 * @param event
 *
 */
private function btnGPSMouseClickHandler(event:Event):void
{
```

continues

LISTING 9-8 *(continued)*

```
            event.stopPropagation();
            GoogleMaps.pointToCoordinates(latitude, longitude);
        }


        /**
         * Click handler for text input
         *
         * @param event
         *
         */
        private function tiAddressClickHandler(event:Event):void
        {
            event.stopPropagation();
        }


        /**
         * Click handler for stage
         *
         * @param event
         *
         */
        private function stageClickHandler(event:Event):void
        {
            btnAddress.setFocus();
        }


    }
```

Android: Setting Permissions

You first need to enable your app for accessing the Internet and geolocation services. To do so, add
the android.permission.INTERNET and android.permission.ACCESS-FINE-LOCATION parameters to your application descriptor file (MapServices-app.xml):

```
<android>
  <manifestAdditions>
    <manifest>
      <data>
      <![CDATA[
        <uses-permission android:name="android.permission.INTERNET"/>
        <uses-permission android:name="android.permission.ACCESS_FINE_LOCATION"/>
      ]]>
      </data>
    </manifest>
  </manifestAdditions>
</android>
```

Running the App

Figure 9-17 shows the `MapServices` app running on an Android phone with an address entered, and Figure 9-18 shows the result when the Map Address is displayed.

For the iPhone app, Figure 9-19 shows the MapServices app running with an address entered, and Figure 9-20 shows the result when the Map Address is displayed. Figure 9-21 shows my current location based on the GPS info obtained from iPhone's geolocation sensor.

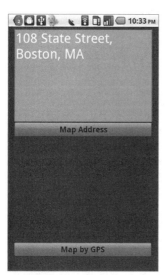

FIGURE 9-17

FIGURE 9-18

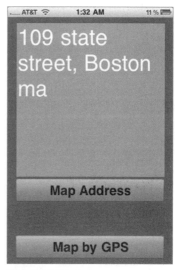

FIGURE 9-19

FIGURE 9-20

FIGURE 9-21

SUMMARY

The focus of this chapter was to integrate with Android and iPhone services using URL protocols. I began the chapter by showing you how to abstract URL calls through a MobileServices AS3 class. I then created subclasses of the MobileServices class to add certain functionality, including calling the phone, sending an SMS message, sending an e-mail message, and pointing to a location on a Google Map. In the following chapter, I'll continue the discussion of integration, but look at direct API level support specifically for Android.

10

Android Camera, Camera Roll, and Microphone

WHAT'S IN THIS CHAPTER?

➤ Accessing the camera

➤ Using the camera roll

➤ Working with the microphone

AIR for Android enables you to go beyond the URL-based integration that I discussed back in Chapter 9. You can also integrate directly with core parts of the Android device. In this chapter, I'll show you how you can work with the Camera, the Camera Roll, and the Microphone inside of your Flash apps.

Note that each of the four sample apps I cover are based on the `AndroidAppTemplate.fla`. So, to ensure identical results, be sure to download the `AndroidAppTemplate.fla` from the book's website before beginning to code these examples.

> *At the time of writing this book, Adobe Flash's iPhone support does not include support for the features covered in this chapter. However, in the event that Adobe revises the Packager for iPhone in the future, I am anticipating that the AIR for Android API discussed in this chapter will be quite similar in support.*

CAMERAUI: LAUNCH AND RETURN

You use the `CameraUI` class to access the still camera and video cam of an Android device. You can then use this class to launch the built-in camera, enable the user to take a picture, automatically save the file, and return the user to your app. Table 10-1 shows the details of the `CameraUI` class.

TABLE 10-1: CameraUI Members

MEMBER	DESCRIPTION
`CameraUI()`	Constructor
`isSupported()`	Indicates whether `CameraUI` is supported on the device
`launch(MediaType.IMAGE | MediaType.VIDEO)`	Launches the still or video camera, depending on the parameter
`addEventListener(MediaEvent.COMPLETE)`	Assigning an event listener to dispatch when the camera returns control to the app

To illustrate the basic interaction between a Flash app and a camera device, this chapter creates an app that launches the still or video camera and then returns the filename on the SD card that the camera saved. The next chapter deals with the actual image.

To follow along, start with the `AndroidAppTemplate.fla` and customize it for this app (by renaming it to `SnapAPic.fla` and the document class to `SnapAPic`).

Because this is an ActionScript 3 (AS3)-based app, go ahead and open the `SnapAPic` class inside your preferred editor and update the class and constructor names appropriately. Although there is some boilerplate code from the template, you customize it for your purposes.

To begin, add several `import` statements inside the package. Most are from the core AS3 packages, but you can also add an `import` line to the Android components:

Available for download on Wrox.com

```
import com.kevinhoyt.components.*;

import flash.display.Sprite;
import flash.display.StageScaleMode;
import flash.display.StageAlign;
import flash.events.MouseEvent;
import flash.media.CameraUI;
import flash.media.MediaType;
import flash.display.SimpleButton;
import flash.events.*;
import flash.text.TextFormat;
import flash.text.TextField;
import flash.filesystem.File;
```

Code snippet SnapAPic.as

Inside the class, you are ready to declare a handful of properties — one a reference to `CameraUI` and the others to UI components:

```
private var btn:Button;
private var ftr:Footer;
private var lbl:Label;
private var ttl:Title;
private var txt:TextInput;
private var cameraUI:CameraUI;
```

Next, you need to define the constructor. You can customize the existing boilerplate code to work for your needs of this app. Note that the code snippet here creates Image and Video buttons on the bottom footer:

```
stage.scaleMode = StageScaleMode.NO_SCALE;
stage.align = StageAlign.TOP_LEFT;

ttl = new Title( "SnapAPic" );
addChild( ttl );

lbl = new Label( "Click a button to snap a picture/video" );
lbl.x = 9;
lbl.y = 52;
addChild( lbl );

ftr = new Footer( "Image", "Video" );
ftr.y = 683;
addChild( ftr );
```

Code snippet SnapAPic.as

Once the UI is defined, you are ready to create your `CameraUI` instance. However, because not all devices may have a camera, always check using the `isSupported()` method first. If support is available, you are ready to create your `cameraUI` instance and assign event handlers:

```
// Camera support?
if (CameraUI.isSupported)
{
    cameraUI = new CameraUI();
    cameraUI.addEventListener(MediaEvent.COMPLETE, mediaCompleteHandler);
    cameraUI.addEventListener(ErrorEvent.ERROR, errorHandler);
    cameraUI.addEventListener(Event.CANCEL, errorHandler);

    ftr.addEventListener(FooterEvent.OK, imageButtonClickHandler);
    ftr.addEventListener(FooterEvent.CANCEL, videoButtonClickHandler);

}
else
{
    lbl.text = "Unable to access Camera.";
```

Code snippet SnapAPic.as

In the preceding code, the `cameraUI` instance is created and listeners are assigned to the key events associated with the `CameraUI` class. The Footer's button handlers are also assigned to respond to the Image and Video button `click` events. You begin filling out these handlers, starting with the buttons.

The Footer's Image and Video button click handlers launch the device's camera application. The Image button launches the still camera using `launch()` and the `MediaType.IMAGE` parameter:

```
private function imageButtonClickHandler(event:FooterEvent):void
{
    cameraUI.launch(MediaType.IMAGE);
}
```

The Video button changes the parameter to `MediaType.VIDEO` to launch the video cam:

```
private function videoButtonClickHandler(event:FooterEvent):void
{
    cameraUI.launch(MediaType.VIDEO);
}
```

Both of these pass control to the camera app to allow the user to interact with the camera as desired. However, the core part of `SnapAPic` is to appropriately handle the user returning from the camera app to your app. When the user takes an image or video shot and returns successfully to `SnapAPic`, the `MediaEvent.COMPLETE` event is dispatched. The `mediaCompleteHandler()` function is set up to deal with this event:

```
private function mediaCompleteHandler(event:MediaEvent):void
{
    var file:File = event.data.file;
    lbl.text = file.url;
}
```

For this simple example, the handler pulls the `File` object associated with a `MediaPromise` object being returned as `event.data`. (A `MediaPromise` object, similar to a `FilePromise`, is a commitment that the media file exists without actually checking.) The file's URL is then assigned to the label.

If the user cancels the process while accessing the camera or something goes awry, trap for these cases using the `errorHandler()` function:

```
public function errorHandler(event:Event):void
{
    lbl.text = event.type;
}
```

The `SnapAPic` document class is now good to go. Save it and return to the `SnapAPic.fla` file.

You are now ready to publish the app. Although you need to add a `<uses-permission android:name="android.permission.CAMERA" />` permission statement in the app descriptor file if you want to directly access the camera, launching the `CameraUI` doesn't require this same permission. Therefore, no additional permission is required.

Figure 10-1 shows the `SnapAPic` app when it is launched. Once you click the Image button, the `Camera` app is displayed (see Figure 10-2). The user can then take a picture and, once satisfied, click OK to return to the `SnapAPic` app. The name of the image file is shown in the user interface (UI). See Figure 10-3.

Listing 10-1 shows the full source code to the `SnapAPic.as`.

FIGURE 10-1

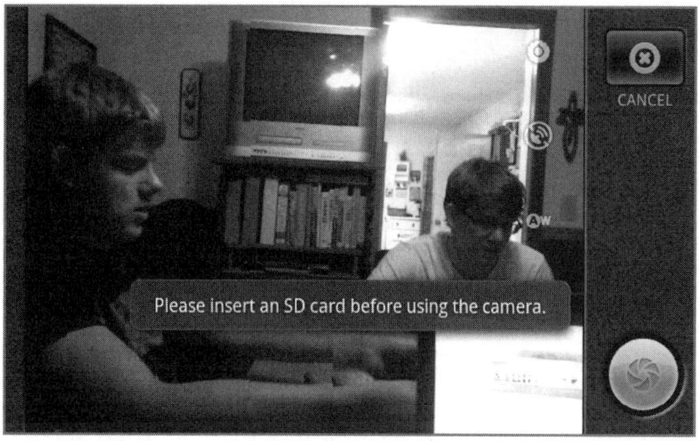

FIGURE 10-2

FIGURE 10-3

LISTING 10-1: SnapAPic.as

```
package
{
    import com.kevinhoyt.components.*;

    import flash.display.Sprite;
    import flash.display.StageScaleMode;
    import flash.display.StageAlign;
    import flash.events.MouseEvent;
    import flash.media.CameraUI;
    import flash.media.MediaType;
    import flash.display.SimpleButton;
    import flash.events.*;
    import flash.text.TextFormat;
    import flash.text.TextField;
    import flash.filesystem.File;

    /**
     * Document class for SnapAPic application.
     * AIR for Android sample app
     *
     * @author Rich Wagner
     *
     */
    public class SnapAPic extends Sprite
    {
        private var btn:Button;
        private var ftr:Footer;
        private var lbl:Label;
        private var ttl:Title;
        private var txt:TextInput;
        private var cameraUI:CameraUI;

        /**
         * Constructor
         *
         */
        public function SnapAPic()
        {

            super();

            stage.scaleMode = StageScaleMode.NO_SCALE;
            stage.align = StageAlign.TOP_LEFT;

            ttl = new Title( "SnapAPic" );
            addChild( ttl );

            lbl = new Label( "Click a button to snap a picture/video" );
            lbl.x = 9;
            lbl.y = 52;
            addChild( lbl );

            ftr = new Footer( "Image", "Video" );
```

```
        ftr.y = 683;
        addChild( ftr );


        // Camera support?
        if (CameraUI.isSupported)
        {
            cameraUI = new CameraUI();
            cameraUI.addEventListener(MediaEvent.COMPLETE,
mediaCompleteHandler);
            cameraUI.addEventListener(ErrorEvent.ERROR, errorHandler);
            cameraUI.addEventListener(Event.CANCEL, errorHandler);

            ftr.addEventListener(FooterEvent.OK, imageButtonClickHandler);
            ftr.addEventListener(FooterEvent.CANCEL, videoButtonClickHandler);

        }
        else
        {
            lbl.text = "Unable to access Camera.";
        }

    }


    /**
     * Launches the image camera
     *
     * @param event
     *
     */
    private function imageButtonClickHandler(event:FooterEvent):void
    {
        cameraUI.launch(MediaType.IMAGE);
    }

    /**
     * Launches the video camera
     *
     * @param event
     *
     */
    private function videoButtonClickHandler(event:FooterEvent):void
    {
        cameraUI.launch(MediaType.VIDEO);
    }

    /**
     * Displays media file name in the label
     *
     * @param event
     *
     */
    private function mediaCompleteHandler(event:MediaEvent):void
```

continues

LISTING 10-1 *(continued)*

```
        {
            var file:File = event.data.file
            lbl.text = file.url;
        }

        /**
         * Displays error details
         *
         * @param event
         *
         */
        public function errorHandler(event:Event):void
        {
            lbl.text = event.type;
        }

    }
}
```

CAMERA: CREATING A LIVE VIDEO FEED

In addition to launching the Camera app, you can get tighter integration by actually bringing the camera into your own application and capturing video using the Camera object. You'll learn how you can use Camera, in combination with the Video object, to create a live video feed in your app without embedding the video into your app.

One important note about capturing video in your app: to use Camera inside your app, you need to use landscape orientation. Otherwise, your video feed is displayed at a –90 degree angle, no matter what you do.

You begin the app by doing the following:

1. Create a new Flash project, name it LiveFeed, and assign it to your d:\android-dev\ LiveFeed directory.

2. Add a copy of the AndroidAppTemplate.fla template to the LiveFeed subdirectory.

3. Customize the AndroidAppTemplate.fla for this app — renaming it to LiveFeed.fla and changing the name of the document class to LiveFeed.

4. For reasons that will be explained in a moment, you change the dimensions to landscape orientation (800×480px) by adjusting the size via the Properties panel.

5. In the AIR Android Settings dialog (accessible from the Properties panel), change the Aspect ratio to Landscape and check the Fullscreen check box.

Because this is an AS3-based app, you open the LiveFeed class inside your preferred editor and update the class and constructor names. There is boilerplate code from the template, but most is not too relevant for this project.

You start by adding several `import` statements just inside the package:

```
import com.kevinhoyt.components.*;
import flash.display.Sprite;
import flash.display.StageAlign;
import flash.display.StageScaleMode;
import flash.events.TimerEvent;
import flash.media.Camera;
import flash.media.Video;
import flash.utils.Timer;
```

Code snippet LiveFeed.as

Next, you declare two class properties inside the `LiveFeed` class:

```
private var lbl:Label;
private var timer:Timer;
```

In the constructor, you create the basic UI shell:

```
stage.scaleMode = StageScaleMode.NO_SCALE;
stage.align = StageAlign.TOP_LEFT;

var ttl:Title = new Title( "Live Feed" );
addChild( ttl );

lbl = new Label( "" );
lbl.x = 9;
lbl.y = 52;
addChild( lbl );
```

Code snippet LiveFeed.as

You then check to see if Ca camera is available on the device using the `Camera.isSupported()` method:

```
// Camera support?
if (Camera.isSupported)
{
    timer = new Timer(1000);
    timer.addEventListener(TimerEvent.TIMER, timerHandler);

    var camera:Camera = Camera.getCamera();
        // Create a video object, enhancing its normal size
        // to fill more of the screen
    var video:Video = new Video(camera.width*2.6, camera.height*2.6);
    video.x = 320;
    video.y = 52;
    video.attachCamera(camera);
    video.smoothing = true;
    addChild(video);

    timer.start();
}
else
{
```

```
        lbl.text = "Camera is not supported on this device.";
    }

}
```

If the device supports a camera, you create a timer that will constantly update the label with statistical information about the camera feed. You also get a pointer to the camera through `Camera .getCamera()`, which you can then use in combination with the `Video` component to display in the app UI. The two are connected by using the Video object's `attachCamera()` method to attach the device's camera to the video and play it within the dimensions of the `Video` object's rectangular box.

The live video feed is already set to go, but you can add a handler for the timer to update the label with information about the camera feed:

```
private function timerHandler(event:TimerEvent):void
{
    lbl.text = "Camera Specifications:" + "\n" +
    "activityLevel: " + camera.activityLevel + "\n" +
    "bandwidth: " + camera.bandwidth + "\n" +
    "currentFPS: " + Math.round(camera.currentFPS) + "\n" +
    "fps: " + camera.fps + "\n" +
    "height: " + camera.height + "\n" +
    "index: " + camera.index + "\n" +
    "keyFrameInterval: " + camera.keyFrameInterval + "\n" +
    "loopback: " + camera.loopback + "\n" +
    "motionlevel: " + camera.motionLevel + "\n" +
    "muted: " + camera.muted+ "\n" +
    "name: " + camera.name + "\n" +
    "quality: " + camera.quality+ "\n" +
    "width: " + camera.width + "\n";
}
```

That's all that's necessary for the `LiveFeed` document class. Save and return to the `.fla` document.

Before publishing, you need to add the camera `permission` tag to your app descriptor file in the Android permissions section:

```
<android>
 <manifestAdditions>
  <manifest>
   <data>
     <![CDATA[
     <uses-permission android:name="android.permission.CAMERA" />
     ]]>
   </data>
  </manifest>
 </manifestAdditions>
</android>
```

You are now ready to publish and run the LiveFeed app. Figure 10-4 shows the app capturing live video.

Live Feed

Camera Specifications:
activityLevel: -1
bandwidth: 16384
currentFPS: 15
fps: 15
height: 120
index: 0
keyFrameInterval: 15
loopback: false
motionlevel: 50
muted: false
name: Default
quality: 0
width: 160

FIGURE 10-4

Listing 10-2 shows the full source code listing for LiveFeed.as.

Available for download on Wrox.com

LISTING 10-2: LiveFeed.as

```
package
{
    import com.kevinhoyt.components.*;
    import flash.display.Sprite;
    import flash.display.StageAlign;
    import flash.display.StageScaleMode;
    import flash.events.TimerEvent;
    import flash.media.Camera;
    import flash.media.Video;
    import flash.utils.Timer;


    /**
     * Document class for LiveFeed application.
     * AIR for Android sample app
     *
     * @author Rich Wagner
     *
     */
    public class LiveFeed extends Sprite
    {
        private var lbl:Label;
        private var timer:Timer;

        /**
         * Constructor
         *
```

continues

LISTING 10-2 *(continued)*

```
 */
public function LiveFeed()
{
    stage.scaleMode = StageScaleMode.NO_SCALE;
    stage.align = StageAlign.TOP_LEFT;

    var ttl:Title = new Title( "Live Feed" );
    addChild( ttl );

    lbl = new Label( "" );
    lbl.x = 9;
    lbl.y = 52;
    addChild( lbl );


    // Camera support?
    if (Camera.isSupported)
    {
        timer = new Timer(1000);
        timer.addEventListener(TimerEvent.TIMER, timerHandler);

        var camera:Camera = Camera.getCamera();
        // Create a video object, enhancing its normal size to
        // fill more of the screen
        var video:Video = new Video(camera.width*2.6, camera.height*2.6);
        video.x = 320;
        video.y = 52;
        video.attachCamera(camera);
        video.smoothing = true;
        addChild(video);

        timer.start();
    }
    else
    {
        lbl.text = "Camera is not supported on this device.";
    }

}


/**
 * Listener for timer routine
 *
 * @param event
 *
 */
private function timerHandler(event:TimerEvent):void
{
    lbl.text = "Camera Specifications:" + "\n" +
    "activityLevel: " + camera.activityLevel + "\n" +
    "bandwidth: " + camera.bandwidth + "\n" +
    "currentFPS: " + Math.round(camera.currentFPS) + "\n" +
```

```
               "fps: " + camera.fps + "\n" +
               "height: " + camera.height + "\n" +
               "index: " + camera.index + "\n" +
               "keyFrameInterval: " + camera.keyFrameInterval + "\n" +
               "loopback: " + camera.loopback + "\n" +
               "motionlevel: " + camera.motionLevel + "\n" +
               "muted: " + camera.muted+ "\n" +
               "name: " + camera.name + "\n" +
               "quality: " + camera.quality+ "\n" +
               "width: " + camera.width + "\n";
         }
    }


    }
```

TAPPING INTO THE CAMERA ROLL

AIR for Android enables you to access not just the device's camera, but its camera roll (image media library) through the CameraRoll class. Table 10-2 lists the key members for the CameraRoll class:

TABLE 10-2: Key CameraRoll Members

MEMBER	DESCRIPTION
CameraRoll()	Constructor
supportsBrowseForImage	Indicates whether the device allows image browsing
browseForImage()	Opens CameraRoll image dialog to allow a user to select an image
supportsAddBitmapData	Indicates whether you can save images on the camera roll
addBitmapData(bitmapData: BitmapData)	Saves a bitmap image to the camera roll
addEventListener(MediaEvent .CSELECT)	Assigns an event listener to dispatch when an image is selected from the camera roll.

To demonstrate how to access the camera roll, you create a sample app that allows a user to select an image from the camera roll and then display that image inside your app. You begin by doing the following:

1. Create a new Flash project and name it GetThatImage, and then assign it to your d:\ android-dev\GetThatImage directory.

2. Add a copy of the AndroidAppTemplate.fla template to the GetThatImage subdirectory.

3. Customize the AndroidAppTemplate.fla for this app — renaming it to **GetThatImage.fla** and changing the name of the document class to **GetThatImage**.

Like the others in this chapter, this app is an AS3 app, so the core programming logic is added to the document class `GetThatImage`, which you can open in your preferred editor to update the class and constructor names appropriately.

You begin by adding several `import` statements inside the package:

```
import com.kevinhoyt.components.*;
import flash.display.Sprite;
import flash.display.StageScaleMode;
import flash.display.StageAlign;
import flash.events.MouseEvent;
import flash.media.CameraRoll;
import flash.media.MediaType;
import flash.media.MediaPromise;
import flash.display.SimpleButton;
import flash.display.Sprite;
import flash.events.*;
import flash.text.TextFormat;
import flash.text.TextField;
import flash.filesystem.File;
import flash.display.Loader;
import flash.display.Bitmap;
```

Code snippet GetThatImage.as

Several class properties need to be added inside the `GetThatImage` class, related to both the UI and the camera-related aspects of the app:

```
private var btn:Button;
private var ftr:Footer;
private var lbl:Label;
private var ttl:Title;
private var cameraRoll:CameraRoll;
private var loader:Loader;
private var image:Bitmap;
```

Code snippet GetThatImage.as

The constructor both defines the UI and sets up the core functionality of the app. The core UI is created with the following code:

```
stage.scaleMode = StageScaleMode.NO_SCALE;
stage.align = StageAlign.TOP_LEFT;

ttl = new Title( "Title" );
addChild( ttl );

lbl = new Label( "Click a button to begin your session" );
lbl.x = 9;
lbl.y = 52;
addChild( lbl );

ftr = new Footer( "Load", "Cancel" );
ftr.y = 680;
ftr.addEventListener(FooterEvent.OK, loadButtonClickHandler);
addChild( ftr );
```

Code snippet GetThatImage.as

The app uses the Kevin Hoyt components to create a title bar, label, and footer with two buttons. These UI components are added to the stage using `addChild()`. The Load button on the footer is assigned an event handler to respond when the user wants to load an image from the camera roll onto the stage.

The next part of the constructor sets up the core functionality of the app as long as the `CameraRoll.supportsBrowseForImage` property returns `true`:

```
if (CameraRoll.supportsBrowseForImage)
{

        loader = new Loader();
        loader.contentLoaderInfo.addEventListener(Event.COMPLETE,
contentLoadedHandler);
        image = new Bitmap();

        cameraRoll = new CameraRoll();
        cameraRoll.addEventListener(MediaEvent.SELECT, mediaSelectHandler);
        cameraRoll.addEventListener(ErrorEvent.ERROR, errorHandler);
        cameraRoll.addEventListener(Event.CANCEL, errorHandler);


}
else
{
    lbl.text = "Unable to access Camera Roll.";
}
```

Code snippet GetThatImage.as

In this code, a `Loader` instance is created, and you add an event listener to the `contentLoaderInfo` property. The `Loader` instance loads the image data it receives from the camera roll. A `Bitmap` instance is created, which will be used later. Next, the `CameraRoll` instance is created and has several listeners assigned to it based on what the user does in the `CameraRoll` app.

If the user selects an image, the `mediaSelectHandler()` function is called. If the user cancels or some other error occurs, the `errorHandler()` function is called.

You now need to define the event handlers that were specified in the constructor. First, add the Load button click handler, which launches the `CameraRoll` app when called:

```
private function loadButtonClickHandler(event:FooterEvent):void
{
    cameraRoll.browseForImage();
}
```

Once the user selects an image in the `CameraRoll` app, the `mediaSelectHandler()` function is called:

```
private function mediaSelectHandler(event:MediaEvent):void
{

    var mediaPromise:MediaPromise = event.data;

    var imageFile:File = mediaPromise.file;
    lbl.text = imageFile.url;

    loader.unload();
```

```
        loader.loadFilePromise(mediaPromise);

    }
```

In this code, the `data` property of the `MediaEvent` object is cast to a `MediaPromise` object. This object can then be used to discover properties of the image that was selected. The URL of the image file is assigned to the label.

To load an image selected from the camera roll, use the `loader.loadFilePromise()` method, with `MediaPromise` as the parameter.

If you recall, you assigned a handler to the `loader.contentLoaderInfo`'s `Event.COMPLETE` event:

```
    private function contentLoadedHandler(event:Event):void
    {

        if (stage.contains(image))
        {
            stage.removeChild(image);
        }

        image.bitmapData = Bitmap(event.currentTarget.content).bitmapData
        image.scaleX = 0.15;
        image.scaleY = 0.15;
        image.x = 10;
        image.y = 80;
        stage.addChild(image);
    }
```

Code snippet GetThatImage.as

The first thing that you do in this function is check whether the image is currently on the stage. If it is, you want to remove it to prevent multiple images from being displayed.

Next, the `event.currentTarget.content` is cast as a `Bitmap`, so you can get its `bitmapData`, which is assigned to the `bitmapData` of your `image` variable. You then reduce the scale of the image so that it can fit inside the viewport. After giving it an x, y coordinate value, you add `image` to the stage. After saving the document class, you are ready to publish.

When you publish and run the app, Figure 10-5 shows the `GetThatPic` after launching. When you click the Load button, the camera roll is displayed, as shown in Figure 10-6. If your device has multiple image library managers, you are prompted to select which one you want to use. Figure 10-7 displays the results in the `GetThatPic` app after you select an image.

Listing 10-3 lists the full source code for `GetThatImage.as`.

FIGURE 10-5

FIGURE 10-6

FIGURE 10-7

LISTING 10-3: GetThatImage.as

```
package
{
    import com.kevinhoyt.components.*;
    import flash.display.Sprite;
    import flash.display.StageScaleMode;
    import flash.display.StageAlign;
    import flash.events.MouseEvent;
    import flash.media.CameraRoll;
    import flash.media.MediaType;
    import flash.media.MediaPromise;
    import flash.display.SimpleButton;
    import flash.display.Sprite;
    import flash.events.*;
    import flash.text.TextFormat;
    import flash.text.TextField;
    import flash.filesystem.File;
    import flash.display.Loader;
    import flash.display.Bitmap;


    /**
     * Document class for SnapAPic application.
     * AIR for Android sample app
     *
     * @author Rich Wagner
```

continues

LISTING 10-3 *(continued)*

```
         *
         */
        public class GetThatImage extends Sprite
        {
            private var btn:Button;
            private var ftr:Footer;
            private var lbl:Label;
            private var ttl:Title;
            private var cameraRoll:CameraRoll;
            private var loader:Loader;
            private var image:Bitmap;

            /**
             * Constructor
             *
             */
            public function GetThatImage()
            {
                super();

                stage.scaleMode = StageScaleMode.NO_SCALE;
                stage.align = StageAlign.TOP_LEFT;

                ttl = new Title( "Title" );
                addChild( ttl );

                lbl = new Label( "Click a button to begin your session" );
                lbl.x = 9;
                lbl.y = 52;
                addChild( lbl );

                ftr = new Footer( "Load", "Cancel" );
                ftr.y = 680;
                ftr.addEventListener(FooterEvent.OK, buttonClickHandler);
                addChild( ftr );

                // Camera support?
                if (CameraRoll.supportsBrowseForImage)
                {

                    loader = new Loader();
                    image = new Bitmap();

                    cameraRoll = new CameraRoll();
                    cameraRoll.addEventListener(MediaEvent.SELECT, mediaSelectHandler);
                    cameraRoll.addEventListener(ErrorEvent.ERROR, errorHandler);
                    cameraRoll.addEventListener(Event.CANCEL, errorHandler);

                    loader.contentLoaderInfo.addEventListener(Event.COMPLETE,
contentLoadedHandler);

                }
                else
```

```
            {
                lbl.text = "Unable to access Camera Roll.";
            }
    }



        /**
         * Launches the camera
         *
         * @param event
         *
         */
        private function buttonClickHandler(event:FooterEvent):void
        {
            cameraRoll.browseForImage();
        }

        /**
         * Called when an image is selected from the camera roll
         *
         * @param event
         *
         */
        private function mediaSelectHandler(event:MediaEvent):void
        {

            var mediaPromise:MediaPromise = event.data;

            var imageFile:File = mediaPromise.file;
            lbl.text = imageFile.url;

            loader.unload();
            loader.loadFilePromise(mediaPromise);

        }


        /**
         * Called when content is done loading by loader
         *
         * @param event
         *
         */
        private function contentLoadedHandler(event:Event):void
        {

            if (stage.contains(image))
            {
                stage.removeChild(image);
            }

            image.bitmapData = Bitmap(event.currentTarget.content).bitmapData
            image.scaleX = 0.15;
            image.scaleY = 0.15;
```

continues

LISTING 10-3 *(continued)*

```
                image.x = 10;
                image.y = 80;
                stage.addChild(image);

        }


        /**
         * Called when an error occurs
         *
         * @param event
         *
         */
        public function errorHandler(event:Event):void
        {
            lbl.text = event.type;
        }


    }
}
```

CAPTURING SOUNDS WITH THE MICROPHONE

The microphone is another important hardware feature on a mobile device that you can take advantage of in your AIR for Android applications. To capture audio from a microphone, you'll use the AIR `Microphone` class.

By creating an app called `SpeakItHearIt`, you will learn how to capture audio data in an Android app and play it back in the same session. This example works with the audio locally. However, if you want to pass this audio data to a Flash Media Server, use the `NetConnection` and `NetStream` classes.

The setup for the app may be a familiar process by now:

1. Create a new Flash project named `SpeakItHearIt`, and assign it to the `d:\android-dev\SpeakItHearIt` directory.

2. Add a copy of the `AndroidAppTemplate.fla` template to the `SpeakItHearIt` subdirectory.

3. Customize `AndroidAppTemplate.fla` for this app by renaming it to **SpeakItHearIt.fla** and changing the name of the document class to **SpeakItHearIt**.

Given that it is an AS3-based app, you open the `SpeakItHearIt` class inside your preferred editor and update the class and constructor names to `SpeakItHearIt`.

Inside the document class, begin by adding several `import` statements just inside the package:

Available for download on Wrox.com

```
import com.kevinhoyt.components.*;
import flash.display.Sprite;
import flash.display.StageAlign;
import flash.display.StageScaleMode;
import flash.events.*;
import flash.events.MouseEvent;
import flash.events.SampleDataEvent;
```

```
import flash.media.MediaType;
import flash.media.Microphone;
import flash.media.Sound;
import flash.utils.ByteArray;
```

Code snippet SpeakItHearIt.as

Five class properties are defined inside the `SpeakItHearIt` class declaring the UI and core objects that the app uses:

Available for download on Wrox.com

```
private var ftr:Footer;
private var ttl:Title;
private var lbl:Label;
private var microphone:Microphone;
private var soundBytes:ByteArray;
```

Code snippet SpeakItHearIt.as

Inside the constructor, you need to define the UI, initiate the microphone, and assign event handlers for the app. The UI definition is standard, based on the `AndroidAppTemplate.fla` template with labels customized for this app:

Available for download on Wrox.com

```
stage.scaleMode = StageScaleMode.NO_SCALE;
stage.align = StageAlign.TOP_LEFT;

ttl = new Title( "SpeakItHearIt" );
addChild( ttl );

lbl = new Label( "Record something, then hear it" );
lbl.x = 9;
lbl.y = 52;
addChild( lbl );

ftr = new Footer( "Speak It", "Hear It" );
ftr.y = 683;
ftr.addEventListener(FooterEvent.OK, speakItHandler);
ftr.addEventListener(FooterEvent.CANCEL, hearItHandler);
addChild( ftr );
```

Code snippet SpeakItHearIt.as

Like the `Camera` object, the `Microphone` object has an `isSupported` property that you can use to test whether the device has a useable microphone. If `true`, the Microphone object is instantiated using the `Microphone.getMicrophone()` method:

Available for download on Wrox.com

```
if (Microphone.isSupported)
{
    microphone = Microphone.getMicrophone();
    microphone.setSilenceLevel(0, 3000);
    microphone.gain = 100;
    microphone.rate = 44;
    soundBytes= new ByteArray();
    lbl.text = "Ready to record and play";
}
else
{
    lbl.text = "Unable to access Microphone.";
}
```

Code snippet SpeakItHearIt.as

The setSilenceLevel() method determines silence levels. The first parameter specifies the minimum audio level to be considered a sound. I set mine to 0 to pick up everything. The second parameter specifies the amount of silence (in ms) to determine when silence has begun. The gain and rate properties of the Microphone instance are also set.

A ByteArray is created to capture the audio stream when the app records.

With the constructor ready to go, turn your attention to the event handlers. When you click the Speak It button, the speakItHandler() function is triggered:

```
private function speakItHandler(event:FooterEvent):void
{
    microphone.addEventListener(SampleDataEvent.SAMPLE_DATA, sampleDataHandler)
}
```

It adds a SampleDataEvent event handler that receives all sounds that are captured from the microphone. The handler retrieves all the data it receives from the SampleDataEvent and writes it to the soundBytes ByteArray:

```
private function sampleDataHandler(event:SampleDataEvent):void
{
    while(event.data.bytesAvailable)
    {
        var sample:Number = event.data.readFloat();
        soundBytes.writeFloat(sample);
    }
}
```

Code snippet SpeakItHearIt.as

The Hear It button has a second handler that plays everything recorded so far:

```
private function hearItHandler(event:FooterEvent):void
{
    microphone.removeEventListener(SampleDataEvent.SAMPLE_DATA,
    sampleDataHandler);
        soundBytes.position = 0;
        var sound:Sound = new Sound();
        sound.addEventListener(SampleDataEvent.SAMPLE_DATA, playbackSampleHandler);
        sound.play();
}
```

Code snippet SpeakItHearIt.as

When called, it stops the sound collection by removing the event listener. It then resets soundByte's position to the start, creates a new Sound object, and then plays it. The sound's SampleDataEvent handler is triggered when the sound is played back:

```
private function playbackSampleHandler(event:SampleDataEvent):void
{
    for (var i:int = 0; i < 8192 && soundBytes.bytesAvailable > 0; i++)
    {
        var sample:Number = soundBytes.readFloat();
```

```
            event.data.writeFloat(sample);
            event.data.writeFloat(sample);
        }
```

Code snippet SpeakItHearIt.as

The `SpeakItHearIt` document class is complete. However, before publishing, you need to add the
`RECORD_AUDIO` permission to the app descriptor file:

```xml
<android>
  <manifestAdditions>
    <manifest>
      <data>
        <![CDATA[
        <uses-permission android:name="android.permission.RECORD_AUDIO" />
        ]]>
      </data>
    </manifest>
  </manifestAdditions>
</android>
```

Code snippet SpeakItHearIt-app.xml

Figure 10-8 shows the app when it is run.

FIGURE 10-8

Listing 10-4 shows the full source code listing for the `SpeakItHearIt` app.

LISTING 10-4: SpeakItHearIt.as

```
package
{
    import com.kevinhoyt.components.*;
    import flash.display.Sprite;
    import flash.display.StageAlign;
    import flash.display.StageScaleMode;
    import flash.events.*;
    import flash.events.MouseEvent;
    import flash.events.SampleDataEvent;
    import flash.media.MediaType;
    import flash.media.Microphone;
    import flash.media.Sound;
    import flash.utils.ByteArray;


    /**
     * Document class for SpeakItHearIt application.
     * iPhone Development with Flash sample app
     *
     * @author Rich Wagner
     *
     */
    public class SpeakItHearIt extends Sprite
    {
        private var ftr:Footer;
        private var ttl:Title;
        private var lbl:Label;
        private var microphone:Microphone;
        private var soundBytes:ByteArray;

        /**
         * Constructor
         *
         */
        public function SpeakItHearIt()
        {
            stage.scaleMode = StageScaleMode.NO_SCALE;
            stage.align = StageAlign.TOP_LEFT;

            ttl = new Title( "SpeakItHearIt" );
            addChild( ttl );

            lbl = new Label( "Record something, then hear it" );
            lbl.x = 9;
            lbl.y = 52;
            addChild( lbl );

            ftr = new Footer( "Speak It", "Hear It" );
            ftr.y = 683;
            ftr.addEventListener(FooterEvent.OK, speakItHandler);
```

```
                    ftr.addEventListener(FooterEvent.CANCEL, hearItHandler);
                    addChild( ftr );

                    // Camera support?
                    if (Microphone.isSupported)
                    {
                        microphone = Microphone.getMicrophone();
                        microphone.setSilenceLevel(0, 4000);
                        microphone.gain = 100;
                        microphone.rate = 44;
                        soundBytes= new ByteArray();
                        lbl.text = "Ready to record and play";
                    }
                    else
                    {
                        lbl.text = "Unable to access Microphone.";
                    }


                }


            /**
             * Called when Speak button is clicked
             *
             * @param event
             *
             */
            private function speakItHandler(event:FooterEvent):void
            {
                microphone.addEventListener(SampleDataEvent.SAMPLE_DATA,
sampleDataHandler)
            }


            /**
             * Called when Hear button is clicked
             *
             * @param event
             *
             */
            private function hearItHandler(event:FooterEvent):void
            {
                microphone.removeEventListener(SampleDataEvent.SAMPLE_DATA,
sampleDataHandler);
                soundBytes.position = 0;
                var sound:Sound = new Sound();
                sound.addEventListener(SampleDataEvent.SAMPLE_DATA,
playbackSampleHandler);
                sound.play();
            }


            /**
             * Begins recording session
```

continues

LISTING 10-4 *(continued)*

```
     *
     * @param event
     *
     */
    private function sampleDataHandler(event:SampleDataEvent):void
    {
        while(event.data.bytesAvailable)
        {
            var sample:Number = event.data.readFloat();
            soundBytes.writeFloat(sample);
        }
    }

    /**
     * Plays back audio data in stored in memory
     *
     * @param event
     *
     */
    private function playbackSampleHandler(event:SampleDataEvent):void
    {
        for (var i:int = 0; i < 8192 && soundBytes.bytesAvailable > 0; i++)
        {
            var sample:Number = soundBytes.readFloat();
            event.data.writeFloat(sample);
            event.data.writeFloat(sample);
        }
    }

    }
}
```

SUMMARY

In this chapter, you explored the nuts and bolts of working with the camera, camera roll, and the microphone of Android devices. You began by creating an app that launched the camera, allowed a user to take a picture, and then returned to your app. You next created a live video feed app, followed by an app that accessed the camera roll. The chapter concludes with a look at how to capture audio using the phone microphone.

PART III
Data

11

File Management

WHAT'S IN THIS CHAPTER?

➤ Exploring File I/O in Android and iOS

➤ Identifying the I/O differences between Android and iOS

➤ Read and write files

A critical part of any native OS application, whether on the desktop or on a mobile device, is the ability to read and write files and work with the local file system. This chapter introduces you to working with files and directories in your Android or iOS application. It shows you the `File` object and what you can use it for in Android/iOS, such as performing standard file operations. The chapter then discusses how to read and write data to a file by creating a plain vanilla text editor.

UNDERSTANDING THE ANDROID FILE AND DIRECTORY STRUCTURE

When you work with files in your Android app, you can access files and directories on both internal and external storage (such as an SD [Secure Digital] card). For internal storage, there are several system directories (such as `/acct`, `/dev`, or `/etc`) that you normally do not have to concern yourself with. However, when your application is installed onto the device, it is installed into the `/data/data` directory by default. Your application storage and temporary storage are there as well.

Every Android device also supports external storage that your app and potentially other apps can read. In addition, users may copy files from an external storage medium to a desktop computer.

Beyond application-specific directories that you may want to add to external storage, you can use public directories that are not specific to any application. These include the following:

➤ `/sdcard/Music/` for music files

➤ `/sdcard/Podcasts/` for podcasts

➤ `/sdcard/Ringtones/` for ringtones

➤ `/sdcard/Alarms/` for alarm clock sounds

➤ `/sdcard/Notifications/` for notification sounds

➤ `/sdcard/Pictures/` for photos (not including those taken with the device's camera)

➤ `/sdcard/Movies/` for videos for photos (not including those taken with the device's video camera)

➤ `/sdcard/Download/` for downloads

Since iOS devices do not have an external storage SD card, you don't deal with these extra directories in the same way, as shown in the next section.

WORKING WITH DIRECTORIES, FILES, AND FILE STREAMS

When you're working with files and file input/output (IO), you work primarily with two classes: `File` and `FileStream`. `File` represents a file or a directory on the file system and is used for basic file and directory management tasks. On the other hand, `FileStream` is used for actually reading and writing data from a file. Both are contained in the `flash.filesystem` package.

Working with Directories

There is no "Directory" class in AS3. Instead, a `File` object points to either a directory or a file. You have access to several special directories through alias-style properties of the `File` object (see Table 11-1). These are the directories you would typically work with.

As you can see from the table, iOS provides much less support for directories than does Android. You have access to the application directory and the application storage directory, but not to other standard AIR directories, such as desktop or documents directory.

TABLE 11-1: Special Directories Available through the Alias-Style Properties of the File Object

PROPERTY/METHOD	DIRECTORY	ANDROID	IOS SUPPORT
`File.applicationDirectory`	Directory in which the app is installed (read-only)	`/data/data/app .appID/app/assets`	Supported
`File.application StorageDirectory`	Private storage directory for the app	`/data/data/app .appID/AppName/ Local Store`	Supported

PROPERTY/METHOD	DIRECTORY	ANDROID	IOS SUPPORT
`File.userDirectory`	User's home directory	`/sdcard`	`Not supported`
`File.documentsDirectory`	User's document directory	`/sdcard`	`Not supported`
`File.desktopDirectory`	User's desktop directory	`/sdcard`	`Not supported`
`File.createTempDirectory()`	Temporary storage directory	Created in `/data/data/app.appId/cache`	`Supported`
`File.createTempFile()`	Temporary file	Created in `/data/data/app.appId/cache`	`Supported`

For example, if you wanted to get the application storage directory, you'd use this:

```
private var storeDir:File = File.applicationStorageDirectory;
```

Once there, you can use the `resolvePath()` method to access a subdirectory or file inside of it. So, for example, to point to a `preferences.xml` file, you'd enter this:

```
private var storeDir:File = File.applicationStorageDirectory;
private var prefXML:File = storeDir.resolvePath("preferences.xml");
```

Because `File` is a static object, you can write more simply:

```
private var prefXML:File =
   File.applicationStorageDirectory.resolvePath("preferences.xml");
```

Using these alias properties is usually much easier than working with the specific directory paths. Also, it enables you to avoid writing OS-specific code. However, if you need to, you can work with the native file system directly using `File.nativePath`. For example:

```
private var sdpath:File = new File();
sdpath.nativePath = "/sdcard/mypath";
```

You can also point to directories and files using the `File.url` property. For local files, use the `file:///` protocol. So, to assign a `url` property instead of `nativePath`, you would use this:

```
private var sdpath:File = new File();
sdpath.url = "file:///sdcard/mypath";
```

Because the `url` property returns the path as a URI-encoded string, be sure to substitute spaces with `%20`.

AIR also supports some URL-based shortcuts when referencing special AIR directories. The `app:/` notation points to the application directory, whereas `app-storage:/` points to the application storage directory for your app. For example:

```
app:/default.sql
app-storage:/preferences.xml
```

To demonstrate these directory references, you'll create a simple app that outputs the special alias directories in a `TextField`. Begin by setting up the project:

1. Within the target source directory, create a new Flash document using the Android or iOS template and name it `DirFile.fla`.

2. In the Properties panel, enter **DirFile** as the document class, and click the pencil button to edit the class definition in your preferred editor.

3. Inside the package and above the `DirFile` class definition, add the following `import` statements for each of the AS3 classes you'll be referencing:

```
import flash.display.MovieClip;
import flash.filesystem.File;
import flash.display.StageAlign;
import flash.display.StageScaleMode;
import flash.text.TextField;
import flash.text.TextFormat;
```

4. Next, inside the `DirFile()` constructor, set up the stage and create a `TextField` that covers most of the stage:

```
// Set up the stage
stage.scaleMode = StageScaleMode.NO_SCALE;
stage.align = StageAlign.TOP_LEFT;

// Create TextField
tfInfo = new TextField();
var format:TextFormat = new TextFormat("Helvetica", 24);
format.color = 0x000000;
tfInfo.defaultTextFormat = format;
tfInfo.border = true;
tfInfo.wordWrap = true;
tfInfo.multiline = true;
tfInfo.x = 10;
tfInfo.y = 10;
tfInfo.height = stage.stageHeight - 20;
tfInfo.width = stage.stageWidth - 20;
addChild(tfInfo);
```

5. Finally, add the following calls, which output the `nativePath` and `url` values for several of the special aliases:

```
tfInfo.text = "applicationDirectory: " + File.applicationDirectory.nativePath
  + "\n\n";
tfInfo.appendText( "applicationStorageDirectory: " +
  File.applicationStorageDirectory.nativePath + "\n\n");
tfInfo.appendText( "userDirectory: " + File.userDirectory.nativePath + "\n\n");
```

```
tfInfo.appendText( "documentsDirectory: " + File.documentsDirectory.nativePath
    + "\n\n");
tfInfo.appendText( "desktopDirectory: " + File.desktopDirectory.nativePath
    + "\n\n");

tfInfo.appendText( "applicationDirectory URL: " + File.applicationDirectory.url
    + "\n\n");
tfInfo.appendText( "desktopDirectory URL: " + File.desktopDirectory.url +
    "\n\n");
```

If you are creating an iOS app, then you can edit out the aliases not supported:

```
tfInfo.text = "applicationDirectory: " + File.applicationDirectory.nativePath + "\n\n";
tfInfo.appendText( "applicationStorageDirectory: " + File.applicationStorageDirectory.
nativePath + "\n\n");
tfInfo.appendText( "applicationDirectory URL: " + File.applicationDirectory.url +
"\n\n");
```

You can save the file and return to the Flash document to publish it. When you run the file, you'll see what's shown in Figure 11-1 (if you run under Android).

File System Operations

The `File` object provides several methods for performing file system operations.

Creating a Directory

You can use the `File.createDirectory()` method to create a new directory. You first need to use `resolvePath()`, passing in the new directory location, to identify where you want to create, and then you must call the `createDirectory()` method. For example, the following code snippet creates a `data` subdirectory inside the `applicationStorage` directory:

```
var dataDir:File = File.applicationStorageDirectory.resolvePath("data");
dataDir.createDirectory();
```

Before you create the new directory, `File.createDirectory()` checks to see if that directory already exists. If it does, the call is ignored. If it's not there, the directory is created.

Creating a Temporary Directory or File

You can also create a temporary directory or file using two methods of the `File` object. The `File.createTempDirectory()` creates a uniquely named subdirectory inside the app's temporary directory. (For Android apps, that will be located in `/data/data/app.appId/cache`.) For example:

```
var tmpDir:File = File.createTempDirectory();
```

In this example, the `tmpDir` variable is assigned a pointer to the new directory.

You can also create a temporary file in the same location (`/data/data/app.appId/cache` for Android apps) using the `File.createTempFile()` method. In this example, the `tmpFile` variable points to the new file created:

```
var tmpFile:File = File.createTempFile();
```

A few usage notes on these two methods:

➤ These methods are intended as time-saver routines. This way you don't have to ensure that you have a unique name for the file or directory you want to create.

➤ `File.createTempFile()` or any other new file object simply points to a file reference; it doesn't create a file with actual data in it. You have to do that yourself, such as through use of `FileStream` (discussed later in this chapter).

➤ Be sure to clean up your temporary files and directories when you are finished with them or when the app closes. They aren't removed automatically.

FIGURE 11-1

Copying and Moving

The `File` object supports copy and move operations. You can perform these operations either synchronously or asynchronously, depending on your needs. If you set the operation to be *synchronous*, your app suspends execution until it receives word from the OS that the task has been completed. In contrast, if you set the operation to be *asynchronous*, your app continues executing and dispatches an event when the OS has completed the task.

Synchronous Operations

You can synchronously copy a file or an entire directory using the `File.copyTo()` method. For example, if you're developing for Android, suppose you want to copy a directory from your `applicationStorage` directory to the `documents` directory:

```
var sourceFolder:File = File.applicationStorageDirectory.resolvePath("data");
// Note: documentDirectory not supported under iOS
var targetFolder:File = File.documentsDirectory.resolvePath("data");
sourceFolder.copyTo(targetFolder);
```

In this code, the `data` subdirectory is copied synchronously to a new location inside the `document` folder. If there is an existing data directory in that target location, the process stops. However, if you prefer to overwrite the existing directory, add an optional `overwrite` flag to the `copyTo()` method:

```
sourceFolder.copyTo(targetFolder, true);
```

When the overwrite parameter is set to true, the call deletes the target file or directory and copies the one you specify.

The moveTo() method works much the same way, except that the source directory is removed once the copy operation has been performed. The following example moves the images directory from applicationDirectory to a subdirectory under applicationStorageDirectory:

```
var sourceFolder:File = File.applicationDirectory.resolvePath("images");
var targetFolder:File =
  File.applicationStorageDirectory.resolvePath("assets/images");
sourceFolder.moveTo(targetFolder)
```

When you want to copy or move files synchronously, you do so in the same way that you do directories. The following example copies a template file from the application directory to the user's applicationStorage directory:

```
var sourceFile = File.applicationDirectory.resolvePath("templates/sample-
template.xml");
var targetFile =
File.applicationStorageDirectory.resolvePath("templates/sample-template.xml");
sourceFile.copyTo(targetFile);
```

Asynchonous Operations

You can also copy and move asynchronously using the copyToAsync() and moveToAsync() methods. Once these operations are finished, an event is dispatched letting your app know. Typically, you would add listeners to these events to determine what to do once the process completes successfully or how to deal with a failed operation.

For example, the following sample creates a backup copy of the application's main database file:

```
public function createBackupCopy():void
{
  // Note: documentDirectory not supported under iOS
  var originalFile:File = File.documentDirectory.resolvePath("MyApp/data.sql");
  var backupCopy:File =
    File.applicationStorageDirectory.resolvePath("Backup/backup01.sql");

  originalFile.addEventListener(Event.COMPLETE, copyCompleteHandler);
  originalFile.addEventListener(IOErrorEvent.IO_ERROR, copyErrorHandler);
  originalFile.copyToAsync(backupCopy);
}

public function copyCompleteHandler(event:Event):void
{
  trace("Backup operation completed successfully");
}

public function copyErrorHandler(event:IOErrorEvent):void
{
  trace("Operation failed.");
}
```

Deleting Files and Directories

When using AIR for desktop operating systems, you have the option of deleting a file (`deleteFile()` and `deleteFileAsynch()`) or sending it to the Trash/Recycle Bin (`moveToTrash()` and `moveToTrashAsync()`). However, because there is no Trash/Recycle Bin concept in the Android OS or iOS, the `moveToTrash()` and `moveToTrashAsync()` methods behave in the same manner as their `delete` counterparts.

The following code evaluates a file to determine if it's a file or directory. It then issues the appropriate delete command:

```
var tempFile:File = File.createTempFile();
// do something with tempFile, then...

if (tempFile.isDirectory() == true)
    tempFile.deleteDirectory(true)
else
    tempFile.deleteFile();
```

Or, if you use `deleteFileAsync()`, you should assign a handler to the complete event when the deletion process is finished.

READING AND WRITING FILES

So far, this chapter has talked about how to work with files, but it has not discussed what you can do with the data inside of them. The `FileStream` class is used for read and write operations with files. As with other file operations, you can work with a file stream synchronously or asynchronously.

Whenever you read or write to a file stream, you open it by using the `open()` or `openAsync()` method. These methods take two parameters: `File` and `FileMode`. `FileMode` is a static class that specifies the permissions open to the `FileStream` object during the operation. There are four possible `file` modes:

➤   `FileMode.READ` indicates that the file is open for reading only.

➤   `FileMode.WRITE` specifies that the file is open for write access. If the file already exists, its contents are deleted. If the file does not exist, it is created.

➤   `FileMode.APPEND` specifies that the file is to be opened in "append mode" — in other words, new data is added to the end of the file rather than overwriting existing data. If the file does not exist, it is created.

➤   `FileMode.UPDATE` indicates that the file is open for both reading and writing. This mode is used when you need random read/write access to the file. When you write to the file, only the bytes at the current location are overwritten, not the entire file. If the file does not exist, it is created.

Table 11-2 summarizes the differences between these four `file` modes.

TABLE 11-2: Possible File Modes

MODES	READABLE	WRITEABLE	IF FILE EXISTS	IF FILE DOESN'T EXIST
`FileMode.READ`	X			
`FileMode.WRITE`	X	X	Contents are deleted.	File is created.
`FileMode.APPEND`	X	X	Contents are preserved. Writing begins at end of file.	File is created.
`FileMode.UPDATE`	X	X	Contents are preserved. Writing occurs at current position.	File is created.

For example, consider the following code snippet, which opens a synchronous read/write stream to a preferences file:

```
var file:File = File.applicationStorageDirectory.resolvePath("preferences.xml");
var fileStream:FileStream = new FileStream();
fileStream.open(file, FileMode.WRITE);
```

Reading a File

When you read from a file, you often choose the manner to use based on the type of data you are reading:

➤ If you are working with ordinary text files that use a UTF-8 character set, use `readUTFBytes()`.

➤ If you need multibyte support, use `readMultiByte()`, which reads based on a character set specified as a parameter.

➤ If you are working with a byte array, use the more generic `readBytes()`.

➤ If you are working with AMF serialized objects, use `readObject()`.

➤ If you are working with a particular numeric data type, consider `readDouble()`, `readFloat()`, `readInt()`, `readShort()`, `readUnsignedInt()`, or `readUnsignedShort()`.

To synchronously read a file and assign the data to a variable using `readMultiByte()`, consider the following code:

```
var file:File = File.documentsDirectory.resolvePath("myapp/text1.txt");
var fileStream:FileStream = new FileStream();
```

```
fileStream.open(file, FileMode.READ);
var s:String = fileStream.readMultiByte(file.size, File.systemCharset);
trace(s);
fileStream.close();
```

In this example, the `FileStream open()` method opens the `text1.txt` file for reading. Using `FileMode.READ` specifies that the `FileStream` instance can read from the file but not write to it.

The `readMultiByte()` method reads a multibyte string from the `FileStream` using the character set specified by `File.systemCharset`, which returns the default encoding used by Android. The total size of the file stream is indicated by the `file.size` property. The `close()` method closes the file stream when it's finished.

Writing to a File

You can also write to a file using a set of write-related counterpart methods to the read methods discussed in the previous section. These include `writeUTFBytes()`, `writeMultiByte()`, `writeBytes()`, `writeObject()`, `writeDouble()`, `writeFloat()`, `writeInt()`, `writeShort()`, `writeUnsignedInt()`, and `writeUnsignedShort()`.

To demonstrate, the following code synchronously writes a multibyte string to a file:

```
var file:File= File.documentDirectory. resolvePath("myApp/text1.txt");
var fileStream:FileStream = new FileStream();
fileStream.open(file, FileMode.WRITE);
var s:String = "This text is being written."
fileStream.writeMultiByte(s, File.systemCharset);
fileStream.close();
```

Android Case Study: Jots

To provide a fuller demonstration of how you can read and write files in an Android app, this section walks through creating a basic text editor called `Jots`. `Jots` provides a TextArea for inputting text, a Save button for saving onto the Android device, and an Open button for loading the file saved previously.

Before diving into the ActionScript code, you need to set up the Flash project as follows:

1. Within the target directory, create a new Flash document based on the AIR for Android template and name it `Jots.fla`.

2. In the Properties panel, enter **Jots** as the document class.

 While the UI portion of this example is Android-specific, the File I/O portions of the Jots document class will function as is under iOS.

Adding Minimal Comps Set

This app also demonstrates how to use a set of open-source Flash-based UI components called Minimal Comps, which you can download from www.minimalcomps.com. Although these are not necessarily targeted for Android, they provide an alternate example of UI implementation beyond what you've seen elsewhere in this book.

Although this section doesn't fully "Androidize" the components, you do need to tweak the default font and size before you can use them on Android devices. Therefore, follow these steps to add and customize the component set for the purposes of Jots:

1. Download the Minimal Comps lightweight third-party components from www.minimalcomps.com.

2. Unzip the file into a master backup directory.

3. Copy the assets and com subdirectories (under src), and paste them into your Jots project directory.

4. Locate the DroidSans.ttf font file and add it to the assets directory for embedding in your application.

5. Open the Component.as file in the com.bit101.components package in your editor of choice.

6. Comment out the Flex 4 Embed reference to the PF Ronda Seven font, and add the following just below it:

   ```
   // Standard Minimal Comps font
   //[Embed(source="/assets/pf_ronda_seven.ttf", embedAsCFF="false",
   fontName="PF Ronda
    Seven", mimeType="application/x-font")]
   // Replacing with Droid Sans for Android deployment
   [Embed(source="/assets/DroidSans.ttf", embedAsCFF="false",
   fontName="Droid Sans",
    mimeType="application/x-font")]
   ```

7. Save and close the Component.as file.

8. Open the Style.as in the same package inside of your favorite editor.

9. Change the fontName and fontSize properties to the following:

   ```
   public static var fontName:String = "Droid Sans";
   public static var fontSize:Number = 22;
   ```

10. Save and close the Style.as file.

Therefore, although the Minimal Comps components are not optimized for Android, now they are at least usable on Android devices for your sample app purposes — and they make life a little easier.

You can return to the .fla document and then, in the Properties panel, click the pencil button to edit the Jots class definition in your preferred editor.

Coding the Document Class

As you begin to edit the `Jots` document class, the first thing you might want to do is add several import statements for both the Minimal Comps components you intend to use as well as the file-related classes you want to use for reading and writing. Here's the list needed for this example:

```
// Base
import flash.display.MovieClip;

// Events
import flash.events.MouseEvent;
import flash.events.IOErrorEvent;
import flash.events.Event;

// Minimal Comps components
import com.bit101.components.PushButton;
import com.bit101.components.TextArea;

// File-related
import flash.filesystem.File;
import flash.filesystem.FileMode;
import flash.filesystem.FileStream;

// Stage setup
import flash.display.StageAlign;
import flash.display.StageScaleMode;
```

Code snippet Jots.as

Inside the `Jots` class, begin by declaring four private properties for UI and file-related purposes:

```
private var ta:TextArea;
private var openBtn:PushButton;
private var saveBtn:PushButton;
public var file:File;
```

Code snippet Jots.as

Filling the Constructor Function

Next, inside the constructor function, create your user interface. Then create a pointer to the text file you will be reading and writing from. Here's the code:

```
public function Jots() {

// Set up the stage
stage.scaleMode = StageScaleMode.NO_SCALE;
stage.align = StageAlign.TOP_LEFT;

// Create TextField
ta = new TextArea();
ta.x = 10;
ta.y = 10;
ta.height = stage.stageHeight - 120;
ta.width = stage.stageWidth - 20;
```

```
addChild(ta);

// Create Open button
openBtn = new PushButton();
openBtn.label = "Open";
openBtn.x = 10;
openBtn.y = stage.stageHeight - 100;
openBtn.height = 70;
openBtn.width = 200;
openBtn.addEventListener(MouseEvent.CLICK, openBtnClickHandler);
addChild(openBtn);

    // Create Save button
    saveBtn = new PushButton();
    saveBtn.label = "Save";
    saveBtn.x = 240;
    saveBtn.y = stage.stageHeight - 100;
    saveBtn.height = 70;
    saveBtn.width = 200;
    saveBtn.addEventListener(MouseEvent.CLICK, saveBtnClickHandler);
    addChild(saveBtn);

    // Create pointer to file
    file = File.applicationStorageDirectory.resolvePath("MyDataFile.txt");
}
```

Code snippet Jots.as

In this code, you can begin by setting up the stage, followed by creating a `TextArea` (Minimal Comps version, not built-in version) instance. Assign it to take up all but 120 pixels of the height and all but 20 pixels of the width of the viewport.

Continue by creating two `PushButton` instances: one for opening the file and one for saving it. Assign `MouseEvent` handlers to these buttons to respond to user clicks.

Finally, create a pointer to the file `MyDataFile.txt`, which is located in the `applicationStorage` directory.

Saving a File

You want the `Jots` app to save the contents of the `TextArea` to a file when you click the Save button. File saving is handled through the `saveBtnClickHandler()` method, which is the event handler for the `saveBtn` click event. The code is shown here:

```
private function saveBtnClickHandler(event:MouseEvent):void
{
    var fileStream:FileStream = new FileStream();
    fileStream.open(file, FileMode.WRITE);
    fileStream.addEventListener(IOErrorEvent.IO_ERROR, ioWriteErrorHandler);
    var s:String = ta.text;
    s = s.replace(/\r/g, "\n");
    s = s.replace(/\n/g, File.lineEnding);
    fileStream.writeUTFBytes(s);
    fileStream.close();
}
```

You open a file stream for writing using the synchronous open() method. You then assign the content of the TextArea to the s variable. Before calling writeUTFBytes(), replace any new line characters (\n) with a platform-specific line ending character using File.lineEnding. Once the file stream is written to the MyDataFile.txt, call its close() method to close it.

As shown in the example, an event listener is added to the FileStream instance to deal with any IO errors. You can handle them using a trace() call:

```
private function ioWriteErrorHandler(evt:Event):void
{
    trace("Unable to save");
}
```

Opening a File

Jots needs to be able to open a previously saved MyDataFile.text file. Clicking the Open button calls the openBtnClickHandler() method. This function uses openAsync() to open the file stream asynchronously. Because you are opening asynchronously, define handlers to be called when the file has been read or an IO error occurs:

Available for
download on
Wrox.com

```
private function openBtnClickHandler(event:MouseEvent):void
{
    var fileStream:FileStream = new FileStream();
    fileStream.openAsync(file, FileMode.READ);
    fileStream.addEventListener(Event.COMPLETE, completeHandler);
    fileStream.addEventListener(IOErrorEvent.IO_ERROR, ioReadErrorHandler);
}
```

Code snippet Jots.as

The file is being read asynchronously, so place the FileStream's read routine inside the Event.COMPLETE handler. Specifically, call readUTFBytes(), which assigns the contents of the file stream to the s variable. This string's value is assigned to the text property of the TextArea. Here's the code:

Available for
download on
Wrox.com

```
    private function completeHandler(event:Event):void
{
    var fileStream:FileStream = event.target as FileStream;
    var s:String = fileStream.readUTFBytes(fileStream.bytesAvailable);
    ta.text = s;
    fileStream.close();
}
```

Code snippet Jots.as

Finally, add an event handler in case an IO error occurs in the open process:

```
private function ioReadErrorHandler(event:Event):void
{
    trace("Unable to open" + file.nativePath);
}
```

Listing 11-1 shows the complete listing for Jots.as.

LISTING 11-1: Jots.as

```
package  {

    import flash.display.MovieClip;

    // Events
    import flash.events.MouseEvent;
    import flash.events.IOErrorEvent;
    import flash.events.Event;

    // Minimal Comps components
    import com.bit101.components.PushButton;
    import com.bit101.components.TextArea;

    // File-related
    import flash.filesystem.File;
    import flash.filesystem.FileMode;
    import flash.filesystem.FileStream;

    // Stage setup
    import flash.display.StageAlign;
    import flash.display.StageScaleMode;

    /**
     * Document class for Jots application.
     * Sample code for Professional Flash Mobile Development
     *
     * @author Rich Wagner
     *
     */
    public class Jots extends MovieClip {

        private var ta:TextArea;
        private var openBtn:PushButton;
        private var saveBtn:PushButton;
        public var file:File;

        public function Jots() {

            // Set up the stage
            stage.scaleMode = StageScaleMode.NO_SCALE;
            stage.align = StageAlign.TOP_LEFT;

            // Create TextField
            ta = new TextArea();
            ta.x = 10;
            ta.y = 10;
            ta.height = stage.stageHeight - 120;
            ta.width = stage.stageWidth - 20;
            addChild(ta);

            // Create Open button
            openBtn = new PushButton();
```

continues

LISTING 11-1 *(continued)*

```
            openBtn.label = "Open";
            openBtn.x = 10;
            openBtn.y = stage.stageHeight - 100;
            openBtn.height = 70;
            openBtn.width = 200;
            openBtn.addEventListener(MouseEvent.CLICK, openBtnClickHandler);
            addChild(openBtn);

            // Create Save button
            saveBtn = new PushButton();
            saveBtn.label = "Save";
            saveBtn.x = 240;
            saveBtn.y = stage.stageHeight - 100;
            saveBtn.height = 70;
            saveBtn.width = 200;
            saveBtn.addEventListener(MouseEvent.CLICK, saveBtnClickHandler);
            addChild(saveBtn);

            // Create pointer to file
            file = File.applicationStorageDirectory.resolvePath("MyDataFile.txt");


        }

        private function openBtnClickHandler(event:MouseEvent):void
        {
            var fileStream:FileStream = new FileStream();
            fileStream.openAsync(file, FileMode.READ);
            fileStream.addEventListener(Event.COMPLETE, completeHandler);
            fileStream.addEventListener(IOErrorEvent.IO_ERROR, ioReadErrorHandler);
        }

        private function completeHandler(event:Event):void
        {
            var fileStream:FileStream = event.target as FileStream;
            var str:String =
                fileStream.readUTFBytes(fileStream.bytesAvailable);
            ta.text = str;
            fileStream.close();
        }

        private function ioReadErrorHandler(event:Event):void
        {
            trace("Unable to open" + file.nativePath);
        }

        private function saveBtnClickHandler(event:MouseEvent):void
        {
            var fileStream:FileStream = new FileStream();
            fileStream.openAsync(file, FileMode.WRITE);
            fileStream.addEventListener(IOErrorEvent.IO_ERROR, onIOWriteError);
            var str:String = ta.text;
            str = str.replace(/\r/g, "\n");
```

```
            str = str.replace(/\n/g, File.lineEnding);
            fileStream.writeUTFBytes(str);
            fileStream.close();
        }


        private function ioWriteErrorHandler(event:Event):void
        {
          trace("Unable to save");
        }


    }

  }
```

Running Jots

Once you compile the Flash project and install the `.apk` file onto your Android device, you can run it. Figure 11-2 shows the `Jots` app with notes in it.

SUMMARY

In this chapter, you explored how to work with file I/O inside of your Android and iOS applications. You discovered how to work with the File object. You also learned how the directories you can access differ between Android and iOS devices. Finally, I walked you through a sample application that showed how to read and write to a text file.

FIGURE 11-2

12

Local Databases

WHAT'S IN THIS CHAPTER?

➤ Introducing SQLite

➤ Opening a database connection

➤ Selecting records from the database

➤ Inserting or updating records

Although you can use XML or binary files to store application or user data, you also can make full use of relational SQL databases right inside your Android and iOS applications. This chapter introduces you to working with local relational databases in your Android and iOS apps.

All operations you perform on the database are not done with AS3, but SQL (Structured Query Language), which is the standard query and data management language for relational databases. Using SQL, you can create tables, perform queries, and insert or modify records.

WORKING WITH A SQLITE DATABASE

One component of the underlying Adobe Integrated Runtime (AIR) engine that is part of AIR for Android run time and compiled into Flash-based iOS apps is SQLite, a SQL relational database engine. As a result, you can use the SQL database library API that is part of AIR to work with a local database in your mobile application.

SQLite is a lightweight open-source database engine that stores relational database data in a local file (often with a .db extension) that you can specify. (For more information on SQLite, go to www.sqlite.org.)

For example, using SQLite, you can create database-oriented apps that run offline and sync with a back-end server periodically when the user is connected to the Internet. You may also want to use the database as an alternative to storing application data in a local XML or binary file.

OPEN A DATABASE CONNECTION

To work with a local database in your Android or iOS app, you need to establish a connection to the database file using the SQLConnection object. Much like file input/output (see Chapter 11), you can connect to the database synchronously or asynchronously.

When you open a *synchronous connection*, the SQL statements you specify are executed sequentially based on the order in which they occur in your AS3 code. The application waits on the database operations to finish before processing more code.

On the other hand, when you open an *asynchronous connection*, SQL statements are passed to the database engine, which in turn executes the commands on the database. In this case, however, the application doesn't wait for the results of the SQL operation before continuing. Instead, event listeners are set up to handle results when they are completed.

Be thoughtful when selecting the type of connection you want to establish with the database. If you are working with a lot of data or are executing a complex query, you will probably want to use an asynchronous connection so you don't tie up the rest of the application while you're waiting on results. However, if your data set is modest and your queries are simple, a synchronous connection may be your smartest move, because it is easier to maintain and debug.

No matter which option you choose, be sure that you place any code that depends on the results of the database operation in the right location. For synchronous connections, you just need to have it appear below the SQL statements you perform in logical sequence. For asynchronous connections, be sure dependent code is placed in the event handler that is dispatched when the operation is completed.

Creating a Synchronous Connection

To create a synchronous connection, you use the SQLConnection.open() method. To illustrate, the following code opens a synchronous connection to a database file called vheissu.db, located in the application storage directory of my application:

```
var sqlConnection:SQLConnection = new SQLConnection();
var databaseFile:File = File.applicationStorageDirectory.resolvePath("vheissu.db");
sqlConnection.open(databaseFile);
```

After the SQLConnection instance is instantiated, vheissu.db is assigned to the databaseFile object. The databaseFile variable is passed as the parameter to the open() method.

When you call open(), your app looks for the specified file and opens a connection with it. If your app can't find that file, it creates the file for you automatically unless you specify otherwise.

Creating an Asynchronous Connection

To open an asynchronous connection to the database, use the openAsynch() of the SQLConnection object. For example:

```
private var sqlConnection:SQLConnection;

private function initDatabase(): void
{
```

```
    var databaseFile:File =
      File.applicationStorageDirectory.resolvePath('vheissu.db');
    sqlConnection = new SQLConnection();
    sqlConnection.addEventListener(SQLEvent.OPEN, databaseOpenHandler);
    sqlConnection.addEventListener(SQLErrorEvent.ERROR, databaseErrorHandler);
    sqlConnection.openAsync(databaseFile);

    // Code not dependent on database could be placed here

}

private function databaseOpenHandler(event:SQLEvent): void
{
  // Add dependent code here
}

private function databaseErrorHandler(event:SQLErrorEvent): void
{
    trace(event.error.message, "Details:", event.error.details);
}
```

The two event listeners are assigned to be triggered either when the database is opened or in the case of a database error. The openAsynch() method is then called to open the Vheissu.db database file. Once the connection is established, you can place any dependent code inside the databaseOpenHandler() function, such as performing a SELECT statement on a table within the database.

CREATING TABLES

Because the database may or may not exist when you try to open it, you can't assume that the tables you want to work with exist. Therefore, the first initialization routine that I perform when accessing a database is issuing a CREATE TABLE statement to the database.

To illustrate, consider the following code:

```
// Create connection to SQLite database. Create, if not found.
_connection = new SQLConnection();
//var dbFile:File = File.applicationStorageDirectory.resolvePath('Vheissu.db');
var dbFile:File = File.applicationDirectory.resolvePath('Vheissu.db');
_connection.open(dbFile, "create");

// Create tables if they don't exist

// Feeds table
var createTable1: SQLStatement = new SQLStatement();
createTable1.sqlConnection = _connection;
createTable1.text =
    "CREATE TABLE IF NOT EXISTS feeds (" +
    "    uid INTEGER PRIMARY KEY, " +
    "    url TEXT UNIQUE, " +
    "    name TEXT, " +
    "    logoUrl TEXT, " +
    "    lastFetched DATE " +
```

```
    ")";
createTable1.execute();

// Feed entries table
var createTable2: SQLStatement = new SQLStatement();
createTable2.sqlConnection = _connection;
createTable2.text =
    "CREATE TABLE IF NOT EXISTS feedEntries (" +
    "    guid TEXT PRIMARY KEY, " +
    "    url TEXT, " +
    "    feedId INTEGER, " +
    "    title TEXT, " +
    "    text TEXT, " +
    "    timestamp DATE, " +
    "    thumbnailUrl TEXT, " +
    "    author TEXT, " +
    "    authorUrl TEXT, " +
    "    category TEXT, " +
    "    wasRead BOOLEAN " +
    ")";
createTable2.execute();
```

Code snippet LocalFeedStore.as (though structured differently)

As shown in the previous code, a connection is opened to a database called `Vheissu.db`. If the database is not found, a new file is created. A `SQLStatement` instance is created, and a `CREATE TABLE` SQL command is assigned to its `text` property. This SQL statement is sent to the database engine using `execute()`. The SQL command checks to see if the `feeds` table exists. If it does exist, nothing is executed. If it doesn't exist, the table is created. A similar procedure is performed for the `feedEntries` table.

In the example, text, integer, and date fields are defined. However, as Table 12-1 shows, you can actually use several types of data.

TABLE 12-1: SQLite Data Types

TYPE	DESCRIPTION
TEXT	Normal text.
NUMERIC	Real, integer, or null values.
INTEGER	Integer values.
REAL	Floating point numbers.
BOOLEAN	True or false values.
DATE	Date values.
XML	XML text. (Use `XML()` to typecast the incoming data into an XML object.)
XMLLIST	XML list. (Use `XMLList()` to typecast the incoming data into an XML list.)

TYPE	DESCRIPTION
OBJECT	For storing JavaScript or ActionScript object instances. Data is serialized in AMF3 format.
NONE	Data is inserted into the field without conversion.

Next, you need to create indexes if they don't exist using the following code:

```
var createIndex1: SQLStatement = new SQLStatement();
createIndex1.sqlConnection = _connection;
createIndex1.text =
    "CREATE INDEX IF NOT EXISTS idxFeedEntriesById ON feedEntries
(feedId, wasRead, timestamp)";
createIndex1.execute();

var createIndex2: SQLStatement = new SQLStatement();
createIndex2.sqlConnection = _connection;
createIndex2.text =
"CREATE INDEX IF NOT EXISTS idxFeedEntriesByUrl ON feedEntries (url)";
createIndex2.execute();
```

As you can see from the tables, this database stores RSS feeds and feed entries (articles). There is a one-to-many relationship between the tables linked by `feedId` as the foreign key in the `feedEntries` table. The source code has matching AS3 classes, as shown in Listings 12-1 and 12-2.

LISTING 12-1: Feed.as

```
package com.richwagner.feed
{

    /**
     * Feed is a model class for RSS feeds.
     *
     * @author Rich Wagner
     *
     */
    public class Feed
    {

        private var _uid:int;
        private var _url:String;
        private var _entries:Vector.<FeedEntry>;
        private var _lastFetched:Date;
        private var _logoUrl:String;
        private var _name:String;

        /**
         * Constructor
         *
         */
```

continues

LISTING 12-1 *(continued)*

```actionscript
public function Feed()
{
    _entries = new Vector.<FeedEntry>();
}

/**
 *
 * Getters and Setters
 *
 */

public function get uid():int
{
    return _uid;
}

public function set uid(value:int):void
{
    _uid = value;
}

public function get entries():Vector.<FeedEntry>
{
    return _entries;
}

public function set entries(value:Vector.<FeedEntry>):void
{
    _entries = value;
}

public function get url():String
{
    return _url;
}

public function set url(value:String):void
{
    _url = value;
}

public function get lastFetched():Date
{
    return _lastFetched;
}

public function set lastFetched(value:Date):void
{
    _lastFetched = value;
}

public function get logoUrl():String
{
```

```
                return _logoUrl;
        }

        public function set logoUrl(value:String):void
        {
            _logoUrl = value;
        }

        public function get name():String
        {
            return _name;
        }

        public function set name(value:String):void
        {
            _name = value;
        }

    }
}
```

LISTING 12-2: FeedEntry.as

```
package com.maark.feed
{

    /**
     * FeedEntry is a model class for an RSS feed entry
     *
     * @author Rich Wagner
     *
     */
    public class FeedEntry
    {
        public var guid:String;
        public var url:String;
        public var feedId:int;
        public var title:String;
        public var text:String;
        public var timestamp:Date;
        public var thumbnailUrl:String;
        public var author:String;
        public var authorUrl:String;
        public var category:String;
        public var wasRead:Boolean = false;

        /**
         * Constructs a feed item from a generic
         * object with fields corresponding to the
         * names of the various item properties.
         */
        public function FeedEntry(itemInfo:Object)
        {
            if (itemInfo)
```

continues

LISTING 12-2 *(continued)*

```
                    {
                        guid = itemInfo.guid;
                        url = itemInfo.url;
                        title = itemInfo.title;
                        text = itemInfo.text;
                        timestamp = itemInfo.timestamp;
                        thumbnailUrl = itemInfo.thumbnailUrl;
                        author = itemInfo.author;
                        authorUrl = itemInfo.authorUrl;
                        category = itemInfo.category;
                        wasRead = itemInfo.wasRead;
                    }
                }


            }
        }
```

MAKING A SQL QUERY

When you run a SELECT query on your database, you execute a SQLStatement in a process similar to
the one you used when you created a table in the first place. However, what's different about a query is
that you need to process the resulting records that are returned to your program from the database.

Suppose, for example, that you want to retrieve all the entries for a given feed. You could do that
with a SELECT statement like this:

```
SELECT * FROM feedEntries WHERE feedId = 100
```

However, to make the call more generic, you would want to use a parameter to represent the feedId:

```
SELECT * FROM feedEntries WHERE feedId = :feedId
```

You can then assign a value to the feedId in your AS3 code and use that for your SELECT query.

To use that SELECT query in your app, you can use the following code:

```
public function fetch(feed:Feed):void
{
    const SELECT_ENTRIES_BY_FEED_ID:String =
        "SELECT * FROM feedEntries WHERE feedId = :feedId";

var sqlStatement:SQLStatement = new SQLStatement();
sqlStatement.sqlConnection = _connection;
sqlStatement.text = SELECT_ENTRIES_BY_FEED_ID;
sqlStatement.parameters[":feedId"] = feed.uid;
sqlStatement.execute();

// For each record in result set, add as a feedEntry instance
    var sqlResult:SQLResult = sqlStatement.getResult();
    var entries:Array = sqlResult.data;
    var entry:FeedEntry;
```

```
        if (entries)
        {
            for (var i:int=0; i<entries.length; i++)
            {
                entry = new FeedEntry(entries[i]);
                entry.feedId = feed.uid;
                feed.entries.push(entry);
            }
        }
    }
```

In this code, the SQLStatement instance is assigned the SELECT query defined in the SELECT_
ENTRIES_BY_FEED_ID constant. As you can see, the :feedId is defined as a parameter in the SQL
command. As a result, you need to assign a value to it before the query is executed. To do so, assign
the value through the SQLStatement instance's parameter property.

After the query is executed, the results are assigned to a SQLResult instance. You can then assign its
data property to an Array instance called entries. Finally, iterate through the entries array and
create new FeedEntry instances and assign them to the Feed object's entries property.

INSERTING AND UPDATING RECORDS

When you want to insert new records in a database, execute an INSERT INTO statement. For example:

```
INSERT INTO feeds (uid, url, name, logoUrl, lastFetched)
VALUES (100, 'www.me.com/rss.xml','My Feed', 'www.me.com/logo.png', '03/31/2011' )
```

Or, if the record may or may not already exist (based on its primary key), use REPLACE INTO. When
you use it in a SQL statement, the database attempts to insert a record using the values provided.
But if the key already exists, it replaces the existing values of that record with the new values. (You
can also use the UPDATE command to update a record, but it does not do anything unless the record
already exists in the table.)

The following code does an insert/replace into the feeds and feedEntries tables:

```
public function save(feed:Feed):void
{
    const ADD_FEED:String =
        "REPLACE INTO feeds (uid, url, name, logoUrl, lastFetched) " +
    "VALUES (:uid, :url, :name, :logoUrl, :lastFetched)";

    const ADD_ENTRY:String =
        "REPLACE INTO feedEntries (guid, url, feedId, title, text,
timestamp, thumbnailUrl, author, authorUrl, category, wasRead) "
        +"VALUES (:guid, :url, :feedId, :title, :text, :timestamp
 :thumbnailUrl, :author,
:authorUrl, :category, :wasRead)";

    // Batch up all the following updates.
    _connection.begin();

    // Insert Feed record
```

```
var is1:SQLStatement = new SQLStatement();
is1.sqlConnection = _connection;
is1.text = ADD_FEED;
is1.parameters[":uid"] = feed.uid;
is1.parameters[":url"] = feed.url;
is1.parameters[":name"] = feed.name;
is1.parameters[":logoUrl"] = feed.logoUrl;
is1.parameters[":lastFetched"] = feed.lastFetched.toUTCString();
is1.execute();

// Insert feedEntry records
var is2:SQLStatement = new SQLStatement();
is2.sqlConnection = _connection;
is2.text = ADD_ENTRY;
var feedEntry:FeedEntry;

// For each enty
for (var i:int=0; i<feed.entries.length; i++)
{
    feedEntry = feed.entries[i];
    is2.parameters[":guid"] = feedEntry.guid;
    is2.parameters[":url"] = feedEntry.url;
    is2.parameters[":feedId"] = feedEntry.feedId;
    is2.parameters[":title"] = feedEntry.title;
    is2.parameters[":text"] = feedEntry.text;
    is2.parameters[":timestamp"] = feedEntry.timestamp.toUTCString();
    is2.parameters[":thumbnailUrl"] = feedEntry.thumbnailUrl;
    is2.parameters[":author"] = feedEntry.author;
    is2.parameters[":authorUrl"] = feedEntry.authorUrl;
    is2.parameters[":category"] = feedEntry.category;
    is2.parameters[":wasRead"] = feedEntry.wasRead;
    is2.execute();
}

_connection.commit();
}
```

The first SQLStatement uses the ADD_FEED constant to define its REPLACE INTO statement. It assigns the values of the incoming feed variable's properties as the query parameters. The command then executes.

The second SQLStatement iterates through the entries property of the feed instance and adds each FeedEntry instance as a record using the REPLACE statement defined in the ADD_ENTRY constant.

Listing 12-3 shows the full source code listing for the LocalFeedStore class.

LISTING 12-3: LocalFeedStore.as

```
package com.richwagner.store
{
    import com.richwagner.feed.Feed;
    import com.richwagner.feed.FeedEntry;

    import flash.data.SQLConnection;
```

```
import flash.data.SQLResult;
import flash.data.SQLStatement;
import flash.filesystem.File;

/**
 * LocalFeedStore is a database access class for storing and
 * retrieving RSS feeds.
 *
 * @author Rich Wagner
 *
 */
public class LocalFeedStore
{
    // SQL Connection
    private var _connection:SQLConnection;

    /**
     * Constructor
     *
     */
    public function LocalFeedStore()
    {
        initialize();
    }


    /**
     * Initializes database engine and creates database as needed
     *
     */
    public function initialize():void
    {
        // Create connection to SQLite database. Create, if not found.
        _connection = new SQLConnection();
        //var dbFile:File =
        //    File.applicationStorageDirectory.resolvePath('Vheissu.db');
        var dbFile:File = File.applicationDirectory.resolvePath('Vheissu.db');
        _connection.open(dbFile, "create");
        // Create tables if they don't exist
        createTables();

    }

    /**
     * Fetches the entries of the Feed from the database
     *
     * @param feed - Feed instance to fetch the entries
     *
     */
    public function fetch(feed:Feed):void
    {
        const SELECT_ENTRIES_BY_FEED_ID:String =
            "SELECT * FROM feedEntries WHERE feedId = :feedId";

        var sqlStatement:SQLStatement = new SQLStatement();
```

continues

LISTING 12-3 *(continued)*

```
            sqlStatement.sqlConnection = _connection;
            sqlStatement.text = SELECT_ENTRIES_BY_FEED_ID;
            sqlStatement.parameters[":feedId"] = feed.uid;
            sqlStatement.execute();

            // For each record in result set, add as a feedEntry instance
            var sqlResult:SQLResult = sqlStatement.getResult();
            var entries:Array = sqlResult.data;
            var entry:FeedEntry;

            if (entries)
            {
                for (var i:int=0; i<entries.length; i++)
                {
                    entry = new FeedEntry(entries[i]);
                    entry.feedId  = feed.uid;
                    feed.entries.push(entry);
                }
            }
        }


        /**
         * Saves the feed and all of its entries to the database
         *
         * @param feed - Feed instance to save
         *
         */
        public function save(feed:Feed):void
        {
            const ADD_FEED:String =
                "REPLACE INTO feeds (uid, url, name, logoUrl, lastFetched) " +
                "VALUES (:uid, :url, :name, :logoUrl, :lastFetched)";

            const ADD_ENTRY:String =
                "REPLACE INTO feedEntries (guid, url, feedId, title, text,
timestamp, thumbnailUrl, author, authorUrl, category, wasRead) " +
"VALUES (:guid, :url, :feedId, :title, :text, :timestamp, :thumbnailUrl,
 :author, :authorUrl, :category, :wasRead)";

            // Batch up all the following updates.
            _connection.begin();

            // Insert Feed record
            var is1:SQLStatement = new SQLStatement();
            is1.sqlConnection = _connection;
            is1.text = INSERT_FEED;
            is1.parameters[":uid"] = feed.uid;
            is1.parameters[":url"] = feed.url;
            is1.parameters[":name"] = feed.name;
            is1.parameters[":logoUrl"] = feed.logoUrl;
            is1.parameters[":lastFetched"] = feed.lastFetched.toUTCString();
```

```
        is1.execute();

        // Insert feedEntry records
        var is2:SQLStatement = new SQLStatement();
        is2.sqlConnection = _connection;
        is2.text = INSERT_ENTRY;
        var feedEntry:FeedEntry;

        // For each enty
        for (var i:int=0; i<feed.entries.length; i++)
        {
            feedEntry = feed.entries[i];
            is2.parameters[":guid"] = feedEntry.guid;
            is2.parameters[":url"] = feedEntry.url;
            is2.parameters[":feedId"] = feedEntry.feedId;
            is2.parameters[":title"] = feedEntry.title;
            is2.parameters[":text"] = feedEntry.text;
            is2.parameters[":timestamp"] = feedEntry.timestamp.toUTCString();
            is2.parameters[":thumbnailUrl"] = feedEntry.thumbnailUrl;
            is2.parameters[":author"] = feedEntry.author;
            is2.parameters[":authorUrl"] = feedEntry.authorUrl;
            is2.parameters[":category"] = feedEntry.category;
            is2.parameters[":wasRead"] = feedEntry.wasRead;
            is2.execute();
        }

        _connection.commit();
    }


    /**
     * Wipes the feed and all entries of the specified feed from the
local cache
     *
     * @param feed - Feed instance to wipe
     *
     */
    public function wipe(feed:Feed):void
    {

        // Batch up all the following updates.
        _connection.begin();

        // Delete the feed and its items from the database.
        var deleteFeed:SQLStatement = new SQLStatement();
        deleteFeed.sqlConnection = _connection;
        deleteFeed.text = "DELETE FROM feedEntries WHERE feedId = :feedId";
        deleteFeed.parameters[":feedId"] = feed.uid;
        deleteFeed.execute();

        // Delete the feed and its items from the database.
        var deleteFeed2:SQLStatement = new SQLStatement();
        deleteFeed2.sqlConnection = _connection;
        deleteFeed2.text = "DELETE FROM feeds WHERE uid = :uid";
```

continues

LISTING 12-3 *(continued)*

```
        deleteFeed2.parameters[":uid"] = feed.uid;
        deleteFeed2.execute();

        // Batch up all the following updates.
        _connection.commit();

    }


    /**
     * Creates tables (if needed) in the database
     *
     */
    private function createTables():void
    {
        // Create our tables if they don't already exist.

        // Feeds table
        var createTable1: SQLStatement = new SQLStatement();
        createTable1.sqlConnection = _connection;
        createTable1.text =
            "CREATE TABLE IF NOT EXISTS feeds (" +
            "    uid INTEGER PRIMARY KEY, " +
            "    url TEXT UNIQUE, " +
            "    name TEXT, " +
            "    logoUrl TEXT, " +
            "    lastFetched DATE " +
            ")";
        createTable1.execute();

        // Feed entries table
        var createTable2: SQLStatement = new SQLStatement();
        createTable2.sqlConnection = _connection;
        createTable2.text =
            "CREATE TABLE IF NOT EXISTS feedEntries (" +
            "    guid TEXT PRIMARY KEY, " +
            "    url TEXT, " +
            "    feedId INTEGER, " +
            "    title TEXT, " +
            "    text TEXT, " +
            "    timestamp DATE, " +
            "    thumbnailUrl TEXT, " +
            "    author TEXT, " +
            "    authorUrl TEXT, " +
            "    category TEXT, " +
            "    wasRead BOOLEAN " +
            ")";
        createTable2.execute();

        var createIndex1: SQLStatement = new SQLStatement();
        createIndex1.sqlConnection = _connection;
        createIndex1.text =
```

```
"CREATE INDEX IF NOT EXISTS idxFeedEntriesById ON feedEntries
(feedId, wasRead, timestamp)";
            createIndex1.execute();

            var createIndex2: SQLStatement = new SQLStatement();
            createIndex2.sqlConnection = _connection;
            createIndex2.text =
"CREATE INDEX IF NOT EXISTS idxFeedEntriesByUrl ON feedEntries (url)";
            createIndex2.execute();
        }

    }
}
```

SUMMARY

Because of the capabilities of AIR for Android and Packager for iPhone, you can work with databases right inside your app without requiring external library support. In this chapter, you explored how to work with SQLite databases inside your Android and iOS applications. You began by connecting to databases and then performed common database operations, including creating tables, selecting records, and inserting and updating records.

PART IV
Testing and Debugging

13

Remote Debugging

WHAT'S IN THIS CHAPTER?

➤ Debugging on your mobile device

➤ Enabling Android devices for debugging

➤ Remote debugging inside of the Flash IDE

One of the major operations of any application development project is debugging. However, mobile apps pose a special problem on this ubiquitous development task — your runtime environment is located on a different machine from your development IDE. Therefore, you need to set up your debugging environment before you can debug on your Android and iOS devices.

In this chapter, I'll walk you through the steps you need to take to set up your development environment and devices for remote debugging.

ESTABLISHING A WIFI CONNECTION

Although your Android or iOS device will already be connected to your development computer via USB, remote debugging is actually done over WIFI. However, there's one condition for WIFI remote debugging to work — you'll need to connect both your development computer and device to the same WIFI network.

Some developers who have problems connecting to an existing WIFI network have had success by turning their Android device into a WIFI hotspot and then connect their development computer to it. To enable, go to Settings ➪ Wireless And Networks ➪ Tethering & Portable Hotspot and configure your device according to your needs.

You'll also need to know the IP address (or hostname) of your development computer. You can find it in Windows by running ipconfig in a Windows command line window. Or, if you're running a Mac, go to System Preferences ➪ Network. The Network Settings page displays your IP address.

USING THE AIR DEBUG LAUNCHER

If you're using Flash Professional, you can perform a quick debug on your development machine right inside of the IDE. While it won't be the same as testing on the device itself, the AIR Debug Launcher is a handy first pass debugging tool. Then, once you've got the kinks worked out, you can move on to remote debugging on the device itself.

To run, open your .fla file in the Flash IDE and then choose Debug ➪ Debug Movie ➪ In AIR Debug Mobile Launcher (Mobile). The app is launched in a separate window. (See Figure 13-1.)

ANDROID DEBUGGING

When you debug your Android apps on your Android device, you first need to make sure your phone is enabled for debugging. Therefore, in order enable remote debug, you need to do the following:

1. On your Android device, enable debugging by going to Settings ➪ Applications ➪ Development and enabling USB debugging. (See Figure 13-2.)

2. If it is not already enabled, make sure that USB Storage is enabled for your device.

   The Android device will need to connect to TCP port 7935.

FIGURE 13-1

FIGURE 13-2

Remote Debugging inside the Flash IDE

The easiest way of debugging your Android app is to remote debug directly from inside of the Flash IDE. To do so:

1. Click the AIR Android Settings dialog box on the Properties panel.

2. Click the Deployment panel. (See Figure 13-3.)

3. Select Debug for the Android deployment type.

4. Select the Install Application On The Connected Android Device check box.

5. Deselect the Launch Application On The Connected Android Sevice check box.

6. Click the Permissions tab.

7. Select the `INTERNET` Permissions check box to enable the `android:permission.INTERNET` permission in your app descriptor file.

8. Click Publish.

   The app is compiled, published, and installed onto your device. But has not yet been launched on your device.

9. Close out the dialog box.

10. Select the Debug ➪ Begin Remote Debug Session ➪ ActionScript 3 from the menu.

    The Flash Professional IDE enters debug mode and displays a "Waiting for Player to connect" message in the Output panel.

11. Launch your app on the Android device.

12. If prompted, enter the IP address or hostname of your development computer (see Figure 13-4) and click OK.

You are now in debug mode. You can now trace or step through your code as needed.

FIGURE 13-3

FIGURE 13-4

Remote Debugging from the Command Line

You can also use the command line Flash Debugger (`fdb.exe`) which is included with Flash Builder and the Flex SDK. Before you begin, you should make sure that your Flex SDK bin directory is in your environment path. If not, you'll need to add the directory information to each of the commands line used in this section.

To do so, follow these steps:

1. In your application descriptor file (e.g., `MyApp-app.xml`), enable INTERNET permissions by adding following XML code:

```
<android>
    <manifestAdditions>
        <manifest>
            <data><![CDATA[ <uses-permission
android:name="android.permission.INTERNET" /> ]]></data>
        </manifest>
    </manifestAdditions>
</android>
```

2. In a command prompt window, change to the directory in which your application source code is located.

3. Compile the application with the `amxmlc` (`amxmlc.bat`) tool (located in the Flex SDK's bin directory) using **amxmlc -debug MyApp.as.**

The `amxmlc` tool will compile and create an `.apk` file.

4. Package the `.apk` you just created using the `adt` command-line tool. (See Appendix B for more details on publishing with the command-line ADT tool.)

You'll want to include a `-connect` option to specify the IP address or hostname of your development machine. Type the following: **adt -package -target apk-debug -connect 192.168.1.9 -storetype pkcs12 -keystore MyCert.p12 MyApp.apk MyApp-app.xml MyApp.swf.**

5. Use the adt tool to install the application onto your device: **adt -installApp -platform android -platformsdk /programs/android-sdk -package MyApp.apk**

Keep this command line window open as you'll come back to it in Step 6.

6. In a new command line window, launch the command-line debugger tool by typing **fdb**.

The Flash Debug window is displayed, and will show the status message "Waiting for Player to connect."

7. From your first command line window, launch the application using the adt tool by typing **adt -launchApp -platform android -platformsdk /programs/android-sdk -appid MyApp.**

Your app will launch on your Android device.

8. If prompted, enter the IP address or hostname of your development computer (refer to Figure 13-4) and click OK.

Debugging with Android SDK's Logcat

You can also use the Android SDK logcat utility to view the `trace()` output of your app. To do so, make sure you create, install, and launch a debug version of your app by following the instructions of the previous section. Then, you can run logcat with the following command:

```
adb logcat
```

(This assumes your Android SDK tool directory is in your environment path.)

In the Logcat window your trace output will be displayed, alongside other Android statements. You can also access the Logcat window from the Dalvik Debug Monitor. To do so, choose Device ➪ Run logcat.

IOS DEBUGGING

If you're using Flash Professional, you can debug on your iOS device following a similar process to what you use for Android. However, iOS does have a special diagnostic tool that comes in handy. I'll explain both in this section.

Remote Debugging inside the Flash IDE

To debug your iOS app from inside of Flash Professional, follow these steps:

1. Click the iPhone Settings dialog box on the Properties panel.

2. Click the Deployment panel (see Figure 13-5).

3. Select Quick publishing for device debugging as the iPhone deployment type.

4. Click Publish.

The app is published and installed onto your device.

5. Close out the dialog box.

6. Select the Debug ➪ Begin Remote Debug Session ➪ ActionScript 3 from the menu.

The Flash Professional IDE enters debug mode and displays a "Waiting for Player to connect" message in the Output panel.

7. Launch your app on your iPhone or other iOS device.

8. If prompted, enter the IP address or hostname of your development computer and click OK.

You are now in debug mode. You can now trace or step through your code as needed.

FIGURE 13-5

Viewing GPU Rendering Diagnostics

One of the handiest debugging tricks that you can perform with iOS apps is being able to view GPU rendering diagnostics. If you have an application that uses GPU rendering, you can use this debugging feature to assess the extent to which your app uses hardware acceleration.

To use this debugging tool, you need to compile the app from the command line (see Appendix B for full details), but include the `-renderdiagnostics` parameter just after the `-package` parameter. For example:

```
pfi -package -renderingdiagnostics -target ipa-debug -connect  192.168.1.9 -
storetype pkcs12 -keystore RichWagnerDev.p12" -storepass gh0stQ21a
"build\CatMan.ipa" "CatMan-app.xml" "CatMan.swf" "Default.png"
"icons\29x29.png" "icons\57x57.png" "icons\512x512.png"
```

When enabled, the GPU rendering diagnostic transforms the app UI into a diagnostic environment. Display objects have color-coded rectangular masks on top of them for the initial four screen refresh cycles. Colors include:

➤ A blue rectangle indicates a display object that is being rendered.

➤ A green rectangle is a display object that is a bitmap (or is being cached as a bitmap) and is being uploaded to the GPU.

➤ A red rectangle signifies a display object that is a bitmap (or cached as bitmap) and is being re-uploaded to the GPU.

You can use this diagnostic information to help optimize your app. For example, if you see blue being used for an object that doesn't change, you can optimize by caching as a bitmap. If green keeps reappearing for a display object, then your code might be re-creating identical objects when it doesn't need to. If red, then enable the `cacheAsBitmapMatrix` property for normal 2D display objects so that they don't need re-rendering during scale or rotation operations.

SUMMARY

Debugging a mobile app can be more challenging to perform than when developing for the Web or desktop AIR. However, once you get your device properly connected with your development machine over WIFI, then you can set breakpoints, step through your code, and evaluate your code just like you're used to. In this chapter, you learned how to configure your development environment for debugging Android and iOS applications.

14

Submitting Your App to the App Store

WHAT'S IN THIS CHAPTER?

➤ Preparing your Android app

➤ Submitting to the Android Market

➤ Getting iOS Credentials

➤ Submitting to the Apple App Store

You've designed and programmed your app, as well as tested and debugged it. You've got an `.apk` or `.ipa` that you've signed with your digital certificate. Now, you're ready to distribute your app to others.

Maybe you've got a great app that will make you the next Bill Gates. Or maybe you just put together an app you want to share with a few people who have interests similar to yours. Whatever the case, your last step is to publish your app to the Android Market or Apple App Store.

PREPARING YOUR ANDROID APP

Before you submit your app to the Android Market or distribute it on the Web, keep the following requirements in mind:

➤ Make sure that you have the following items in your app descriptor XML file: `<android:versionCode>` and an `<android:versionName>` attribute in the `<manifest>` element of its manifest. The server uses `<android:versionCode>`

as the basis for identifying the application internally and handling updates, and it displays `<android:versionName>` to users as the application's version.

➤ Your application must define both an `android:icon` and an `android:label` attribute in the `<application>` element of its manifest.

Getting a Screenshot

When you submit your app to the Android Market, you're asked to present screenshots. The easiest way to get a screenshot is to do the following:

1. Connect your Android device to your computer using a USB cord.

2. Start the Dalvik Debug Monitor (`tools/ddms.bat` in your Android SDK directory).

Figure 14-1 displays the monitor.

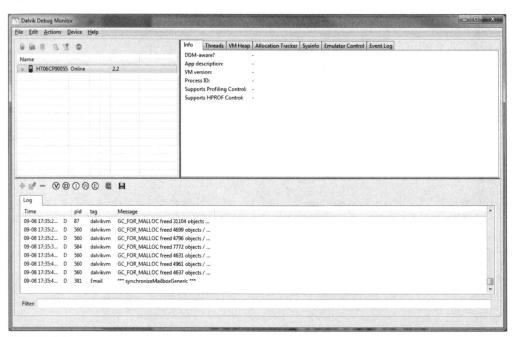

FIGURE 14-1

3. Select your device from the list.

4. Select Device ⇨ Screen Capture from the top menu.

A Device Screen Capture window appears and displays a screenshot of your Android device. (See Figure 14-2.)

5. On your device, launch your app and set it up for a screenshot.

6. Click the Refresh button in the Device Screen Capture window to refresh the image.

7. If you're satisfied with the screenshot, click the Save button.

8. Repeat Steps 5–7 for each screenshot you want to take.

9. Click Done when you've finished.

If you are submitting to the Android Market, you need to upload in one of two sizes:

➤ 320×480

➤ 480×854

If your screenshot is a different size, you'll need to scale it in Photoshop or another image editing tool to one of these two sizes.

SUBMITTING YOUR APP TO THE ANDROID MARKET

The Android Market is the storefront for Android apps. Android users can easily search for and download apps to their Android devices through the

FIGURE 14-2

Android Market. If you are familiar with iPhone's popular App Store, think of the Android Market as the equivalent.

Registering Your Developer Profile

To register your developer profile, follow these steps:

1. Go to market.android.com/publish.

   To submit your app to the Android Market, first register with Google and pay the $25 registration fee.

   Then create the developer profile that identifies you.

2. Enter your name and contact info in the boxes provided, and click Continue. (See Figure 14-3.)

3. You're asked to pay for your registration using Google Checkout in the next two steps.

   After your transaction is complete, you're asked to return to the Android Market Developer Site to complete the registration process.

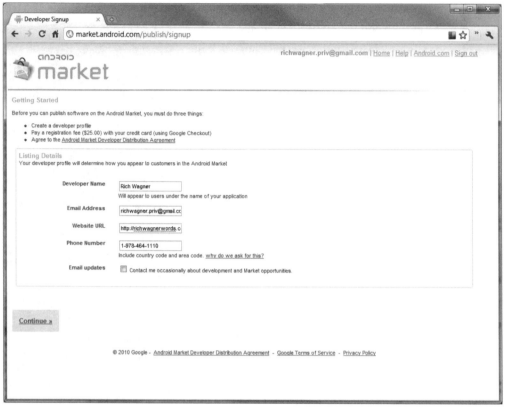

FIGURE 14-3

4. Click the Android Market Developer Site link to continue.

    The Android Market Developer Distribution Agreement is displayed. You're asked to agree to the agreement and to associate your credit card and account registration with the terms of service.

5. Click the check box, and then click the I Agree, Continue link to continue.

    You are taken to the Android Market home page, as shown in Figure 14-4.

After you complete this registration, you're ready to upload and publish your apps.

Submitting Your App

Once you have an approved developer profile and have a debugged, tested, and finished app, you are ready to submit it to the Android Market.

1. Go to `market.android.com/publish`.

2. Click the Upload an Application link.

    The Upload an Application page is displayed, as shown in Figure 14-5.

FIGURE 14-4

FIGURE 14-5

3. Upload your .apk file by selecting it from your hard drive and clicking the Upload button.

The file is uploaded, and app info is displayed. The page also highlights the permissions that users will be warned about. Be sure to check these over and remove any that are not essential to the running of the application. (See Figure 14-6.)

FIGURE 14-6

Your app must be signed with a .p12 digital certificate that has a validity period ending after October 22, 2033.

4. Upload two screenshots of your app in the Screenshots section.

See the "Getting a Screenshot" section earlier in this chapter for details on how to obtain screenshots of your Android device. You need to specify either 0 or 2 screenshots.

5. If desired, add an optional promotional image.

6. If you choose to opt out of any third-party marketing activities, check Marketing Opt-Out.

7. Enter the name, description, promotional text, type, and category in the Listing Details section.

The Price field is marked as free unless you have a Merchant Account with Google Checkout. (You can click the Merchant Account link to get started with the sign-up process.)

8. Choose whether to have copy protection in the Publishing Options section.

It's not recommended that you use this option. Google recommends using its newer licensing service instead. Click the Licensing Service link to get started.

9. Check the Locations in which you want to list.

10. Enter contact information in the Contact Information box.

11. Read the Android Content Guidelines. If you're satisfied that your app meets these guidelines, check the box.

12. Check the box indicating your agreement that your app is subject to U.S. export and related laws.

13. Click the Save button to save your work without publishing. Or click the Publish button to upload your submittal to the Android Market.

PREPARING YOUR IOS APP

Before you submit, check out Apple's App Store Review Guidelines, which is a plainly worded document that tells you what Apple considers when determining whether to approve an app. You can find the guidelines at `https://developer.apple.com/appstore/resources/approval/guidelines.html`.

When you're satisfied that your app meets these guidelines, you're ready to begin.

Getting a Distribution Certificate

Similar to what you did when you obtained a developer certificate to develop and install your apps on your own device for testing, for a final release, you need to get a distribution certificate that Flash uses when it compiles the app into an `.ipk` file. To do so, follow these steps:

1. Log in to the iOS Dev Center at `developer.apple.com`.

2. Click the iOS Provisioning Portal link.

The iOS Provisioning Portal page is displayed, as shown in Figure 14-7.

3. Click the Certificates link on the left sidebar.

4. Click the Distribution tab.

A list of current certificates is displayed, as shown in Figure 14-8.

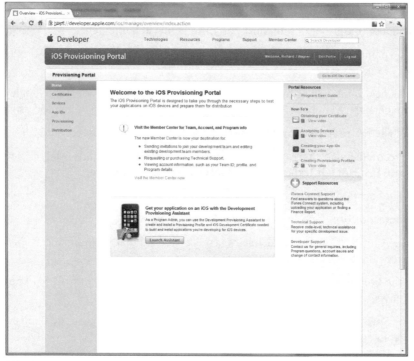

FIGURE 14-7

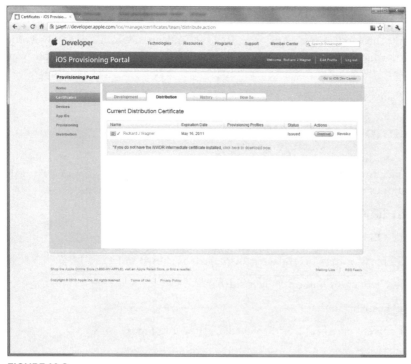

FIGURE 14-8

5. If you have a certificate ready, click the Download button.

If you don't, follow the on-screen instructions to create a certificate. Once it is created, then you can download the .cer file and continue.

6. After you download the .cer file, you need to convert the file to a .p12 certificate format so you can sign it in Flash CS5. To do so, see the instructions provided in Chapter 2 (in the "Getting an iPhone Developer Certificate" section).

You now have the .p12 certificate ready for use when you publish your distribution version.

Creating a Distribution Provisioning Profile

Once you have the .p12 file, you are ready to obtain a distribution provisioning profile. To do so, follow these steps:

1. Log in to the iOS Dev Center at developer.apple.com.

2. Click the iOS Provisioning Portal link.

The iOS Provisioning Portal page is displayed. (Refer to Figure 14-7.)

3. Click the Provisioning link on the left sidebar.

4. Click the Distribution tab to display the list of distribution provisioning profiles.

If this is the first time you've selected this tab, this area is blank.

5. Click the New Profile button.

The Create iOS Distribution Provisioning Profile is displayed (see Figure 14-9).

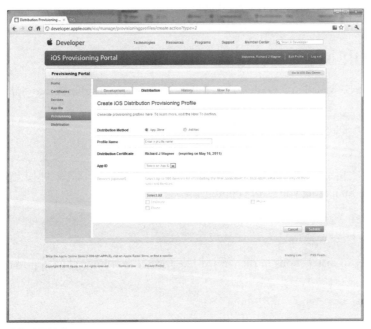

FIGURE 14-9

6.   Fill out the profile form for the application you want to submit, and click the Submit button when you are satisfied with the inputs.

Your provisioning profile is added to the list, with a Pending status.

7.   Refresh the browser in a minute a two, and you should see the status changed to Active and a Download button displayed.

8.   Click the Download button to download the `.mobileprovision` file.

9.   Save this in a handy location on your hard drive.

Publishing a Distribution Release of Your App

Now that you have all the preliminaries completed, you are ready to publish the final distribution release of your iOS app. Follow these steps:

1.   Open your app in Flash Professional.

2.   In the iPhone Settings dialog box, click the Deployment tab.

3.   Update the certificate used in the publishing process to point to the newly created `.p12` distribution file.

4.   Update the Provisioning profile file to point to your new `.mobileprovision` file.

5.   Select the Deployment ⇨ Apple App Store option in the iPhone Deployment Type group.

6.   Click the Publish button to publish the app using these settings.

7.   Before submitting to the App Store, you need to rename the `.ipa` extension to `.zip`. Go ahead and do it now so you're ready to go later.

SUBMITTING YOUR APP TO THE APPLE APP STORE

Once you have your app compiled and ready to go, follow these steps to submit your app to the Apple App Store.

1.   Log in to the iOS Dev Center at `developer.apple.com`.

2.   Click the iTunes Connect link.

You are taken to the iTunes Connect website, as shown in Figure 14-10. This is the website that you use for managing your store content.

3.   Click the Manage Your Applications link.

4.   Click the Add a New App link.

5.   Follow the series of instructions in the wizard-like format to submit your app to the App Store.

FIGURE 14-10

When you fill out the submission forms for your app, be sure to be as open and complete as possible. Doing so lessens the chance of red flags or roadblocks that might delay or block your app from being approved by Apple.

Now just be patient and wait for Apple to review your app. Some approvals take a few days, whereas others take a few weeks.

SUMMARY

In this final chapter, I walked you through the final steps to take for your app by submitting it to the Android Market and the Apple App Store. You discovered the process of preparing, registering your developer profile with Google, and submitting your app. I then showed you how to get the necessary credentials in place for iOS apps as well as how to submit it to the Apple App Store.

A

Application Descriptor Settings

WHAT'S IN THIS APPENDIX?

➤ Application Descriptor Settings for Android

➤ Application Descriptor Settings for iPhone

If you have created AIR apps using Flash or Flex, you are probably familiar with the application descriptor file for your project. The *application descriptor file* is an XML file that provides metadata — such as application name and version — about your project. The compiler reads and uses this data during the compilation process.

By convention, the application descriptor filename is *projectName*-app.xml. For example, the application descriptor file for the FindMeAPizza project is named FindMeAPizza-app.xml.

In this appendix, I'll describe the application descriptor settings for both Android and iPhone.

ANDROID APPLICATION DESCRIPTOR SETTINGS

Flash CS5 automatically creates and maintains the app descriptor file for you inside the environment. You can modify several of the properties of the file via the AIR for Android dialog box (see Figure A-1) or you can do it manually working with the app descriptor file.

When you manually modify the application descriptor file, don't open the AIR for Android dialog box until you have closed the file.

FIGURE A-1

Sample Android Application Descriptor File

Listing A-1 provides a sample application descriptor file.

LISTING A-1: Sample application descriptor file

```xml
<?xml version="1.0" encoding="UTF-8" standalone="no"?>
<application xmlns="http://ns.adobe.com/air/application/2.5">

    <id>example.FindMeAPizza</id>

    <versionNumber>1.0.0</versionNumber>

    <versionLabel>Beta</versionLabel>

    <filename>FindMeAPizza</filename>

    <description>Finds the nearest Pizza shop based on your location.</description>

    <name>FindMeAPizza</name>
```

```
  <copyright>Copyright ©2010, Rich Wagner</copyright>

  <initialWindow>
    <content>FindMeAPizza.swf</content>
    <systemChrome>standard</systemChrome>
    <transparent>false</transparent>
    <visible>true</visible>
    <fullScreen>false</fullScreen>
    <aspectRatio>portrait</aspectRatio>
    <renderMode>auto</renderMode>
    <autoOrients>false</autoOrients>
  </initialWindow>

  <icon>
    <image36x36>assets/36x36.png</image36x36>
    <image48x48>assets/48x48.png</image48x48>
    <image72x72>assets/72x72.png</image72x72>
  </icon>

  <customUpdateUI>false</customUpdateUI>

  <allowBrowserInvocation>false</allowBrowserInvocation>
<android>
  <manifestAdditions>
    <manifest>

    <!-- Define permissions -->
    <data>
        <![CDATA[
         <uses-permission android:name="android.permission.INTERNET" />
         <uses-permission
android:name="android.permission.ACCESS_FINE_LOCATION" />
         <uses-permission android:name="android.permission.WAKE_LOCK" />
         <uses-permission android:name="android.permission.DISABLE_KEYGUARD" />
         <uses-permission android:name="android.permission.READ_PHONE_STATE" />
         <uses-permission android:name="android.permission.CAMERA" />
         <uses-permission android:name="android.permission.RECORD_AUDIO" />
         <uses-permission
android:name="android.permission.WRITE_EXTERNAL_STORAGE" />
        ]]>
    </data>

    <!-- Install on external card -->
    <!--attribute name="android:installLocation" value="preferExternal"/-->

    <!-- Not display on installation -->
    <application>
      <!--attribute name="android:enabled" value="false"/-->
    </application>

     <launcherActivity>

       <!-- Exclude from recently ran apps list -->
```

continues

```
<!--attribute name="android:excludeFromRecents" value="true"/-->

<!-- Optionally specify invoke actions -->
<data>
    <![CDATA[
    <intent-filter>
    <action android:name="android.intent.action.EDIT"/>
    <category android:name="android.intent.category.BROWSABLE"/>
    <category android:name="android.intent.category.DEFAULT"/>
    <data android:scheme="fmap"/>
    </intent-filter>
    ]]>
</data>
</launcherActivity>

</manifest>
</manifestAdditions>
</android>

</application>
```

Basic Properties

The following list discusses the properties you are most likely to use:

<application>

Root element of the application descriptor file. For Android apps, it needs to have the AIR 2.0 namespace.

➤ **Value** — `String`

➤ **Example** — `<application xmlns="http://ns.adobe.com/air/application/2.5">`

<id>

This is the application ID of your application. The typical App ID is often a reverse-domain string.

➤ **Value** — `String`

➤ **Example** — `<id>com.richwagner.myapp</id>`

<versionNumber>

This is the version number of the application and is required. The format should adhere to *xx[.xx[.xx]]*, where *x* is a digit 0–9. Subversions inside the brackets are optional. This property is used to determine application upgrades, as an upgrade must have a higher version number than the earlier version.

➤ **Value** — `String`

➤ **Example** — `<versionNumber>1.0.12</versionNumber>`

<versionLabel>

This is an optional tag that enables you to display a string value to the user and associate it with the version.

➤ **Value** — String

➤ **Example** — `<versionLabel>Alpha</versionLabel>`

<filename>

This is the filename of the compiled `.apk` file. Don't add an extension. The compiler supplies that.

➤ **Value** — String

➤ **Example** — `<filename>FindMeAPizza</filename>`

<name>

The official name of the application is the name your Android device uses.

➤ **Value** — String

➤ **Example** — `<name>FindMeAPizza</name>`

<copyright>

Use this standard copyright line to protect your intellectual property.

➤ **Value** — String

➤ **Example** — `<copyright>Copyright ©2010, Rich Wagner</copyright>`

<description>

Here you provide a helpful description of the application and what it does.

➤ **Value** — String

➤ **Example** — `<description>Finds the nearest pizza shop.</description>`

<initialWindow>

This is the container of several child elements that indicate the settings for the initial display at startup.

The `<systemChrome>`, `<transparent>`, and `<visible>` elements, used when compiling desktop AIR apps, are not applicable for AIR for Android apps.

Here is an example:

```
<initialWindow>
  <aspectRatio>portrait</aspectRatio>
  <autoOrients>false</autoOrients>
```

```
        <content>FindMeAPizza.swf</content>
        <fullScreen>true</fullScreen>
        <renderMode>auto</renderMode>
    </initialWindow>
```

<aspectRatio>

Here you indicate the initial aspect ratio (portrait or landscape) of the application. Its value is either `portrait` or `landscape`.

<autoOrients>

Here you indicate whether auto-orientation support is enabled. (See Chapter 7 for more information) Its possible values are `true` or `false`.

<content>

This is the main SWF that the compiler uses for the application. Its value is

`String`.

<fullScreen>

Here you indicate whether to display the application in the entire viewport of the Android device or whether to display the top bar. Its possible values are

`true` or `false`.

<renderMode>

This setting determines the way display objects are rendered. If the default `auto` is used, the compiler makes the call. If `gpu` is used, hardware graphics acceleration is explicitly used. See Chapter 5 for more details on how and when to use hardware acceleration. Its possible values are `auto` or `gpu`.

<supportedProfiles>

By defining supported files, you can limit the project to be compiled only for specific platforms. For Android apps, either don't add the element or use `mobileDevice`.

- ➤ **Value** — `mobileDevice` (`desktop` or `extendedDesktop` available for AIR contexts)
- ➤ **Example** — `<supportedProfiles>mobileDevice</ supportedProfiles>`

<icon>

This contains the child elements that define the icon files for the application, as shown in this example:

```
<icon>
  <image36x36>assets/36x36.png</image36x36>
  <image48x48>assets/48x48.png</image48x48>
  <image72x72>assets/72x36.png</image72x72>
</icon>
```

These are the image options:

➤ <image36x36> — This image is used for low-density Android devices. It has the value String.

➤ <image48x48> — Image used for medium-density Android devices. Its value is String.

➤ <image72x72> — Image used for high-density Android devices. Its value is String.

Android Settings

The Permissions tab (see Figure A-2) of the AIR Android Application & Installer Settings dialog box contains several Android specific permissions settings that you can enable for your application.

FIGURE A-2

Requesting Device Permissions

The Android security model specifies that each application must ask for permission from the OS to use the security or privacy-related features of the device. You have to ask for these up front when the application is installed, not when the application is running.

Inside of an AIR for Android application, you request permission inside of the `<android>` element, which itself has descendants that must also be specified: `<manifestAdditions>` and `<data>`.

Here's the basic structure:

```
<android>
  <manifestAdditions>
    <manifest>
      <data>
        <![CDATA[
          <uses-permission android:name="android.permission.NAME_OF_PERMISSION" />
        ]]>
      </data>
    </manifest>
  </manifestAdditions>
</android>
```

Inside of the `<data>` element, you can add permission tags. These tags must be enclosed in a CDATA tag.

➤ **Enabling internet access** — To enable internet access, use
  `<uses-permission android:name="android.permission.INTERNET" />`.

  To perform remote debugging, make sure your descriptor file has this enabled.

➤ **Enabling geolocation services** — To enable GPS support and utilize the Geolocation class, use
  `<uses-permission android:name="android.permission.ACCESS_FINE_LOCATION" />`.

➤ **Disabling sleep** — To disable the device from sleeping (when playing video or using the `SystemIdleMode` class). For example, `<uses-permission android:name="android.permission.WAKE_LOCK" />` and `<uses-permission android:name="android.permission.DISABLE_KEYGUARD" />`.

➤ **Muting audio for phone call** — To mute audio when an incoming phone call is received use
  `<uses-permission android:name="android.permission.READ_PHONE_STATE" />`.

➤ **Enabling camera access** — To enable access to the camera, use
  `<uses-permission android:name="android.permission.CAMERA" />`.

➤ **Enabling microphone access** — To enable your app to access the device's microphone, use
  `<uses-permission android:name="android.permission.RECORD_AUDIO" />`.

➤ **Writing to external memory card** — To enable write access to the device's external memory card, use `<uses-permission android:name="android.permission.WRITE_EXTERNAL_STORAGE" />`.

Installing to an External Card

You can also specify additional settings for your application inside of the `<manifest>` element. While applications are normally installed to the device's internal memory, you can also request to install to external storage instead (for larger apps, for example):

```
<android>
  <manifestAdditions>
    <manifest>
```

```
        <attribute name="android:installLocation" value="preferExternal"/>
      </manifest>
    </manifestAdditions>
  </android>
```

Not Displaying an Application on Install

If you have an application that should not be displayed when it is installed, then set the value of the android:enabled attribute to false:

```
<android>
  <manifestAdditions>
    <manifest>
      <application>
        <attribute name="android:enabled" value="false"/>
      </application>
    </manifest>
  </manifestAdditions>
</android>
```

Adding Launcher Settings

You can specify certain application-specific settings related to the Android Launcher.

➤ **Excluding an application from recently ran lists** — If you want to disable your application's entry into the Launcher's recently ran application list, use the android:excludeFromRecents attribute:

```
<android>
  <manifestAdditions>
    <manifest>
      <launcherActivity>
        <attribute name="android:excludeFromRecents" value="true"/>
      </launcherActivity>
    </manifest>
  </manifestAdditions>
</android>
```

➤ **Enabling your application to be launchable from other applications** — The <launcherActivity> element also can contain an optional <data> section that enables you to specify a custom URI for launching from other Android apps or a browser. To do so:

1. Specify the data URI using the <data android:scheme/> tag.

2. Specify the action that should be performed using the <action> tag.

Add additional info about which components handle the activity using a <category> tag.

For example, to open up my application to edit data using an rwapp:// protocol:

```
<android>
  <manifestAdditions>
    <manifest>
      <launcherActivity>
        <data>
```

```
<![CDATA[
<intent-filter>
  <data android:scheme="rwapp"/>
  <action android:name="android.intent.action.EDIT"/>
  <category android:name="android.intent.category.BROWSABLE"/>
  <category android:name="android.intent.category.DEFAULT"/>
</intent-filter>
]]>
        </data>
      </launcherActivity>
    </manifest>
  </manifestAdditions>
</android>
```

For more info on intents, go to `http://developer.android.com/guide/topics/intents/intents-filters.html`.

IPHONE APPLICATION DESCRIPTOR SETTINGS

Flash CS5 automatically creates and maintains the application descriptor file for you inside of the environment. You can modify the properties of the file via the iPhone OS Settings dialog box, shown in Figure A-3.

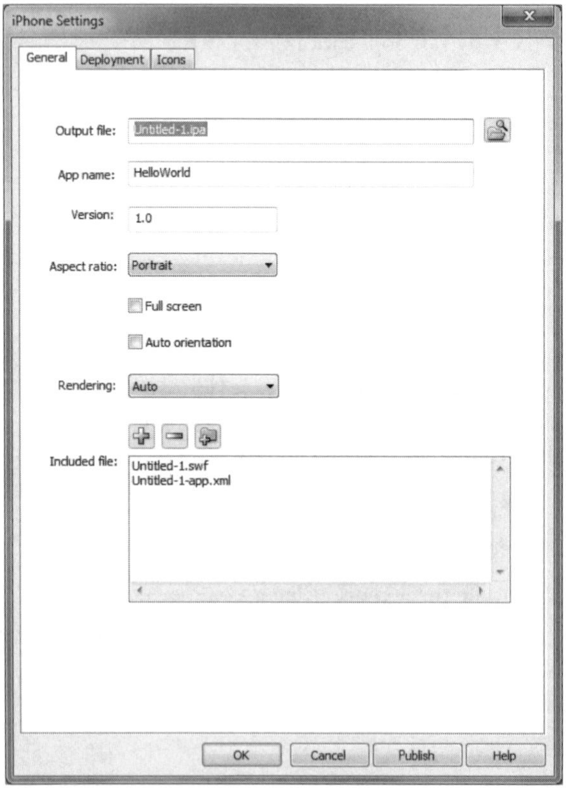

FIGURE A-3

However, there are also some properties in the application descriptor file that are not visible in the iPhone OS Settings dialog box. Use this appendix as a guide to each property.

When you manually modify the application descriptor file, don't open the iPhone OS Settings dialog box until you have first closed the file.

Sample iPhone Application Descriptor File

Listing A-2 provides a sample application descriptor file.

LISTING A-2: Sample application descriptor file

```xml
<?xml version="1.0" encoding="UTF-8" standalone="no" ?>
<application xmlns="http://ns.adobe.com/air/application/2.0">

  <id>DDK533SVDK.FindMeAPizza</id>

  <version>1.0</version>

  <filename>FindMeAPizza</filename>

  <name>FindMeAPizza</name>

  <copyright>Copyright ©2010, Rich Wagner</copyright>

  <description> Finds the nearest pizza shop.</description>

  <initialWindow>
    <content>FindMeAPizza.swf</content>
    <systemChrome>standard</systemChrome>
    <transparent>false</transparent>
    <visible>true</visible>
    <fullScreen>true</fullScreen>
    <aspectRatio>portrait</aspectRatio>
    <renderMode>auto</renderMode>
    <autoOrients>false</autoOrients>
  </initialWindow>

  <icon>
    <image29x29>assets/29x29.png</image29x29>
    <image57x57>assets/57x57.png</image57x57>
    <image512x512>assets/512x512.png</image512x512>
  </icon>

  <iPhone>
    <InfoAdditions>
    <![CDATA[
      <key>AutoLogin</key>
      <string>true</string>
      <key>Username</key>
      <string>John Doe</string>
    ]]>
```

continues

LISTING A-2 *(continued)*

```
        </InfoAdditions>
      </iPhone>

  </application>
```

Properties

The following sections show the properties of the iPhone OS application descriptor file.

<application>

This is the root element of the application descriptor file. For iPhone applications, it needs to have the AIR 2.0 (or higher) namespace.

➤ **Value** — String

➤ **Example** — <application xmlns="http://ns.adobe.com/air/application/2.0">

<id>

Typically the application ID of your application is a reverse-domain string. See Chapter 2 for full details on determining the application ID.

➤ **Value** — String

➤ **Example** — <id>com.richwagner.myapp</id>

<version>

The format of the version of the application should adhere to the *xx[.xx[.xx]]* format where *x* is a digit 0-9. Subversions inside of the brackets are optional.

➤ **Value** — String

➤ **Example** — <version>1.0.12</version>

<filename>

This is the filename of the .ipa file. Don't add an extension. That's supplied by the compiler.

➤ **Value** — String

➤ **Example** — <filename>FindMeAPizza</filename>

<name>

This is the official name of the appLication that is the one used by iPhone and iTunes.

➤ **Value** — String

➤ **Example** — <name>FindMeAPizza</name>

<copyright>

Use the standard copyright line to protect your intellectual property.

➤ **Value** — String

➤ **Example** — <copyright>Copyright ©2010, Rich Wagner</copyright>

<description>

Here you provide a helpful description of the application and what it does.

➤ **Value** — String

➤ **Example** — <description> Finds the nearest pizza shop.</description>

<initialWindow>

This is a container of several child elements that indicate the settings for the initial display at startup.

The <systemChrome>, <transparent>, and <visible> elements, used when compiling AIR apps, are not applicable for iPhone applications. Here is an example:

```
<initialWindow>
  <aspectRatio>portrait</aspectRatio>
  <autoOrients>false</autoOrients>
  <content>FindMeAPizza.swf</content>
  <fullScreen>true</fullScreen>
  <renderMode>auto</renderMode>
</initialWindow>
```

<aspectRatio>

This indicates the initial aspect ratio (portrait or landscape) of the application.

portrait or landscape are its only possible values.

<autoOrients>

Here you indicate whether auto-orientation support is enabled. (See Chapter 7). Possible values are true or false.

<content>

This is the main SWF used by the compiler for the application. Its value is

String.

<fullScreen>

This indicates whether to display the application in the entire viewport of iPhone device or whether to display the top bar. Its possible values are

true or false.

\<renderMode\>

This determines the way display objects are rendered. If the CPU is used, the CPU is used for rendering. If the GPU is used, hardware acceleration is used. See Chapter 5 for more details on how and when to use hardware acceleration. The possible values are CPU or GPU.

\<profiles\>

If defined, this setting allows you to limit the project to be compiled for only specific platforms. For iPhone applications, either don't add the element or use mobileDevice.

Value

Use mobileDevice (desktop or extendedDesktop available for AIR contexts) as shown here:

```
<profiles>mobileDevice</profiles>
```

\<icon\>

This is the container of child elements that define the icon files for the application. Here is an example:

```
<icon>
  <image29x29>assets/29x29.png</image29x29>
  <image57x57>assets/57x57.png</image57x57>
  <image512x512>assets/512x512.png</image512x512>
</icon>
```

You have the following options:

➤ \<image29x29\> — Image used in iPhone's Spotlight search list. Its value is String.

➤ \<image57x57\> — Image used as the main icon on the iPhone main screen. Its value is String.

➤ \<image512x512\> — Image displayed in iTunes. (For testing use only). Its value is String.

\<iPhone\>

This contains elements used to define iPhone settings during installation, as shown here:

```
<iPhone>
  <InfoAdditions>
  <![CDATA[
    <key>AutoLogin</key>
    <string>true</string>
    <key>Username</key>
    <string>John Doe</string>
  ]]>
  </InfoAdditions>
</iPhone>
```

\<InfoAdditions\>

Within \<iPhone\> the container \<InfoAdditions\> holds the key-value pairs used in the application's Info.plist preferences file. Children inside of it must be enclosed in a CDATA tag. The \<key\> and \<string\> elements define a key-value pair.

Compiling Applications from the Command Line

If you are working solely in Flash Builder or simply prefer to use the command line, you can compile Android and iOS applications directly from the command line.

COMPILING ANDROID APPLICATIONS

To compile `.apk` files, you use the Adobe Integrated Runtime (AIR) ADT tool from the command line and supply several parameters to it. The ADT (`adt.bat` on Windows) is located in the `bin` subdirectory, inside of the `AIR SDK` folder.

Here's the basic syntax:

```
adt   -package
      -target apk|apk-debug
      -storetype keyType
      -keystore p12File
      -storepass password
      outputPackage
      appDescriptorXMLFile
      inputPackage
```

If you plan to use the ADT from command line, you'll want to be sure to add its path as an environment variable. Table B-1 shows the ADT parameters.

TABLE B-1: ADT Parameters

PARAMETER	DESCRIPTION
`-package`	Tells ADT that you want to create a package
`-target`	`apk` for a final version of your app
	`apk-debug` for a debug version to install on your Android device
`-storetype keyType`	Type of key (e.g., `pkcs12`)
`-keystore p12File`	Path and filename of your `.p12` certificate
`-storepass password`	Password of your .p12 certificate
`"outputPackage"`	Filename of your output `.apk` package
`"appDescriptorXMLFile"`	Path and filename of your application descriptor XML file
`"inputPackage"`	Name of your `.swf` file that will be packaged as a `.apk` file, along with any other files (such as, icons) that you wish to be added to the package

Here's an example:

```
adt
    -package
    -target apk-debug
    -storetype pkcs12
    -keystore "D:\iphonedev\RichWagnerDev.p12"
    -storepass gh0stQ21a
    "build\CatMan.apk" "CatMan-app.xml"
     "CatMan.swf" "icons\36x36.png"
      "icons\48x48.png" "icons\72x72.png"
```

RUNNING THE PACKAGER FOR IPHONE

To compile `.ipa` files for iOS, you call the PFI Packager for iPhone (PFI) tool directly from the command line and supply several parameters to it. The PFI command-line tool (`pfi.jar`) is located in the `PFI/lib` subdirectory, inside of the `Flash CS5` folder.

Here's the basic syntax:

```
java -jar pfiFile
    -package
    -target ipa-test|ipa-debug|ipa-ad-hoc|ipa-app-store
    -provisioning-profile mobileProvisionFile
    -storetype keyType
    -keystore p12File
    -storepass password
    ipaFile
    appDescriptorXMLFile
    sourceFileList
```

For each of the files in the command string, you must specify the full path name. Also, make sure `java.exe` is available in your path, or else reference the full path name in your command line instruction. Table B-2 shows the PFI parameters.

TABLE B-2: PFI Parameters

PARAMETER	DESCRIPTION
`-jar "pfiFile"`	Path and filename of the `pfi.jar` file.
`-target`	ipa-test—for a test version to install on your iPhone.
	ipa-debug—for a debug version to install on your iPhone.
	ipa-ad-hoc—for use in *ad hoc* deployment.
	ipa-app-store—for use when deploying to App Store.
`-provisioning-profile "mobileProvisionFile"`	Path and filename of your `.mobileprovision` file.
`-storetype keyType`	Type of key (e.g., `pkcs12`).
`-keystore p12File`	Path and filename of your `.p12` certificate.
`-storepass password`	Password of your `.p12` certificate.
`"ipaFile"`	Path and filename of your output `.ipa` file.
`"appDescriptorXMLFile"`	Path and filename of your application descriptor XML file.
`sourceFileList`	Path and filename of all of the source files of your application, including `.swf`, `default.png`, icon files. Put each in quotes and separate with spaces (not commas).

Here's an example:

```
java
    -jar "C:\programs\Adobe\Creative Suite 5\Adobe Flash CS5\PFI\lib\pfi"
    -package
    -target ipa-test
    -storetype pkcs12
    -keystore "D:\iphonedev\RichWagnerDev.p12"
    -storepass gh0stQ21a
    "build\CatMan.ipa" "CatMan-app.xml" "CatMan.swf"
    "Default.png" "icons\29x29.png" "icons\57x57.png"
    "icons\512x512.png"
```

INDEX